# FINAL EXAM

## A NOVEL

Peter Green

PublishNation

ISBN: 978-1-291-46899-1

PublishNation.

'You taught me language, and my profit on't

Is, I know how to curse.'

(Caliban in *The Tempest.*)


'The unexamined life is not worth living.'

(Socrates, after choosing death.)

# CONTENTS

# PART 1: CAMBRIDGE, 1961: EXAMINING A MIND

## Chapter 1

ENGLISH TRIPOS, PART II

Tuesday, 23 May 1961, 9 - 12.30

CRITICISM AND COMPOSITION

Answer Question 1 and TWO or THREE others.

1. Assign approximate dates to FIVE of the following passages, giving your reasons:

...(d) Pathless, and dangerous, wand'ring ways it takes,
    Through Error's fenny boggs, and thorny Brakes:
    While the misguided Follower climbs with Pain
    Mountains of Whimsies, heapt in his own Brain,
    Stumbling from Thought to Thought, falls headlong down
    Into Doubt's boundless Sea, where like to drown
    Books bear him up a while, and make him try
    To swim with Bladders of Philosophy,
    In hopes still to o'ertake the skipping Light:
    The Vapour dances, in his dazzled Sight,
    Till spent, it leaves him to Eternal Night.
    Then Old Age, and Experience, hand in hand,
    Lead him to Death, and make him understand,
    After a Search so painful, and so long,
    That all his Life he has been in the wrong...

------

Saturday, 13 May 1961; 5 p.m. (Recalled in 1969.)

I lay with my head on Arabella's thigh, my fingers still deep in the slimy haven of her crotch.

I thought: "'I lay with my head on Arabella's thigh, my fingers still deep in the slimy haven of her crotch'? ...'Crotch' I don't like, non-phonetic spelling and masculine-sounding; but "hole" is too proley-crude, and "vulva" or "vagina" are too bourgeois-technical; "queynte", "quim" and "no-thing" are antiquarian; and other terms, "minge", "cunt" and "fanny", are coarsely derogatory: in the Navy, we called the rubbish-bins "fannies"...'

It was nine days before Finals, and my brain was accordingly well-tuned, verbalising by reflex, digesting experience into – thank you, Education Act of 1944 – linguistic excrement, lingering turds of words.

Starchy jissom faintly perfuming the wide bed; flute music providing an ironically civilised sound-track, melodies abstracted from Couperin's *Les Barricades mystérieuses*. I have the Couperin at home on a harpsichord record that I bought in the Naafi at Kiel with Bafs; and Jack has it on one of his stolen LPs. Now, those phrases, plaintive modulating to proud, are being played on the flute by someone on the sunny Newnham lawn outside. The civilised purity of the music mocks my sprawling state.

Before my chest's sweat had dried, I was plotting the exact timing of my pre-planned defection, my walk out, my betrayal, my symbolic gesture, my stand on principle.

Sometimes an orgasm was a mad midwife, shoving me back rapidly into a dreamless sleep-womb; sometimes, as now, it magicked body into lead but brain into lucidity; and my lucidity told me that in ten minutes – well, twenty at most – I'd be away scot free; cock, stock and barrel; lightened, by an eggspoonful of jissom, for the leap. ('Jissom'? Better than 'seminal fluid' or 'spunk'. American, I guess; Henry Miller? Thanks to Arabella the lissom, an exorcism of jissom.) No apologies, no explanations;

2

just up and out, not wasting breath on words, words, words. Jack's favourite quotation currently: 'Half the words we use have no meaning whatsoever, and of the other half each man understands each word after the fashion of his own folly and conceit': that's Conrad, communicating incomunication eloquently in his third language; like St Paul's paradox of the Cretan who said all Cretans are liars; and possibly useful for three exam papers – not just 'The English Moralists' but also 'Special Period' and the three-hour Essay...

I had time to luxuriate in a last aesthetic stocktaking, a mock-examination of Arabella, while thanking the unknown flautist and Monsieur Couperin for the cool and gracious sound-track. Even Caliban had an ear for airborne music.

If I closed my myopic left eye, the view with my right was dominated in the foreground by my right wrist and hand, three of whose glued fingers would have been invisible from any viewpoint; on a further horizon, beyond the coppery jungle of pubic hair, rose the undersides of her breasts: bulgy, slightly sideways, teased by gravity. Inside her abdomen, blind muscles, gulled, squinged tight for the last time on my knuckles, a friendly appreciative grip, and relaxed. 'Squinge' was Arabella's portmanteau-verb for her orgasmic and post-orgasmic vulvaic contractions. 'Squeeze' copulating with 'twinge', I guess. ('I guess', again? Another Yankeeism? Substitute 'I conjecture'.)

Close right eye, open left.

The view with the left should theoretically have been more extensive, that eye having greater altitude at the time, owing to the angle of repose of my head; but although that view gave a middle-ground of pale belly beyond the pubis, the breasts now didn't have the clarity of outline and the subtlety of texture of the previous survey: myopia gave just sufficient blur, after eighteen inches or so, to (ha!) cruden the edge and surface.

My left was my book-reading eye. My right never focussed on print. (And the verb 'to cruden' I have hereby created.)

I reflected that the myopia was nevertheless a blessing, because of its incentive to compensatory perceptual activity (com-pens*ay*tory I pronounced it in those salad days; now I give it the middle-class stress on *pens*): I made the most of what I *could* see; and this cheering stoicism enjoyed the confidence which possession of one good eye imparts, and entailed no defence of the probably-late Creator's ineffable miscarriages of justice.

My black-rimmed spectacles were serving as a book-marker at my lodgings over a mile away. They marked that heroic passage in the *Treatise of Human Nature* where David Hume, having by logic not only destroyed the causal nexus but also verified solipsism, is reduced to 'philosophical melancholy and delirium'; but he then finds that, though *reason* cannot provide a cure, *nature* can: 'I dine, I play a game of backgammon, I converse, and am merry with my friends.' (I'd stopped reading there because my eyes were prickling with admiration: that passage seemed the *ne plus ultra* of philosophy. '*Ne plus...*'? Some O-level Latin lingers. I just mean 'ultimate point, furthest extreme'; but the Latin pays tribute to Hume, who there makes Sartre seem naive.)

If I'd been a film-director, I'd have rigged the camera up there under the ceiling, vertically two yards above Arabella's neat little navel, the lens freezing our bodies' head-to-thigh pale symmetry against the black velvet bed-cover, my fingers keyed into her, and her fingers locked on my unloaded tool which, although still bloated and glowing from lubricated friction ('Pond's Cold Cream' being the lubricious lubricant), was already beginning to shrink and retract into wrinkles as mental analysis fanned it; analysis prompted by Sterne's pedantic precision and Antonioni's frigid framing. *Tristram Shandy*; *L'Avventura*.

That black bed-cover had previously been spattered half a dozen times that Easter term by the tachiste whitish jettings of my spunk: Arabella had remarked that one day she'd hang the cover as a tapestry on her wall and give it the title 'The Leavis Nocturne', in honour of the famous Doctor's inveighing against irrelevant or superfluous life (in most of Dickens' novels except – we must discriminate, must we not? – *Hard Times* and much of *Dombey*). If I'd owned a luxurious velvet cover I'd probably have hidden it in a wardrobe rather than risk getting it stained; or if it had been on my bed, I'd have posed as nonchalant until

4

the girl had left and then rubbed frantically at it with a cloth soaked in Thawpit in the hope of eradicating the marks. Rank sweat of an enseamèd bed. Never write 'and then': school rule.

Reasoning engines, Rochester calls us. Engine fingers engine.

The first time she'd taken me to her room in Newnham, my pleasure in discharging through her frenziedly milking fist had actually been augmented by the knowledge that I'd be imprinting a whitish spattered tool-print on the cover – there'd been elements of revenge: (i,) revenge against the luxury (both senses) of the room; (ii,) revenge against an Arabella who, ostensibly for the sake of her 'semi-fiancé', preserved a mode of virginity, eschewing penic penetration; (iii, etc.,) revenge against her acquiescence in lechery, against her class, against her *name* that spoke of upper-middle-class christenings and upper-middle-class ignorance (her parents couldn't have read *The Female Quixote* or *Jude the Obscure*). But she hadn't minded the stains: for her, that bed-cover was just another trophy for the collection, I inferred, as were the weathered C.N.D. banner in the corner, the immobile aluminium mobile beneath the lightshade, and, on the wall, the pseudo-Dalí painting that an artistic boy-friend of a past year had painted for her.

In this, my last undergraduate term, the world-conspiracy (as Casey put it) or Sod's Law (as Jack preferred) had cruelly blessed me with two girl-friends. There were now only nine days before Finals started, and a careful rationalisation of my problem would be as follows.

I was determined to win a first-class degree in Finals; therefore, given my pace of revision and resources of memory, et cetera, one of the girl-friends had to go. And go for good, not just for a week or two. I'd been lucky so far, prudence said; but sooner or later Jan would see me with Arabella; and then I might lose both. I needed to dispel that worry. The choice I had made proved (I persuaded myself) my covert capacity for emotional warmth, moral rectitude, blood-consciousness, class-consciousness and all the other virtues that my weekly essays had 'celebrated', or at least publicised, to a readership of two, for years. If I'd paraded Arabella and Jan before an interview-board of ten representative young men *in statu pupillari* and asked the board which I should keep and which I should relinquish, at least nine of them would certainly have said, 'Keep Arabella, she's the obvious choice'. But I, leaden-casket fancier I, unswayed by snobbery and the aesthetic canons that made Arabella outwardly aureate, the Helen chosen by Paris, I, honest Pete, had decided to choose Jan.

I was twenty-four; my political ideal was the cashless, class-less, co-operative society; and, at a time when only one per cent of the population held university degrees, I craved a First.

Arabella sat up, by this move incidentally expelling my fingers, and rubbed her hand briskly on the cover, her breasts wobbling a little as she rubbed. (Jan's would have swung.) She proffered the carved ivory cigarette-box from the bedside table where semi-fiancé Lionel, smartly suited as befitted a Rothschild banker, beamed approvingly from his steel frame. I had to fumble in the box: the Seniors she thoughtfully or patronisingly put in for my benefit were this week buried beneath the menthol-tipped cigarettes she preferred.

'Tobacco's got dry', I grumbled, sitting up; the flame of her lighter was invisible in the hot sunlight from the window. Just one smoke, then go. Just one. She was in mid-yawn, but the mid-yawn abruptly became a Colgate-advert smile.

'You know, you're an ungrateful hog, Pete. Does it soothe your conscience to look every gift horse in the mouth?'

'They'd keep better if you just left them in the packet, that's all. They would.' Carved on the lid of the box was the double head of Janus. 'Gift horse in the mouth': her very enunciation, that low-voiced, partly-seductive, clearly-articulated upper-middle-class diction with its unwittingly patronising inflections, 'horse' becoming 'hawss', 'mouth' with the rounded 'ou' ('How now, brown cow'): all that was part of the gift I'd finally weighed up. (Even when she said 'soothe', the word as she pronounced it had a cooing onomatopoeic note you'd never hear from Jan – or Jack – or Casey, though he'd try.) Anther part of the gift was her beauty, which was self-evident. You could imagine that if she fell down a spiral staircase, she'd still land at last in an

6

elegant pose, subsiding into grace, resembling a poster for something sexy, feminine and expensive.

Once the previous year, immediately after cashing my State
Grant cheque (£110 for the term), I'd bought from the Ted-gear
shop in Rose Crescent a new jacket (black corduroy, no lapels, a
style I'd seen in Kiel) and a pair of tight grey drainpipe trousers,
and, when I paraded in them, Casey had inspected me
thoughtfully, cleared his clear throat, and said: 'The final effect
is still one of... scruffiness, even though the clothes are new.'
'Why, how?', I said. He walked round me, reflected, and
concluded: 'The clothes are neat; your body, alas,... is untidy.'

So, typically, here I sat, navy-blue shirt crumpled up round
my chest; black jeans and white pants in a tangled concertina
round my ankles, and with one of the socks ('Indestructible' brand
from the Co-op, texture of Brillo-pads) exposing through a tiny
chink a *soupçon* of yellowy big-toe-nail; while Arabella, meanwhile, who lacked my proletarian scruples about day-time
nudity, relaxed in casual naked rightness, a model for a modern
Botticelli.

When I smoke, as she'd once pointed out, I smoke like a
starving dog swallowing a dinner – it's just a single-minded
voracity; waste not want not; but with her, you'd scarcely notice
the cigarette because your attention would soon be sidetracked by
the subtle flexions of her full lips and the minute gradations of
tautness in the skin between the corner of her mouth and her
cheekbone. It was typical that as I lifted the fag to my mouth, the
fingers that held it, the fingers that had been right inside her a
minute ago, exuded nothing of the alley-cat reek that Jan would
have steeped them in. Yes, there was a hint of sweat in the smell,
but mostly it was a soapy-scenty odour; I could tell she bathed
seven times a week more often than I did; it was another
obscure cause of resentment; Dr Johnson wasn't keen on clean
linen either; and 'What?', I said.

She repeated: '"Is this a bloody knife I see before me, the
handle towards my hand?"'

'Come again?'

'Yes please; – Pete: your expression', she explained. 'You have your Edmund-Kean-in-*Macbeth* face: you've just been staring at my mouth with an expression of demented horror. Let me know if I've just sprouted a pair of fangs.' She leaned over and – nip! – nibbled – nip! – the flabbier part of my upper arm. This exercise, as a matter of fact, I found surprisingly painful: I could have yelped; but I mustered both the Hollywood stoicism (without blinking, Alan Ladd took the full force of the heroine's slap...) and the self-possession to push her away by ostensibly playful pressure of my free hand to her breast.

'Come on, don't be crabby; cheer up', she cajoled, in that slyly sexy low voice. 'Didn't I do it nicely just now? Do you know you've got paradoxical hands? They look like a navvy's because they're so broad and beefy. Look at your thumb now: it's twice the breadth of mine. And yet they feel like a little girl's, they're so soft. There. You ought to use Johnson's Baby Soap. Really. Phoo, you should do something about these finger-nails, though. Let me give you a manicure.'

I grimaced and turned away, in my humiliation; so no manicure. She got up, washed her hands, and dressed deftly, while I considered the balance-sheet in my head. For the last time. (An embryonic fart, or more politely the soul of the corpus of my canned-bean lunch, Crosse and Blackwell's, swelled in my gut against a tightening sphincter-muscle. Finish this cigarette, dress and go. The repressed fart dwindled; sphincter relaxed. Well, just stay for a coffee, her strong percolated coffee, then go.)

The balance-sheet: a validation of my education, of the syllabus, of the weekly-essay system: for wasn't I, after all, applying to life the comparative method I'd learnt to apply, week by week, to writers down the ages?

All right. So Jan's friendly stolidity might not have made her a pin-up outside a collective farm in Siberia. But against that stolidity, weigh Arabella's insistent liveliness. When I'd first met Arabella, at one of Piggott's parties, I'd been elated by her immediate interest in me, and it had taken me half this term to realise that that loquacious interest was largely just her style, her manner: she'd talk as breezily about a dress, the latest C.N.D. march, her car (a pre-war Austin 7 she called 'Mr Toad'), or any play at the Arts Theatre. She reminded me then of Alexander

Pope's Belinda and her 'puffs, powders, patches, bibles, billet-doux'. Classic example of the decadence of the university: Arabella spouting fluently about the brilliance (yes, 'brilliance', her misnomer) of Lawrence's demonstrations of the corruptions of 'sex in the head', her big blue eyes gleaming like a magpie's with sincerity.

All right: so Jan had read no Lawrence apart (of course) from the newly-liberated *Lady Chatterley* (*everyone*'s read that now); but in her sometimes clumsy and hesitant comments on films we'd seen, or people we'd met, there often seemed more reflectiveness than there'd ever been in Arabella. If – which Yahweh forbid – they were ever to meet, they'd probably get on well at first, with Jan flattered by Arabella's apparent liveliness of interest, as I'd been; but, after a while, Jan would be like an earth neutralising the younger woman's electricity. Jan talked with you; Arabella interviewed you. Men lusted after the beauty of Arabella, but they relaxed in the company of Jan.

Soft crackle of coppery hair as Arabella stood brushing it back over her white shirt-collar, her eyes shut against the sunlight from the window, tugging her head this way and that against the pull of the brush. I found I was watching her out of the corner of my eye, as the dirty old men and the frustrated undergraduates used to watch her when I led her into the Red Lion or the Still & Sugarloaf for a drink on Wednesdays, a besotted Bottom leading a radiant Titania.

Yes, the whole balance-sheet was put in a cruelly ironic perspective when I recalled my own bulging-eyed frustration during the first two terms. Then, in the urgently nagging hope of a sniff of sex, I'd searched intently and usually unrewardingly – apart from a couple of furtive against-wall knee-tremblers – the Rex Ballroom (mainstream jazz on Tuesdays; admission, gents, five bob, ladies two and six), the Masonic Hall (modern jazz on Saturdays; admission, free if you arrive fairly late), and even, one desperate weekend, Little St Mary's Church (traditional God, and Hymns Ancient and Modern on Sundays; silver collection).

Then, it had seemed that with twenty men's colleges to only three women's, if you include New Hall, the ratio of male to female undergraduates being 12:1, and with my handicap of an adequate but not lavish State Grant, a speedy sterilisation, castration therapy, might be the only solution to the problem of reconciling flesh with study. After all, I'd served in the Navy (National Service, two years; Coder Special branch, Russian course) between school and university. If Cambridge harboured an equivalent to Hamburg's Reeperbahn, I hadn't found it. The perennial and increasing stress of exams was bad enough, a clinging private depressive anxiety; but when accentuated by sexual frustration, it was a deranging torment. Mental lucidity required prior gratification. Desire's pressure deranged judgement; sated lust conferred objectivity.

Once, desperate, that first winter, I'd hitch-hiked to London and haggled with a prostitute on a doorstep in Peter Street, Soho, eventually securing a students' reduction (from thirty shillings to twenty-five) for what was accurately termed 'a *short*-time' upstairs, which at least helped me to assess sceptically the purportedly rapturous fornicatory experience of young Stephen Dedalus in *Portrait of the Artist*, who, encountering a pressure 'darker than the swoon of sin', 'all but burst into hysterical weeping'. At *my* encounter, 'It's just a job, son', said the systematically proficient woman. I'd hastily stripped to my trusty Indestructible socks: an action which, her brief suppressed snigger hinted, was not the customary etiquette. She deftly removed her jersey and her skirt – no underwear beneath – and positioned herself on the bed. Kissing was not part of the deal: she averted her face this way and that from my mouth, to make the rule clear. The blazing coal fire in the black Victorian corner-grate made the little room hot as hell. If copulation was just a job for her, it was an essential study-aid for me: to study intensely, I needed lewd interludes. The following week, Piggott had given me an alpha grade for an essay in which I'd criticised Leavis's denunciation of Shelley: I'd argued that whereas Keats's imagery sought to capture the sensuous, Shelley's characteristic imagery was concerned to convey a *process* (the master-process being the Godwinian revolution), and Leavis hadn't allowed for this. 'Where did you get the idea from?', asked Piggott. I was tempted to say, 'A Peter Street whore', but replied 'The poems.'

Pembroke College had been founded in 1347 by a noble lady,

Marie de St. Pol; yet the only women currently on the staff were the bedders, a redoubtable array of vigilant middle-aged women to keep the place tidy; everyone else there, from the matriculands and the kitchen staff to the Master, being male. We students didn't under-estimate the bedders, knowing that, at Magdalene, one of them was responsible for William Empson's banishment from the University, because she had seen contraceptives in his room. Empson, erudite poet and author of *Seven Types of Ambiguity*, was one of our heroes: Jack, Casey and I had found Empson's Ambiguity of the Seventh Type ('that of full contradiction, marking a division in the author's mind') greatly – and ironically, in the circumstances – seminal; a fertile offspring of Blake's 'Without Contraries is no Progression': it suited our characters, each of us being socially, morally and intellectually divided. What's more, it had helped to engender Jack's 'theory of janiformity', the theory that numerous texts, once deemed 'organic wholes', were radically paradoxical or self-contradictory (e.g. *Wuthering Heights* or *Heart of Darkness*); and it had also helped to engender my notion of covert plots: beneath the text's overt plot might lurk a subversive hidden plot, overlooked by critics. Where Casey was concerned, it strengthened his belief that Nietzsche had provided a key to all mythologies when declaring 'Truths are illusions of which we have forgotten that they are illusions'. As Jack had then said, however, snapping his fingers under Casey's nose, 'Okay, brother. But is that aphorism true – and therefore merely illusory?' (Brooding silence from Casey. He clears his throat. Brooding silence prevails.)

In Arabella's room now, the balance-sheet was complicated and four-dimensional; and there were entries in it that didn't become legible to me until long afterwards, long after the drowning, and long after my teaching came to resemble the task of Sisyphus, that first victim of rock'n'roll. While Arabella, subtly undulant, stood brushing the sheeny cascades of her hair, I added a meticulous auditor's rider about the impossibility of accurate balance-sheets for breathing coinage; but the final statement, the bottom line, was the same as it had been yesterday and the day before: one of the two had to go, and it would be Arabella. Morally and politically, wasn't it an admirable conclusion? The only element of doubt lay in my own capacity for a courageous walk-out: I might flinch at the last moment. The Couperin-player had stopped; and the silence over the grassy quadrangle was like a roll of drums that only I could hear.

Yet, after we'd finished the cigarettes and drunk coffee and talked for a while about the impending nuclear holocaust (Cuba, Berlin or a radar error would be the flashpoints, we agreed), I got up to go and walked to the door; and, at that threshold, instead of saying, as I might have, 'See you on Wednesday as usual', I found, with some surprise, that all I said was 'Cheers'; and, with an especially frank and friendly grin, I turned and walked away down the institutionally drab corridor of Newnham. Like Conrad's Lord Jim, 'I had jumped – it seems'. Left, right, left, right, so far, so good, left, relax, left, don't run, left, yes, left, good, left, born again, right, left, hallelujah, left, born again, left, and I my own midwife, left, right...

# Chapter 2

Wednesday, 24 May 1961, 1.30 – 4.30

SPECIAL PERIOD OF ENGLISH LITERATURE FROM 1880
TO 1910

Answer Question 1 and THREE others.

1. Write brief notes on the following passages, showing how they represent or illustrate characteristics of the period:

(a)    Only the gracious air, only the charm,
      And ancient might of true humanities,
      These nor assault of men, nor time, can harm:
      Nor these, nor Oxford with her memories.

      Together we have walked with willing feet
      Gardens of plenteous trees, bowering soft lawn:
      Hills whither Arnold wander'd: and all sweet
      June meadows, from the troubling world withdrawn.

(Lionel Johnson.)

(b)   '...Everything's bought and sold, from the dust of the cinder-heaps to the favour of Heaven – which last little trifle is bid for with all sorts of things, from a piece of plate for the rector, to a new church for St. Paul, it being considered that the Creator of the Universe is peculiarly gratified by small pepper-pots in silver, and big pepper-pots in stucco, as propitiatory and dedicatory offering. Pooh! Everybody's bribed. The only blunder ever made is in the bribe not being suited to the recipient.'

(Ouida.)

---

Saturday, 13 May 1961; early evening.

Before I'd gone many yards from Arabella's room, that late-Victorian corridor smelling of musty wood and wax floor-polish began to instil a little more osmotic guilt and fear into me. Big institutional buildings – schools, churches, hospitals, barracks, colleges – always did that. They still do, occasionally, but now, in my sensible thirties, I almost relish the feeling, and inspect it as a curiosity, an atavistic survival; whereas then, with the brown lino squeaking in quiet sniggers (as if to say 'National Service, National Service') under my Tuff shoes (39 shillings and eleven pence, guaranteed for six months), I had to take retaliatory action, striding more boorishly and whistling (though softly) some Gillespie phrases from 'The Champ'.

'Whatever you do, don't forget to keep your gas-mask close', my mother had said on the first day she'd guided me through the open spike-topped gate of the Infants' School (Highbury, in Grosvenor Street, 1941), 'and if you need to go to the lavatory, you must hold up your hand and ask the teacher and say "Please Miss"...'. And now merely to walk through Newnham, past door after door behind which one girl might be tussling with the phrasing of an essay, another girl might be soaking her stockings in a wash-basin, another perhaps pushing the Tampax box back into a drawer of waxy lipsticks and little scent-bottles, – merely to walk there made me feel I was trampling through invisible cucumber-frames of rules and taboos. I had to remind myself that at quarter past five on a Saturday afternoon in May there was no rule, statute or commandment which forbade a human male – 'human', 'male'? define; crunch! crunch! – get out of those frames! – a human male to be walking through Newnham to the main gate.

And today there was this new, slight but distinct, fear that Arabella, poise abandoned, might come chasing down the corridor after me, jilted Titania pursuing a scruffy Bottom, her coppery hair streaming and undulating in slow motion (dream-sequence from a pretentious Cocteau film, *Orphée* perhaps, saw it in Kiel), tears worming up across her temples in the airflow of her own headlong

14

flight (rain on train window; Shelley, 'West Wind'), to scream (Hollywood, Janet Leigh): 'Don't leave me! I couldn't bear it!' – and a hundred doors would spring open, all down the lengthening corridor (Kafka), and a hundred identical blue-stockings, one in each doorway, all in identical poses of indignation and accusation, would form the perspectived chorus of this balletic melodrama (choreography: Gene Kelly and Hermes Pan). But such an Apocalypse, propitiated as it usually is by my imagining it, and exorcised by analysis, didn't invade reality, evidently; and I marched on, so far, so good ('and the wretch kept marching', Flaubert), past doors that remained shut, as most Newnham doors do most of the time, as I trod the polished lino that squeaked like polished lino.

Staggering up the stairs was no Horseman of the Apocalypse but Dr Victoria Haggerty, known as Hag: a grey-haired adornment of the arts who usually looked as if she were chewing an enamel-stripping mouthful of raw rhubarb.

Once upon a time she'd completed a thesis on Byron which, when condensed, had promptly been published as a book deemed precocious then: 'a wealth of learning, worn lightly, ...compassionate, ...delightful', said the anonymous *Times Lit Sup* review that was later quoted on the jacket; 'sentl, square, punk', I'd entered in my notebook when I'd read it during my first undergraduate year. Her subsequent two books received, I noted with satisfaction, rather disparaging reviews: no new ideas; barren recycling. She had haunted the university for about thirty years, lecturing regularly in the two series advertised as 'Romantic Poetry' and 'The Modern Novel'; she had an unringed finger in a dozen Boards and committees; and now *per ardua* she heaved herself grimly up the staircase, planting her two rubber-tipped aluminium walking-sticks on the step ahead and, with a suppressed grunt, levering her body up between them. My good eye saw that, at each heave, the grey skin round her mouth puckered briefly into wrinkles. Her reputation and status evoked just enough of my forelock-tugging instinct to give impetus to my malice: her every laboured step made me feel young-blooded: so:

'Can – May I give you a hand?' I said, leering, halting two steps above her with my thumbs in my leather belt, knowing she'd refuse and knowing she knew I knew it. Her severe face reminded me of Miss MacDonald, the cane-wielding headmistress of my junior

15

school; so for a moment I imagined kicking a stick away and making Hag lose balance; but –

'I think I'm quite capable of managing, don't you, Mr Peter Green?'; and, wafting the aroma of musty wardrobes, she struggled past me. That was all; but the 'Mr Peter Green' gave the trick to her. I was more discomfited than flattered to learn that she'd got my name card-indexed in her committee-manipulator's memory, even though she'd met me only twice before.

The first time was at a seminar on Romanticism: at question-time, I'd asked, accusingly, why she had said nothing about Godwin's anarchism. 'Keats's nightingale didn't need lessons on libertarianism', she'd testily replied. The second time was at Piggott's party at the start of term, where I'd inflicted on her a drunken harangue (for sentimentalising arrogant Byron as a great defender of liberty – in her war-time book) just before I'd proceeded to meet and gain Arabella.

The prickly thought arose that Hag might even be a member of the Board that was holding, until the Finals' results were known, my pugnaciously-polemical application to do research on Lawrence – in which case, my leer just now might cost me a vote then, which might cost me a Ph.D.; and I wouldn't have been there to leer if I hadn't just left Arabella, and I wouldn't have just left Arabella if I hadn't met her at Piggott's party, therefore Piggott had cost me a Ph.D., therefore - ah, paranoia, sod it. Let's get out and into the sunshine.

Outside, in Sidgwick Avenue, the sun wasted its illumination on the stark new concrete, stone and glass slabs of the 'Raised Faculty Building', a brutally fashionable design (by Sir Hugh Casson) housing the English Faculty. That 'Raised' referred not to resurrected Faculty-members but to the building: it stood on hefty concrete props which seemed to generate draughty gusts. The ceiling of the undercroft consisted of concave concrete slabs: in course of time, surely, they would start to fall, one by one. Further down the road, trees shaded the asphalt where a few cars revved and fumed at the Queens' Road traffic-lights, scenting the warm breeze with carbon monoxide and lead. That pert little red-and-white car is an Austin Nash Metropolitan, brightly stylish among the other vehicles that are mostly black or grey.

Not enough time for me to go back to my lodgings and do some

16

work before dinner. I crossed over into Silver Street, my tongue teasing at a wiry hair caught between two of my teeth, and mentally re-dramatised the way I'd just left Arabella. Abandoning her was intrinsically a moral victory and incidentally a strategic victory over Casey: fascist that he seemed, he'd never understand the moral rectitude of my choice of Jan.

Where the pavement widened, towards the new Silver Street Bridge, I looked out across the scrubby common by the riverside. Litter, picnickers, sunbathers; a few punts gliding on the Mill pool; and just down there, where a sodden packing-case was now floating, I'd swum with Arabella the second time we'd gone out together. It had been an overcast day then, the water cold to me; I'd soon climbed out, all goose-pimples, and felt my foot start to sting: I'd cut it on the broken glass of the river-bed. You never feel an underwater cut till you get out. The mud by the Mill is encrusted with broken glass, centuries of it, beer-mugs, bottles. She had characteristically emerged, shapely in a glossy white costume, unscathed and laughing, shaking her hair leftwards and rightwards to spatter my face.

Misgivings began to condense and germinate in my mind, but before they could take form, they were aborted by Casey, who came into right-eye focus, leaning with his back to the white parapet, his arms folded in a too-tidy pose. With his silvery hair, black corduroy suit, his watch-chain and his little black shoes, he looked like a dwarfish Victorian gent of decadent inclinations. I crossed myself, and he raised his delicate hand in a papal benediction.

He cleared drily his dry throat. 'As you're not wearing your spectacles, it follows that you've wasted the afternoon... attempting to prove your virility', he murmured.

'Ah, piss off, Quasimodo', I responded amiably, swinging myself up to sit on the broad parapet. He knew all about proving virility: he'd long since developed, to a point of self-parody, an apparently ruthless and insatiable sexual avarice which sometimes gave his non-sexual dealings an air of absent-mindedness. He hoarded his complicated campaigns in tight-fisted taciturnity, but occasional glimpses of his predatory virtuosity had given me cause for respect. His past, like mine, was one of back-streets, Grammar School and National Service; though, if I hadn't seen him in uniform at J.S.S.L. Crail (the Joint Services' School for Linguists, where conscripts from

17

the Navy and the Air Force took the Russian course) and later at R.A.F. Wythall (radio training for naval and Air Force men), I'd never have believed that so pallid, wizened and evil-looking a recruit could ever have been allowed by conscientious doctors to survive the forces' medical exam. When he walked down a narrow street, pregnant women crossed the road to avoid him, and men twice his weight stepped into the gutter and turned to stare. He didn't give way; he never would. Alas.

Groups of students wearing gowns, ready for dinner, cycled across the bridge and past the curving red-brick front of Queens', shouting unintelligibly. A few epicurean flies buzzed greedily round my Brylcreemed quiff and long sideburns. Dr David Daiches walked briskly by, glanced at us, recognised us, and waved his pipe briefly in greeting. Casey and I had attended some of his lectures on Elizabethan sonnet-sequences, during which Daiches seemed to be telling us what we knew already, except that we hadn't expressed the knowledge in such lucid words. A pretty woman passed us, and Casey pretended to pursue her for a few yards, doing his Groucho Marx imitation – long low loping pace, lascivious grin, bespectacled eyes rolling, eyebrows undulating. He returned and gave a yearning groan. I leaned down to his ear: 'What you need is the love of a good woman.'

'I had your sister for lunch', he replied. 'Who are you selling now?'

'Miss Arabella is yours for a pint, your need being the greater. Take it or leave it, man.'

'So soon?', he replied in a stage-Jewish accent; 'And for a pint you want I should make her an honest woman or something already? You want–'

Alex Eastbourne approached us, not exactly panting, but radiating as always his spaniel-like eager undiscriminating niceness. Niceness? More precisely, spontaneous endeavour to be pleasant. His fair curly hair and innocent smile even brought angels to mind. He actually said 'Anyone for tennis?' – oh, sure, he said it so you could hear the quotation-marks, but it was still a genuine question, to judge by his outfit and nature. I beamed and replied 'When I want to play with a prick, I'll play with my own'; and Casey simply retorted 'Tennis!' in a way that made it sound like syphilis. Eastbourne shrugged sadly and started to walk away; then he trotted back and, addressing the blue sky above our heads, said melodiously: ' "Ah... woe to the man whose heart has not learned

18

while young to hope, to love – and to put its trust in life!" ' After a gentle smile  at our perplexity, he trotted off towards the traffic-lights.

'The bastard's out-ployed us,' I said. 'Things are getting bad, when a naïve Lancing-College Christian like that starts to answer back. Perhaps he won't fail after all. Let's cut our losses and have a pint.'

Casey, looking irritated, didn't reply for a while: he was trying to identify Eastbourne's quotation. I didn't recall it; Casey reckoned he did, from a Leavis lecture, but couldn't identify the source. '*Yob tvoy-oo maht'*, he murmured: we could both swear in Russian, thanks to National Service. After a minute he said '"He renounces" (*Godot*)', consulted his watch, and concluded whatever devious espionage he'd been conducting from that vantage-point. It's taken me a very long time to perceive that the person he was looking for had, in fact, arrived.

During my first two undergraduate years, when I'd been accom-modated in college, Eastbourne's room was on my landing (top floor of T staircase in the Victorian New Court) at Pembroke, and he had been unfailingly helpful and kind: he had lent me sugar, coffee and milk, and even an umbrella, when I needed them. Again, a week ago, he'd saved us half an hour of bar-billiard time by eagerly taking our three 'creative writing' submissions, together with his own, along to the Exam Office, just before the deadline.

The trouble with angelic Eastbourne was that he was irredeemably *square*, by which I meant, then, tediously innocent, boringly guileless, and ignorant of jazz. Virtue is perennially doomed to be less interesting than vice. Ben Jonson's Volpone is charismatic; his Bonario and Celia are cardboard. Blake's Milton was 'a true Poet and of the Devil's party without knowing it'. At least Mahalia Jackson proved that the Devil doesn't always have the best tunes. But the Devil knows that to accentuate the rhythm, you clap on beats two and four. Eastbourne was doomed to be one of those who kill the rhythm by clapping on one and three. That's the empirical test for separating the square from the cool.

Casey and I proceeded to the Mill: there would be time for our customary game of bar-billiards before the second sitting of college dinner. On the way, as we turned into the alley that leads down to the pub, there was a sudden dry gust of wind, so that on the corner we were caught for a few seconds in a dusty vortex of sweet-papers and

19

lolly-wrappers that swirled round our knees; and, momentarily, there swirled in my head one of my exam-fodder quotations: 'he passed the stages of his age and youth / Entering the whirlpool'; but the Eastbourne quote remained unsourced.

In Mill Lane, Casey, as was his habit, paused to peer into a braked pram. The infant stared back in surprise. 'Curious animal', said Casey, in the vocative rather than the nominative. The infant, as was the habit of infants when Casey addressed them, opened its mouth to scream: briefly its mouth was wedged open by the preparatory big intake of air; then, as we scurried away, the shriek rose in crescendo from the trembling pram.

It had been a good afternoon. Education had borne fruit in life. I'd proven my altruism by choosing Jan, and confirmed my rectitude by rejecting Arabella. Yes, 'proven': there's precision.

I was twenty-four. My political ideal was the cashless, classless, co-operative society. But, as I said, I craved a First.

# Chapter 3

....2. 'Manliness in art, what can it be, as distinct from that which
in opposition to it must be called the feminine quality there, – what
but a full consciousness of what one does, of art itself in the work of
art, tenacity of intuition and of consequent purpose, the spirit of
construction as opposed to what is literally incoherent or ready to fall
to pieces, and, in opposition to what is hysteric or works at random,
the maintenance of a standard?'                                    (PATER.)

**Either** Explain how far the emphasis made here is central to
Pater's view of art in general, and literature in particular.

**Or** Consider the work of any writer of the period who endorsed,
or could have endorsed, these sentiments.

———

Mostly the same Saturday, May 13th, 1961; evening.

All this happened eight years ago, in 1961. Not until December of
that year would the Minister of Health, Enoch Powell, herald the
arrival of the birth-control pill: he would announce that a
contraceptive pill (unfortunately called 'Conovid') would be
available under the National Health scheme for two shillings a week.
That caused a form of revolution; but 'too late for me', as Philip
Larkin says.

Before that time, young British women were warned by a
multitude of voices (at home, church, school, and in women's

21

magazines) to preserve their virginity for marriage and not become 'damaged goods'. Above all, the stigma of becoming a mother of a 'bastard', an illegitimate child, was to be avoided. The phrase 'unmarried mother' was almost synonymous with 'amateur whore'. I sometimes furtively perused the 'advice' columns in women's mags, and in those days even 'petting' (meaning 'caressing') was regarded as dangerous: it could lead to 'heavy petting', and that might lead to 'a loss of control' by the man or the woman or both, and the result would be 'enduring shame'. Besides, young women were supposed to be modest, shy, retiring, and, above all, chaste until wedlock: surely it was the nature of the feminine to be reticent and reluctant; it was the male who, alas, suffered from primitive urges, which the virtuous girl should prudently anticipate and stalwartly repel.

The pill transformed the apparent nature of women. That little oral contraceptive revealed that when females could fornicate without fear, they generally did so with gusto ('Meet Gusto, my randy Italian boy-friend'). One of the great boons conferred by the pill was to soak in irony's sour vinegar the events I'm recalling. Unfortunately, the people most likely to appreciate that irony will be those who, like Arabella, Jan, Casey, Jack and me, were born between 1937 and 1940: which is a further sour irony. Eventually we'll all join the silent majority in Marvell's fine and private place where 'none, I think, do there embrace'.

The *Love's Labour's Won* problem then comes to mind. The *Love's Labour's Won* problem is ready in my head because I've already used it five times this week in five different A-level classes (that repetition's a symptom of my present Sisyphean corruption). I use it to show the students how a sound evaluation of a work is dependent on knowledge of the historical context of the work. The problem, in that form, first came to me on that Saturday evening, when Casey was making his customary tedious preparations for one of his shots.

At the Mill, Casey and I met Jack in the back room where the hefty bar-billiard table stood waiting. The three of us had our usual ritualised argument over whose turn it was to buy the first round of drinks (Tolly beer) and whose turn to pay for the game. At length Jack, exasperated by thirst, had bought the beer (but without conceding he'd lost the argument: he never lost an argument), and I'd

22

reluctantly put a silver tanner in the slot. When it was Casey's turn to shoot, the red was in a very propitious position. He chalked the end of his cue, and took aim in his fidgety way; then he straightened, and chalked the end of his cue again, coughed his nervous cough a few times, and took aim again. Behind his back, big Jack mimed hair-tearing impatience.

'How's the three-week plan going?', Jack asked me, feigning uninterest.

'They call it the rhythm method in Rome; Vatican roulette elsewhere', remarked Casey, who at last completed his feeble but accurate stroke. The red wobbled on the brink of the hundred hole and pitched down onto the runners with a detonating clatter.

'Jammy. – It's four weeks behind schedule, but I've got one scrap of curious knowledge to trade. Fanfare please, ta-rah, ta-rah. It seems the Immortal Bard wrote a comedy that's vanished without trace, called *Love's Labour's Won.*'

'Ah, try again', said Jack, his tone implying 'we all know about that'. 'It's mentioned in *Palladis Tamia.* By Meres. In his list.' Casey, listening and reflecting, accordingly knocked down a peg with his next shot, and Jack seized the cue.

'Fair enough', I said, 'but think of this one, then. Imagine that I find the manuscript of it, and it's the real manuscript, the genuine article. Suppose I find it today, and I'm just about to send it off to a publisher with a note saying "Dear Mate, I've found Shakespeare's long-lost play, what's it worth, mate?". And suppose, instead of sending it straight off, I craftily sit down and type it out word for word and comma for comma, but I just alter the name, so that instead of beginning "*Love's Labour's Won* by William Shakespeare", it begins "*Love's Labour's Won* by Peter Green", and suppose I send the typescript off to a good publisher, Faber say, with a covering note saying "Dear Mate, This is your lucky day, I have just unburdened my soul of one of the world's greatest comedies, so what'll you fork out for it?" –'

'A hundred and twenty', said Jack, playing a fluent series of shots. 'Supposing all that – a hundred and forty, a hundred and seventy. Don't keep us in suspense. Two hundred and ten. I'll save it. There, like ...come on, baby' (he coaxed the red ball to kiss a white and obediently rest) '...that. Mark me two hundred and ten.'

'Well, supposing all that, does the publisher, when he's read the script, hail me as the greatest genius since Shakespeare, or does he sling the script into the fanny, the dustbin, and arrange for me to be carried off to Coney Hatch in a strait-jacket?'

'He...publishes the script in his name... and sends you a rejection-slip signed "William Shakespeare"', suggested Casey. With my thumbnail I prised the reluctant wiry hair at last from between my teeth. Pubic.

'Get on with it. Your turn', said Jack, pushing me with his heavy hand towards the green baize. 'He throws the script in the dustbin to safeguard Shakespeare's name and sends you a rejection-slip signed "Peter Green". But the guy who empties the dustbin is working for MI5 and has you arrested for sending an indecent article through the post.'

Left eye closed, aiming with my good right eye, I made my usual aggressive rapid shots. From all directions the heavy balls went thudding through the holes and rumbling down the racks.

'Perhaps... he publishes it as a... *parody* of a Shakespearian comedy', murmured Casey reflectively. Then he sniggered as I ploughed the black peg and lost all my score. Distracted by the problem, I'd forgotten that the Mill's table slopes up at the top left-hand corner, so the balls rebound faster from the cushion there. (At the Still & Sugarloaf, the table was impeccably level.)

'No, that won't work either', said Jack. 'Think. For first few pages he expects it to be a parody; but by page ten or so, the grin's been wiped off his face: there's no parodic point emerging. He's put up valid critical scaffolding on false premises, viz, to wit and namely, that it's a contemporary work. Result, valid: dustbin. Q.E.D.! – All right, point taken; but a neater way of showing the tacits of criticism is the "'nice' once meant 'foolish', 'nice' later meant 'fastidious', 'nice' now means 'pleasant'" argument.' He snapped a finger and thumb under my nose. 'Borges. Borges is the man you need, Mr Green. Read "Pierre Menard, Author of the *Quixote*" by Borges. Spelt B.O.R.G.E.S. It'll work. Never heard of him, have you? And what made you think of that one, Mr Green, anyway?'

'Association of ideas', said Casey over his shoulder, aiming. 'Via *Love's Labour's Lost*. He tells me he... abandoned Miss Arabella this afternoon. Must be out of his... putative... mind.'

'Likely story.'

'Is true. He just sold her to me half an hour before already. Is it the clap, or has she proven frigid, I ask myself.'

'I tell you, she fucks like a rattlesnake', I lied vehemently. 'She'd wear you out and yell for more.' A minor revenge against her: she'd been deftly expert at mutual masturbation and the occasional gobble, but nothing beyond that; avowedly to be faithful to her Lionel, that minion of mercantilism. After one delectably voracious Venus-fly-trap gobbling, I'd said, 'What would Lionel think of that?', and she had replied: 'Eating cannot be deemed cheating.' 'But it's fellatio, the vice that dare not speak its name –' 'Because its mouth is full!': she'd read Kenneth Tynan, too.

I held up my beer-mug and added: 'The beer here is piss; must be watered.'

'Be logical', said Jack. 'If she's all you claim, then what are you playing at? Trying to save the three-week revision plan, brother?' (It was a Geordie 'brother': 'broothah'.)

Casey completed his cautious break and marked up the score. 'One possibility that occurs to me', he said to Jack as though I weren't there, 'is that Arabella had seen him with Jan somewhere, and gave him the boot.'

'Do me a favour', I grumbled, delving in my mind for some lie that would give me prestige before them, and blushing for fear I'd indicate a lie by blushing, 'It's... it's practical economics. As soon as the exam's out the way, she'd expect to be taken to a May Ball. I can't afford it, I don't fancy it; it's a decadent ritual of the budding bourgeoisie; and what's more, it's a wasted investment, because in the vacation she'll probably go abroad; and next term, if I do manage to get in on the research racket, she'll probably be hundreds of miles away in a job. Miss Jan, on the other hand, lives here all the time. She'll be around this year, next year, the year after that. Besides which, she often pays for her own ale, but Arabella's a parasite.' I paused for breath, surprised by the specious fluency of this improvised argument; it almost convinced me. 'Do you realise how much bloody Arabella's bastard gin-and-tonics cost? They –'

'Cool it', said Jack. 'Cool it. They can hear you in the other bar.'

'Heart-rending, heart-rending', murmured Casey thoughtfully.'The poor lad doesn't have a... clue.'

But he lost the game; I came second; and Jack, as usual, won, and announced the fact (more to himself than us) with deep satisfaction.

It gave me unfeigned pleasure to play my quite violent bar-billiard shots – particularly the far corner-cushion volley which, when I allowed for the slope, repeatedly sent the red, after a double ricochet, into the twenty hole, having tapped a cornered white; and it *was* a little like a sexual gratification to hear the red and the white clattering down the holes into the thud-rumbly wooden belly of the plump table; but I knew that if I'd been playing without the lads watching, half my strokes would have been Caseyesque and crafty. But then, who wants to win a game of solo bar-billiards? What pleasure in defeating an oak scoreboard with brass pointers?

I asked Jack about Eastbourne's quotation, 'Woe to the man whose heart has not learnt while young to love, to hope'. 'No, brother, it's "to hope, to love",' he replied; then, snapping his thumb and middle finger at me: 'Conrad, *Victory*: Leavis quotes that, to show that Conrad is morally wholesome. But the hero of *Victory*, instead of taking the advice, then commits suicide. Leavis still finds a "victory for life". Conrad finds it for nihilism, more like.' 'Aah', said Casey, struggling to recollect, 'The last word... The last word... is..."Nothing!"... Conrad must have read Schopenhauer.' 'Snap', said Jack, nodding, and shaking Casey's hand in congratulation. I tried to take mental note: *Victory*, Schopenhauer. The word *Victory* evoked the Battle of Britain we'd lived through as kids, when Poles were the boldest Spitfire pilots: Conrad, 'Polish Joe' to his fellow-seamen, would have been proud.

After collecting our black gowns from Jack's high-ceilinged room by entrance O in Pembroke's New Court (new in 1881), we attended the inexpensive and nourishing ritual of dinner in the College Hall. That night, the grace, uttered by an aged Fellow at the High Table, was the mercifully brief *'Benedictus benedicat'*. After which: 'Why...do Morris dancers wear bells on their knees?', Casey asked us, irritated by the gowns. 'To annoy blind people too', replied Jack, reaching for the ground ginger.

The starter was exotic to us: sliced melon (though unripe and hard) with ginger; and the main course was a stew flavoured with curry-powder, which imparted a yellowish tinge to the gravy. Between courses, the public-school hearties occasionally shied a few rolls at us ex-grammar-school students; but we, who knew the price of bread-rolls (tuppence each), preferred to stuff our jacket-pockets with them. We remembered how, in war-time, the empty-windowed bakery-shops had no rolls to sell; and the National Loaf, greyish in colour, had always been slightly stale, when rationed out from the stacks beneath the counter, for the government had astutely decreed that, when purchased, the loaf must be at least one day old, so that people would eat less of it. Ha: strife spurs astuteness: usable.

The old waiter hobbled to and fro, bringing the dishes and clearing away the dirty crocks and irons. 'Thanks, mate', 'Ta', 'Thank you', we muttered; but, as usual, the more punctiliously we thanked him, the most worried he looked: sometimes it almost seemed that he'd be happier if, as the other third-year students did, we'd simply treated him as invisible.

Amid the clink and clash of plates and cutlery ('eating-irons' in the Navy), Casey committed a joke about a seemingly-impotent Mr Goldberg and his crafty neighbour, Mr Nathan. (At least this story didn't involve Rabbis and foreskins.) It's the one where Nathan gives Goldberg a tedious rigmarole of instruction about the preparation of the bedroom for Goldberg's honeymoon: soft lights, scented air, room warmed to a temperature of 71 degrees Fahrenheit, rose-petals strewn on the rugs, bouquets on the pillows, champagne in the ice-bucket... 'Yes, yes, and *then* what do I do?', asks Goldberg. Nathan replies: 'And then, you phone for *me.*'

'Fascist', I said.

'Heard it before', said Jack, flicking crumbs from his beard. 'Stereotype: perfidious Jewry. Tubal didn't back Shylock. Hurry up and let's get out of here.' A dour Edmund Spenser stared down at us with distaste from his cracked and darkened canvas on the brown wainscot. Spenser (Pembroke, 1569-76), author of the abominable *Faerie Queene* (which even *he* couldn't finish), had advocated a genocidal final solution to the Irish problem.

Outside, we separated: Jack in the direction of the Arts Cinema, to see the new Antonioni film, *La Notte* (he was a fan of Jeanne Moreau, fascinated by her wide downturned tragic mouth); Casey for an assignation (I guessed) with Mrs Fletcher, his avid landlady; and I

27

towards Jan's flat.

Many times during the year, I'd cycled from College to Jan's on Saturday nights; but, on this particular evening, the first part of the journey was unusually wearisome, as if the resilience of my leg-muscles had been spattered gratuitously over the Newnham bed-cover. Perhaps I owed to Arabella this nagging ache in my thighs as I pedalled the clanking bike past Emmanuel, past the Saturday crowd of jostling teenagers by Drummer Street bus-station, and up towards Midsummer Common. The ache, as I wobbled in the wake of a fumy bus, turned into an old quiet resentment at the role into which Jack and Casey so often seemed to push me.

Casey's manner was generally quiet, neat, fastidious, almost donnish. He'd done his best to eliminate his northern provincial proley accent, whereas Jack and I often flaunted *our* local accents. To define myself against Casey, I sometimes slid into the contrasting role of the vulgar reductive philistine. Jack was big, six feet one and built like a heavyweight wrestler, and aggressively intelligent; so for self-definition I noted his bullying element, and exploited in myself for contrast my vein of jaunty self-pity. And we watched each other, and probed and parried, so that relaxing with them could be hard work. Competition corroded amity.

Sometimes Casey and I sided against Jack: two ex-servicemen against this upstart prodigy, just eighteen when he arrived from Newcastle's Royal Grammar School. He'd never have to do the square-bashing we'd done, National Service having been phased out. Not fair. Not a fair world. Sometimes, instead, Jack and I sided against Casey: two aggressive impatient men against this slow meditative prematurely-old little fellow (he was five foot five, silver-haired and skinny) who couldn't understand jazz. In that respect, far from being cool, Casey was so square as to be cubic: his taste in music led him to Gregorian chants, Mussorgsky, Eric Satie and, inexplicably, Eartha Kitt, a commercial crooner with a tendency to bleat.

Sometimes, though, Casey and Jack sided against me: a Nietzschean and a Pyrrhonist (both book-thieves) in alliance against a part-time libertarian anarchist with a shambling flat-footed walk, greasy hair and a Gloucestershire burr. I grumbled that their book-stealing simply increased the cost of books for honest folk. They replied that since morality was a human artefact with no transcendent guarantor, that kind of honesty was outmoded; their honesty lay in formulating their own independent mode of conduct. In cinemas, therefore, they remained seated during the National Anthem at the end of the show, instead of standing up. I thought that was ludicrous (but was reassured to see their cleverness alloyed with such crassness), and preferred to join most of the patrons in the customary Anthem-evading stampede to the exit.

Where thieving was concerned, I tardily realise, I had been worse than them – correction – than they. During a school exchange in 1953, I'd collected 'souvenirs'. On Bundesbahn trains, I had unscrewed and pocketed some of the little enamelled notices on window-frames which read '*Nicht hinauslehnen*'; and, walking on the outskirts of a village, I had (for my collection) pulled from a post a board bearing in Gothic script the warning '*Hundesperre*'. Only now do I perceive that, for want of those warnings, some insouciant traveller by rail may have been decapitated on leaning out as the train entered a tunnel; and some trusting traveller by road may have died writhing from rabies after patting a red-eyed hound of the village. When stationed in Germany in 1957, another rating and I had stolen a big Humber van from the barracks, visited several bars in Kiel, and, on the way back, had patriotically driven on the left side of the Autobahn, cackling triumphantly as on-coming motorists blared their horns and swerved to avoid us.

Those who can, do; those who can't, teach; and teachers say that literature provides guides to life. We couldn't blame it for our delinquencies. We had known literature as a refuge from life, even a substitute for life. All three of us had learnt, during the stresses of war-time and its drably austere aftermath, that a variety of literary works offered us a magical escape, an exciting refuge, trustworthy friends, instant time-travel, and soaring flights to new opulent lands that gratified the senses and the imagination. We all three knew it; we wouldn't admit it. Sometimes, too, an episode had made my boyish eyes prickle with incipient tears: Robinson Crusoe finding that his escape-boat, built with 'inexpressible labour', was too heavy to be dragged to the sea; or Robin Hood, mortally weakened by the prioress's malicious blood-letting, managing to dispatch, through the window of his cell, one last arrow to mark the place where he should be buried. Our bravado concealed such secret literary emotions.

At Cambridge we'd dutifully attended F. R. Leavis's crowded lectures at Mill Lane, where he, in a white open-necked shirt, whatever the weather, spoke in a conspiratorially quiet voice; and in different ways we were all three repelled by his emphasis on the study of literature as a 'moral discipline', with the critic acting as a policeman, putting some authors under arrest ('Mr Milton: I warn you that anything you say may be taken down and used in evidence...'), letting some off with a caution ('George Eliot: we'll admit your Gwendolen Harleth, but not your Daniel Deronda, an illegal immigrant'), and patting others on the back ('Ho yes, Mr Lawrence, at your best you indeed display a reverent openness before life'). 'Magic' wasn't part of his critical vocabulary; and he spoke of the harmless *Times Literary Supplement* as if it were the organ of Beelzebub. So we preferred – with reservations – the gusto of C. S. Lewis, as he strode up the aisle, with swaggering gait and wild glare, to enact the fearsome Green Knight; C. S. Lewis, who, though polemically Christian, once bitterly remarked to us all that at a time of bereavement, 'Heavenly consolation is no earthly use'. (He had survived the Battle of the Somme.) We also enjoyed, more than we cared to admit, the darkened lecture-room séances of Tom Henn from St Cat's, as he projected Blake etchings on to the screen and, in the gloom, paced about, reciting intensely Blake's 'London' or 'The Sick Rose'. (He'd become a Brigadier in World War 2; now walked with a limp; and declaimed emphatically the accusatory lines 'And the hapless soldier's sigh / Runs in blood down palace walls', in which the dying soldier surrealistically curses the source of his woe, the ruling class.) Such lecturers were haloed by their fame: we had read their books, and, as if we had rubbed the magic lamp, the authors now emerged like genies before us, the words made flesh; tangible transubstantiation.

All three of us distrusted a current orthodoxy of school English and the so-called 'New Critics', that a good literary work should be 'an organic whole', which any reduction or addition could only mar. We, divided beings, thanks partly to the exam system, preferred to think that plenty of good literary works were also divided, being paradoxical or even self-contradictory. Jack's term, 'janiform', honoured Janus, the two-faced god. Our attempts at original literary criticism were thus fragments of transmuted autobiography; but Karl Marx, Sigmund Freud, Bertrand Russell and William Empson, by emphasising inner conflicts, had abetted us.

Another shared feature, related, was that our cultural heroes included not only a range of literary and philosophical eminences but also Buster Keaton, the Marx Brothers of *Duck Soup*, and Peter Sellers of *The Goon Show*; and, when the Pembroke Players had performed Jonson's *The Alchemist* in December 1958, we'd enjoyed the anarchic ad-libbing of a second-year student called Peter Cook, playing Face. Long ago, around A-level exam time, I'd relished the jarring juxtaposition of contrasted joys: for instance, reading Shelley's neoplatonic-surrealistic 'Life, like a dome of many-coloured glass / Stains the white radiance of eternity', while on the radio Bessie Smith was majestically singing 'Gimme a pig-foot an' a bottle of beer...'. And Shelley tells her: 'Until death tramples it to fragments.' Contradiction resolved as (ha!) ironic counterpoint.

Jack, Casey and I had taken the Pembroke Entrance Examination in the Old Library, a mellow dark-panelled room with a big ticking clock, invigilated by an elderly gentleman enshrouded (like a Blake priest) in a long black gown. The three of us found that we were greatly outnumbered by lads from fee-taking schools, the so-called 'public' but really very 'private' schools; most would evade National Service; lads with easy access to theatres, foreign cultural centres, good libraries and opulent art galleries. To be able to buy such privileges was surely a form of cheating: 'the exam system is radically bloody unjust', we agreed: the system resembling a torture-rack, an escape-ladder, and a baited trap.

At home, my father had a library of five hefty books: *The Universal Home Doctor* (with its curiously un-erotic labelled picture of a naked man and woman); *Newnes' Everything Within* (a salmagundi that even imparted the method of reading fortunes in tea-leaves); *Odham's English Dictionary* (to explain 'salmagundi'); *The World's Library of Best Books* (catholic assortment: everything from *Plutarch's Lives* – abridged, but telling you how Brutus's Portia swallowed fire – to *Penguin Island*); and the *Wide World Magazine Annual* for 1929 (true stories of action, adventure and exploration: one of them, about a surveyor marooned on a rocky island, must have been a source – as yet unrecognised – for Golding's *Pincher Martin*.)

31

But these were complemented, of course, by the infinite riches of the public library, that incomprehensibly generous cornucopia: Caliban's dream made true.

One sunny morning, entering College for lunch, we ambled through the 14th-century Old Court: Jack (big) and Casey (little), with me (average, five foot eight) between them. The other two wore black corduroy suits (as on every day of the year); I was wearing a black corduroy jacket and shabby black jeans; and we passed a low open upstairs window where the dog-collared Dean (the Reverend Dr Dooley) was standing with Piggott. Each, framed by the mullioned casement, had a sherry-glass in hand, and they were surveying, proprietorially, the pebble-bordered grass quadrangle.

As we passed by on the flagstoned path, the Dean gestured down towards us, turned to Piggott, and said something indistinct which might have been 'What *is* this place coming to?'. Piggott responded: 'These things of darkness I acknowledge mine.' 'God, man and the Devil, I should say', Dooley proclaimed loudly, with a dry cackle. This proclamation instantly gratified the three of us, below; clearly I was 'man'.

Jack hoped eventually to become a cryptic poet surpassing his current heroes, Wallace Stevens and the Pound of the Pisan Cantos. That might impress Piggott, who boasted that one of his recent undergraduates had been Ted Hughes, no less. Casey (with Rilke and Nietzsche among *his* heroes) dreamt of a career in politics, but in the meantime would be content to translate Anna Akhmatova – thanks to the forces' Russian course and its free post-conscription supplementary tuition. I merely hoped to see my name on the jacket of a book; a digressively realistic novel would do.

At the end of Emmanuel Road I came in sight of Jesus. Jesus College: a nunnery once, now a brick-and-stone blasphemy. 'Jesus'... some connotations: 'Gentle...meek and mild', 'The meek shall inherit the earth', 'Sell all that thou hast, and give to the poor': three years in Cambridge had scrambled those connotations. With its battlemented tower, that fortress of a place sought by its name to assure the world that the rural carpenter's son had given his blessing to the sacred rights of property and élitism.

Parents and religion may say 'Love and co-operate', but, from the first day you enter infants' school, an educational system made by and for the economy says 'Compete; combine when I require you to; compete again.' No wonder there was such an uneasy balance of collaboration and hostility between Jack and Casey and me. We collaborated best when we sensed siege-conditions, when the 'Us versus Them' paradigm seemed to apply: 'Us' versus the mass of middle-class, private school students; 'Us' versus the United Examiners; yet within the collaboration, a gnawing competitiveness. And all the time, above the three of us, hovered that mental thunder-cloud of exam stress.

Car after car overtook my clanking Raleigh (my bid had been £2 for it at the police abandoned-bikes auction, October 1958); and I found I'd forgotten the new name Jack had commended. The shape of it was in my head: it began with a B and had – three? no – two syllables; but the details of its features had vanished. Jack's memory was magnetic, mine slothful. I wouldn't want to prove my amnesia and parasitism by asking Jack to spell the name out again. He probably sensed that his literary name-dropping and widely-ranging ploys dictated more of my academic reading than the lists and recommendations I'd noted at lectures or at Piggott's supervisions.

Casey might look like a don, a sinister wizened don, while Jack looked like a nightclub bouncer, but it was Jack's freebooting mental voracity that offered me the best pickings, the best short-cut to a First, and thus to a continuation of this student-life rather than entry into the world where you sold your autonomy for bread-and-butter and a mortgage. Research meant being my own boss for three funded years, and eventually entry to an academic job where I'd be able to be myself, my own man, for months rather than days of the year. If 'being myself' was no joy-inducing goal, it seemed, on the whole, preferable to the alternatives.

So, burly Jack was my mentor in the world of image-clusters, themes, archetypes, current critical approaches, and American poetry: particularly Stevens and the Black Mountain school, Dorn, Olson, Creeley. He had range plus fine memory plus scepticism; he knew more than I did about rock and pop music and Musica Antiqua. He also mocked my libertarian anarchism ('you Cheltenham Spa revolutionary'). But he sometimes respected *my* range and edge-seeking: I'd persuaded him to visit with me an entrancing Alfred Deller recital at Newnham ('A *counter*-tenor? What the hell's that? A *castrato*?', Jack initially exclaimed); and he would consult me about Aeschylus, Ibsen, *Titus Andronicus,* William Godwin, how Dalí weds Dryden (Augustan satire generates surrealistic imagery) or how Humbert Humbert aids Chekhov (superfluous men, oscillating in mood between self-mockery and self-vindication); and in jazz I was still his mentor, though he was catching up rapidly. Hare to my tortoise.

He'd won an Open Scholarship to Pembroke (£60 a year and accommodation for three years in a room in College), whereas Casey and I had won Open Exhibitions (£40 a year and accommodation for two years in a room in College). All three of us had subsequently been disgusted to find that the Scholarship's £60 and the Exhibition's £40 did not *augment* the State Scholarship (about £330 a year for kids from humble backgrounds like ours) but merely *subsidised* it, so that instead of £330 from State plus £40 from Pembroke, as I'd assumed, I got now £290 from State and £40 from Pembroke. There's no justice.

Silver-haired Casey was my mentor in Nietzsche, German culture, Akhmatova's poetry, and in sexual opportunism. If Casey hadn't arrived at Piggott's party, I probably wouldn't have dared, even with several sherries inside me, to accost the lissom Arabella there; but I knew that if I hesitated he'd home in on her, and do so successfully: he had a knack with women that I didn't understand.

Oddly, Jack's judgement seemed fallible only where Casey was concerned: in that matter he verged on the sentimental. I reckoned Casey had a hard fascistic centre from which stemmed his sexual outlook, his cultural tastes and even his jokes; yet Jack seemed to think that Casey had a soft centre of sensitivity and poetic imaginings, for which his half-jocular political fascism was a transparent compensation or protective carapace. According to the situation, I felt small eddyings of affection for – and hostility to – both of them. I'd had a similar mixture of feelings for several people (mainly relatives) who were boring and dispensable. What did matter was that after two and a half years' close acquaintance at the University, the three of us were less often bored in each other's company than in the company of virtually all the other people we knew; and in common we had our related egoisms, malice, insecurity, class background, and, of course, war-time childhoods.

34

We remembered with lucidity those war years, when the popular songs from the wire-festooned wireless included 'The Last Time I Saw Paris' (written by Jerome Kern, sung by Ann Sothern), 'We'll Meet Again', 'There'll be Bluebirds over / The White Cliffs of Dover' (Vera Lynn) and 'I Don't Want to Set the World on Fire' (the Ink Spots: a popular number around the time when Dresden was destroyed). In those years, on grimy railway-station platforms the red cast-iron slot-machines tauntingly proclaimed 'Nestlé's Chocolate' in fancy scrolled lettering, but contained only cobwebs. Sometimes, on those platforms, low stationary trolleys would bear huge dozing bombs awaiting delivery to air-bases, bombs decorated with chalked defiant slogans and occasionally with peeling rows of War Savings stamps, red, blue, green, gold, when the workers paid for the bomb.

At primary school, teachers showed us pictures in tattered ten-year-old textbooks ('You'll have to share, one book between two') of strange lustrous fruits called 'bananas', 'grapes' and 'pineapples', fruits which had once been real and present in those exotic years of plenty called 'Before the War'. The night sky had shown us not calm constellations but the ceaseless criss-crossing of searchlight beams, sometimes lighting a bulging silvery barrage-balloon. Fuel rationing and shortages had meant that on some wintry days, school or home was cold; food rationing and shortages meant that meals were monotonous and sometimes sparse; but, for Harvest Festival at the school's church, St John's, my dad always mustered for me a fine bunch of carrots from his allotment-patch, well washed and neatly tied with thin white string.

In the years immediately following the war, though we had expected a return to a land of milk and honey, the reality was a grimmer austerity. Rationing for a while became even more severe than in war-time: even furniture and clothes needed coupons. Coal was in short supply; often, when at last the sooty horse-drawn cart called, my parents had to accept a sack or two of mere slack as part of the allocation, 'slack' being coal-grit and glittery black dust. Now and again, later, there were sharp bangs as red-hot bits shot out from the fireplace onto the carpet; because the miners, to speed their output, had been using gunpowder to split the seams, and some powder remained unexploded until it reached the domestic hearth. One afternoon in 1946, Alan Wills told me excitedly that the nearby

35

post office was selling sweets 'off-ration'; so we queued and bought two pennuth, but the sticky red globules in the little paper cone proved to be sugarless cough pastilles.

The myth of the Fall of Man had been made real to us by countless instances of deterioration. Once there was a golden age, without rationing and shortages, where the sun shone on swimming pools with high diving boards and ice-cream parlours, an age of brightness, colour and freedom; but then, through the folly of Man, there came world-wide war and the descent into deprivation. Mitigations: so few cars on the war-time roads that any cul-de-sac would serve for an hour of cricket, the stumps being chalked on a wall; the removal of railings meant that once-private gardens became public places for a soccer match or wild chase-game; and the departure for America of some of the owners of stately homes meant that kids could break in and explore wide-eyed the cobwebbed corridors and high rooms where chandeliers were bagged and furniture lay shrouded in spectral dust-sheets.

And at least, during that war, both my parents were alive and present. Jack's father, navigator in a bomber's crew, had been killed by ack-ack fire in a raid on blazing Hamburg. Casey's father, in the army, eventually didn't come home, having formed a relationship with a young woman of the A.T.S. (Auxiliary Territorial Service), leaving Casey's mother to work as a cleaner to support herself and her lad. We all three had air-raid memories. Casey, from Leeds, recalled sporadic raids, in the Beeston, Headingly and Woodhouse areas; sometimes his mother simply ignored the warnings, or even slept through them. In my recollection, when the nearest siren oscillatingly ululated, my mother would wake up me and my sister, and all three of us would sit or crouch, torch-lit, in the pantry under the stairs, by the red shilling-in-the-slot gas meter (for the lighting as well as the cooker), the set-spring mouse-trap, the Kilner jars of greying plums, the pail of isinglass in which two real eggs were sealed, and the pots and boxes on the shelves. Hitler's bombers rumbled overhead; but they usually proceeded to targets in Gloucester, nine miles to the west. When Cheltenham *was* bombed, the Germans were either accurate or lucky: they destroyed part of the gas-works in Gloucester Road and, lethally, some housing nearby; and one stick of bombs culminated spectacularly at the Pilley road-

36

bridge, which fell as rubble on to the railway line beneath. But Fritz never detected the lofty UCAL (chemical) factory near us, even though the swirly patterns of brown and green paint seemed impotent camouflage of its high windowless walls; so Hewlett Road remained unscathed; and, after a tedious delay, the long level reassuring note of the 'All Clear' siren would sound, and mother would guide us back to bed. ('Hewlett'? Ha: it means 'owl'. Wise mother.)

Jack, in Newcastle-upon-Tyne, had seen and heard far more devastation. Month after month of bombing; streets reduced to rubble-heaps. His home was on New Bridge Street, near the railway station and goods yard: the big warehouse there was stocked with margarine and sugar, so, when it was hit by the Junkers 88 bombers, it burned for several days, filling the air with rich sickly-sweet fumes. In 1944 came the V1s, the doodle-bugs: he said he remembered the huge explosions. And now, perhaps as a consequence, Jack was intermittently deranged: his relaxations at such times took the form of delinquencies. Occasionally, a hurling of bicycles into the Cam; once, a quick crap in the porch of the Congregational Church ('Puerile atheism my arse', he responded to my protest, 'I *needed* that crap'); very frequently, stealing books from Bowes and Bowes or LPs from Miller's Music Shop, Casey being his apprentice and accomplice (distracting the assistant), Sartre his philosophical pretext-monger. Bourgeois morality entailed *mauvaise foi*; and Sartre's definitions made *bonne foi* elusive. 'Property is theft', pronounced conniving Proudhon, having stolen the idea from Godwin. Indeed, Jack seemed capable of breaking someone's neck and experiencing no subsequent agenbite of conscience.

Once, in the Anchor pub, two local teenagers had mocked his Geordie accent. ('How*ee*ah the lads!', they repeated inanely.) At closing time, he quietly followed them outside and suddenly banged their heads together, twice, very hard, before ambling ursinely away. When I passed the youngsters, one was sitting on the kerb, contemplating the gutter in dazed bewilderment; the other was still standing but was trying in vain to staunch the glistening blood that flowed copiously from his broken nose to his chin and green T-shirt.

But those lads hadn't reported Jack, and he seemed to be a peculiarly lucky thief; so the police wouldn't arrest him, I assured myself with flickers of regret. Unless he was arrested, he was almost certain to win a First again. He'd taken a First in the 1959 Prelims and in the 1960 Part One.

Casey had taken a II.ii and a II.i respectively, and what he'd get in Finals was anybody's guess. There would have been great variations between his marks for various papers. I reckon he stood a chance of a First if he'd spend less time gazing meditatively at the ceiling of the exam room and if a sufficient number (ha! I nearly put 'if enough' there) of his scripts happened to go to examiners sympathetic to his perennial preoccupation with writers whose work was hardly central to the English Tripos. Cambridge University harboured so many eccentrics that just possibly one don might share Casey's interest in Nietzsche, Rilke, Hesse, Spengler and Akhmatova. Casey claimed that the final examination should be a time of 'culminative shared meditation, not a regurgitation'. He would probably conclude his general essay with what seemed to be his favourite quotation in recent days: '*Wovon man nicht sprechen kann, darüber muss man schweigen*': 'Whereof one cannot speak, thereof one must be silent': Wittgenstein's *Tractatus.* Not bad for a portable sign-off line that suited his character. But perhaps I could trump that with Fred Ayer: 'What you can't say, you can't say, and you can't whistle it either.' The three of us were simultaneously bound and divided, like fettered contrasting galley-slaves at the same oar; mentally we bore the crisscross scars and perennially suppurating wounds of long years of examination stress. And, like battered gladiators, we found that each apparent victory led us into the ambush of an even more difficult contest; ahead lay Finals.

These reflections gave me a surge of exam-anticipation-panic: the accelerated heart-beat and pulse, prickling armpits, drying mouth. I was tempted to turn my bike round there and then in Victoria Avenue, to pedal wildly back to my digs, open up my files of notes, and start now the revision I'd time-tabled for Sunday.

They say that intelligence-tests only test the ability to cope with intelligence-tests. Certainly such tests can't assess emotional intelligence or moral intelligence, let alone co-operative decency; and they don't allow for variability. In a vacation, sitting in a pub with a pint, I can be bovinely slow-witted, slack as a mariner in Cockayne... like one of those sprawling mariners in the picture-book I read as a child: they recline, stupefied, by the wine-stream, and long tendrils of fried sausages dangle to them from the shady branches overhead. (The tale exemplifies 'Soft Primitivism', as defined by Lovejoy and Boas.) Or if, even after I'd been taught by excellent teachers, I knew that an exam to come was only a mock exam, I'd laze and be dull and dense. But in competitive conditions where the exam mattered, my will would start to transmute malice, fear, resentment and other emotions into mental work, and the result could impress examiners who regarded the resultant essay on, say, Shakespeare as reasoned reflections on Shakespeare, and didn't recognise the covert howl or transmuted whine or stab.

Homeland texts were *Measure for Measure* and *Troilus and Cressida*. Problematic and paradoxical; authority is mocked and nobody emerges unscathed. An ideal homeland for janiform feelings and notions. Those plays weren't plot-driven, or dominated by any one character; they were vivid fierce quarrels. In *Measure for Measure*, the topics seemed to be stern justice versus mercy and, arising from the 'stern justice', attitudes to sex and death. In *Troilus and Cressida*, the topic seemed to be 'order versus appetite'. Caroline Spurgeon, in *Shakespeare's Imagery*, had blundered: she'd seen an abundance of images of food and disease, but hadn't recognised that they could both be sub-categories of the dominant category, appetite; and several meanings of 'appetite' appeared to co-ordinate *Troilus and Cressida*: alimentary greed, illicit sexual desire, anarchic ambition. Casey, when I'd tried this out on him, had reflected, cleared his throat twice, and then said: 'The cannibal banquet... in *Titus Andronicus*... could be a crudely explicit anticipation of that thematic nexus; it's... literal rather than metaphoric'; and Jack, overhearing, added: 'You could call the banquet a "reification", or "explicit thematic prolepsis"; yeah, that'll do; other examples?' He snapped his fingers under our noses. Casey cleared his throat: 'Twins... Twins in *Comedy of Errors* ... anticipate single divided selves in, yes, I think, in some later comedies... Claudio, perhaps.' I couldn't beat that, so I tried to memorise it.

Once, exasperated, Jack had snarled at me: 'You're Mister Both-and-neither!'. When I was writing an essay in my customary style, defining terms, seeking objectivity, the endeavour could seem to me at times an act, a fraud, a game of earnest articulacy by a less articulate, cruder, prolier centre. Yet if I were talking to a navvy in

39

a pub, or a lorry-driver when hitch-hiking, I'd feel that the crude proley conversation I was making was in part another act, another fraud, another hypocrisy: I'm surely more sensitive and articulate centrally than this, I'd feel: I've got my A-levels and Exhibition to prove it. Ah, not to worry. No smoke without fire, no nut without kernel; my heart / blood-consciousness / morality / politics must be in the right place, else why should I be pedalling now (after hesitation) towards Jan?

Thus I reflected, while the lead-smelly cars overtook me repeatedly in Victoria Avenue as they headed away from the city centre, until at last I could freewheel down the quiet footpath across the open breezy greenness of Midsummer Common, towards the foot-bridge over the river. I resolved to stop analysing and here just be an amateur Wordsworth – 'wise passiveness'. That tree, now... whatever it's called. Oak, chestnut? Why didn't they teach me the names of trees at school, instead of rods, poles and perches, measurements used by Cotswold yokels? Arabella would know... She scored a II.i in 1959 but only a third last year... Mind that dog-turd on the path... When I'd asked her what went wrong in 1960, she'd said: 'I told Lionel, it seems so childish, so schoolgirlish, to be still doing the prep and the cramming and mugging up the cribs, and that's what it still mainly amounts to. And when you've been on a C.N.D. march, or helped a sister with her kids, all this paperwork seems a bit irrelevant, don't you think? God knows, teaching's the *last* thing I want to do with my life!' With that attitude, she'd be lucky to get a bare pass this year, and 'bare' would be apt. But even *she* seems to be part of a general change occurring in England these days: a widespread sense that the days of deference to authority are coming to an end, and that the established order can be challenged. The Suez war (scared me, in the Navy then) was surely the sordidly conspiratorial finale of the old imperialist era. The new imperialism, American and Russian, looks more dangerous. Commander Crabb's headless corpse is an omen. A crabby future.

The breeze lifted my soup-stained gown and tugged it out behind me, and I had a momentary picture of Arabella's face under water, the current very green and swirly, so that her staring eyes just seemed emeraldy precipitations of the flow. I hastily recited Eliot's lines about Phlebas the drowned Phoenician entering the whirlpool, which exorcised the inconvenient apparition. Sign of stress perhaps.

Half-way across the foot-bridge, and nobody about. So, as was my custom, I stopped to spit down on the swans that swanned on the river near the Jesus boat-house. I chewed the bread-roll I'd brought in my jacket pocket (waste not, want not) and watched how, when I spat and missed, the swans glided towards the little ripple in the water and deigned to survey the brief bubbles for food. I'd caught a swan once, just after the end of the war, when I'd been out fishing with my father on the Avon at Tewkesbury. Bread-paste bait on a size-16 hook. I'd made an awkward cast with his heavy greenheart rod, and just as the bait touched the water, this great swan had come and – ssnap! – gobbled it down, bread, hook and catgut together, and when I yanked at the line to try to free it, the bird came flapping and hissing off the water at us in a white-feathery fury, and I'd dropped the rod and grabbed my father's arm for shelter, and he'd stood over me swinging his fist and yelling 'Bugger off!'; and, as it went flapping away down the grey river, he cut the line deftly with his old wobbly-bladed penknife. The songless bird flew low into the distance, trailing yards of line. 'Catch anything?', said my mother when we arrived home. 'Only a swan,' I said, '*and* dad said "bugger". *And* it's Sunday.'

I'd cycled over the same route so often in the previous three terms, I could almost have cycled blindfold the last part, over the common; and I reflected that if my reflections seemed to ignore Jan, that might be as it should be. One man's callousness is another man's profound repose of spirit. Hemingway in 'Cat in the Rain', Gary Cooper in *High Noon*, and even F. R. Leavis in 'Literary Criticism' at Mill Lane, had taught me to value the implicit, rather than the explicit that daws can peck at. ('Daws ...peck'? *Othello*?)

I had two pounds in my wallet, and hoped it would be a cheap evening.

# Chapter 4

ENGLISH TRIPOS, PART II

Tuesday, 23 May 1961, 9 – 12.30

CRITICISM AND COMPOSITION

Answer Question 1 and TWO or THREE others.

1. Assign approximate dates to FIVE of the following passages, giving your reasons:

...(g) So that, in short, here was but eightpence a day when they both worked hard, and that not always, and perhaps not often, and all this to maintain a man, his wife, and five small children, and yet they seemed to live very pleasantly, the children looked plump and fat, ruddy and wholesome; and the woman was tall, well-shaped, clean, and (for the place) a very well-looking, comely woman; nor was there anything looked like the dirt and nastiness of the miserable cottages of the poor: though many of them spend more money in strong drink than this woman had to maintain five children with. This moving sight so affected us all that, upon a short conference at the door, we made up a little lump of money, and I had the honour to be the almoner for the company; and though the sum was not great, being at most something within a crown, as I told it into the poor woman's hand, I could perceive such a surprise in her face that, had she not given vent to her joy by a sudden flux of tears, I found she would have fainted away. She was some time before she could do anything but cry; but after that she was abated, she expressed herself very handsomely. ...

———

Jan shared with a pretty but frown-marked girl-friend called Jenny the ground-floor flat of a dingy late-Victorian terrace house in

42

Aylestone Road, not far from the foot-bridge. The first time I'd spent the night there, Jenny had complained haughtily because I'd left my bike on the kerb overnight. 'What *will* the neighbours think?', she said. 'Balls to the neighbours: my old bike won't hurt them.' 'It's easy enough for you to say that', she persisted, 'but *we've* got to live here and you *haven't*, and I don't intend to go through another ordeal of flat-hunting with baby Patrick just because of your thought-lessness.'

All of which was typical of her prickly officiousness. She thought I was vulgar; though how an unmarried mother aged 24, albeit an infant-school teacher, could adopt that self-righteous moralistic tone baffled me. A middle-class infant-school teacher, with an illegitimate kid. I could imagine her, as the afternoon session ended, saying, as my teachers had once said, 'Hands together, children; all eyes closed. Now, say after me: "Lord, keep us safe this night," – louder! – "Secure from all our fears;" – that's better! – "May angels guard us while we sleep, / Till morning light appears."'

Yes, that's how it used to go. I tried to make allowances for Jenny. She was doubtless frustrated, was jealous of Jan's sexual luck, and was venting her mortification on my rusting Raleigh. But this evening, nevertheless, for at least the twentieth time in the academic year, I wheeled the bike into the gravelly strip that made no pretence of being a front garden, and leaned it against the hedge. The leaves were dusty and cobwebby, and a fuzzy caterpillar fell out onto my wrist.

I presented it to Jan. She'd opened the door already, all breathless, pleased, and grinning her uneven toothy grin. In winter, out of doors in her sweater and duffel coat, she'd often seemed to have no more shape than a sack of spuds. ('Sack of spuds'? That's what an angry Chief Petty Officer, Mahoney, had yelled in my ear during square-bashing at Portsmouth, in the blitz-damaged Victoria Barracks: 'You stand to attention like a sack of bloody *spuds*!'. 'Yes, Chief!'. 'Don't call me "*Chief*"! I am *not* a fuckin' *Mohican*!'.) But this evening, in her bright flowery summer dress that squeezed her waist and helped to push her breasts up into a high bulge, 'generous' was a reasonable term for her figure. She even seemed pretty, in a round-faced Shelley-Winters way. After we'd kissed, tonguing, she reflected for a moment, and said 'You had curry tonight in hall, right?' (She was constantly

43

hungry.) 'Nearly', I said. 'There was curry-powder in it, but it was some sort of pukey stew.' 'I wouldn't have minded that. Come in: I've just got to do my lipstick, then I'm ready.' She placed the caterpillar gently on the grimy window-sill by the empty milk-bottles.

Baby Patrick was writhing on the kitchen table, howling like a banshee while his mother struggled to change his nappy. The dowdy room reeked of sour shit. I sat there, trying to breathe sparsely and shallowly, and smiling fixedly in the vague direction of the struggle, to give an impression of tolerance and man-of-the-world-liness.

'Oh, Peter,' shouted Jenny over the uproar, with strained politeness and a smile more artificial than my own, 'Could you possibly do me an awful favour? I know it's vile – Patrick, keep *still*! – but could you possibly just hold his legs in the air for a moment while I clean him up? All you've got to do is hold his ankles – Oh, thanks, thanks. Now, you horrible little man – I shouldn't call him horrible really, he can't help having diarrhoea, can you, poor little pet? Was it the nasty collywobbles, den?' And so on, while I tried to focus on his head, and all the time my vision seemed maliciously to crowd its faculties into the periphery, so I could see she was dabbing at the runny brown mess of his buttocks with the corners of a ragged old nappy and then with a lot of cotton wool, dextrously turning each bit of wool this way and that, so as not to waste any but get the whole tuft plastered slimy-brown except for the tiny part gripped between her finger-tips. And even when at last he was safety-pinned into a clean towelling nappy, even then he howled and howled, decibels of sheer crass male egoistic rage, so that I felt like strangling him, not out of cruelty but out of mere love of quietness. Nevertheless, I acted calmly and dutifully, and kept a tolerant smile on my face: 'No trouble; call me in any time', I said when she thanked me. (Blake was right: 'Helpless, naked, piping loud: / Like a fiend hid in a cloud.' Title? 'Infant' something. 1794.)

And then, thank Nobodaddy, Jan was ready, and I steered her away from the brat before she could start to fuss over him; and she and I went out into the clean warm fresh evening air. Clean, apart from its pollution by nuclear tests. The USA, the USSR, Britain, and now France: crapping on all of us. Soon, Israel. Then widespread proliferation of nuclear weapons, making Armageddon inevitable.

No wonder D. H. Lawrence never had any kids. And angels

44

excrete by evaporation through their pores: 'what redounds, transpires': Milton says so: John Milton, mocked as 'The Lady of Christ's' while at Christ's College, 1625-9; apologist for dictatorship; now being scorned (for verse 'almost as mechanical as bricklaying' – cheers rise from a thousand desks) by Frank Leavis, Emmanuel College, 1919-24, currently supervisor at Downing.

# Chapter 5

1. Assign approximate dates to FIVE of the following passages, giving your reasons:

....(e) He never speaks of himself except when compelled, never defends himself by a mere retort, he has no ears for slander or gossip, is scrupulous in imputing motives to those who interfere with him, and interprets everything for the best. He is never mean or little in his disputes, never mistakes personalities or sharp sayings for arguments, or insinuates evil which he dare not say out. From a long-sighted prudence, he observes the maxim of the ancient sage, that we should ever conduct ourselves towards our enemy as if he were one day to be our friend. He has too much good sense to be affronted at insults, he is too well employed to remember injuries, and too indolent to bear malice... If he engages in controversy of any kind, his disciplined intellect preserves him from the blundering discourtesy of better, though less educated minds; who, like blunt weapons, tear and hack instead of cutting clean, who mistake the point in argument, waste their breath on trifles, misconceive their adversary, and leave the question more involved than they find it. He may be right or wrong in his opinion, but he is too clear-headed to be unjust; he is as simple as he is forcible, and as brief as he is decisive...

———

We'd each had a pint of beer at Jan's local, the Fort St George, walked across the common for another at the George and Dragon (a leafier riverside pub, sheltered by trees and bushes), and then entered

46

the arid warmth of the narrow terraced streets that led us in a winding route towards the city centre. All day the red-brick terraces had been digesting the sun, and now at dusk the bricks and paving-stones and asphalt seemed to radiate soft warmth. My shambling flat-footed stride was a bass to the snare-drum of her pattering stiletto heels. The warmth could soothe and relax you – until you remembered that it wasn't just the sunlight that was being digested by you and the surroundings; it was also the thin but persistent bomb-test radio-activity.

Jan worked in a petrol station. It was one of the experiences we had in common. Between the end of my National Service in March 1958 and beginning at Pembroke in October, I'd worked at the East End Service Station, London Road, Cheltenham; owned by the American firm Mobilgas (splendid signboard aloft: a bright red soaring Pegasus). I wore a badged cap and overalls, and, when a car came in for petrol, I had to trot up to the driver and say 'How many?', pump in the petrol, try to persuade him to have an oil-check (profit on the glass bottles of oil being eight times that on the petrol) or a squirt of Upperlube ('only tuppence, lubricates the cylinders, makes the running even smoother'; 60% profit), take his money to the till, and return to hand him the change. Prices were written on a piece of cardboard over the lever-operated till: 2-star, 4/2½d, 3-star, 4/7½d, 4-star, 5/-, 5-star, 6/-. Five-and-a-half-day week, starting at 8 a.m. and ending at 6 p.m.; Saturday, 8 until noon. Jan's job was just the same, at an Esso petrol station on the outskirts of Cambridge. Same pay: £8 a week. And we'd both been fooled initially by the Ford Zephyr, on which the petrol cap is ingeniously hidden behind the hinged rear number-plate.

So I'd told her about the Asp that solves the problems of *Hamlet.* One day this builder, 'Fat-Head', had come in, driving a car I couldn't identify. The front was like a Ford, the back like an Austin, and the middle like a Hillman. I said: 'What make of car is this?'. He said: 'It's an Asp.' I said: 'You mean, a snake, like Cleopatra's?'. He said, 'No, Pete; it's an Asp: A.S.P.: All Spare Parts.' He'd welded together parts of different old motors and spray-painted the result. And I then realised that when any student reads *Hamlet* in a standard modern edition, the student is reading not *Hamlet, Prince of Denmark*, but *Hamlet the Asp*; because the editor has taken bits of the

47

short First Quarto, bits of the long Second Quarto, and bits of the differing First Folio, and welded them together; and the equivalent of the spray-painting has been the modernising of the spelling, punctuation and stage-directions.

So: that mongrel motor owned by 'Fat-Head' had provided a more useful commentary on *Hamlet* than had A. C. Bradley's *Shakespearean Tragedy*. Hamlet the character and *Hamlet* the play are both asps: palimpsests, hybrids, welded disparates: hence all the critical wrangling. The ancient legend featuring bloody revenge has been welded to an Elizabethan analysis of mortality in Christian and post-Christian perspectives. Our Hamlet lurches between civilised reflections and harsh conduct, because the likeable modern character is repeatedly being manipulated by the old plot and is obliged at times to mimic the nastiness of his ancient namesake. Modern Hamlet says 'There's nothing either good or bad, but thinking makes it so'; but he's also forced to mimic the primitive Hamlet and say: 'Now could I drink hot blood.' Aspish. Janiform.

On this evening, Jan talked about: the working week, which now entailed a Sunday afternoon shift; the punitive price of food, and how for lunch she'd eaten only stuffing (main course) followed by custard (desert); the woeful fact that Jenny's maintenance hadn't arrived, so she hadn't been able to do the shopping while Jan was at work; the curious fact that Jan had been weeing more often recently, and the flow tended to sting; and the obvious practicality of marriage (a favourite topic). She said that Jenny (her prettiness sadly marred by those frown-lines) was worried about breast-feeding Patrick, because the *Guardian* reported that the testing in the atmosphere of nuclear weapons by the USA, the USSR and the UK – a deranged and seemingly unstoppable competition – was polluting pastures with radioactive iodine, which was then poisoning dairy products and thus the mothers' breast-milk; which could lead to thyroid cancer for the offspring; and meanwhile, for decades to come, the poisoned air would generate cancers: if fags didn't give me lung cancer, the tests might give me prostate cancer.

I responded with: the slogan 'Sir: the future of Britain is in your hands', which someone had inscribed above the urinal in the George and Dragon; the rising price of beer (sometimes two shillings a pint now); marriage as a repressive property-relationship; the injustices of capitalism; the likelihood of Armageddon; etc. If the topics were sometimes nightmarish (nuclear warfare between America and Russia being increasingly likely, with life on England, a moored U.S. aircraft-carrier, then sure to be annihilated in the first exchange of atomic missiles), there was pleasure in the companionship of our talking, the counterpointed rhythm of our strolling, and the gentle familiarity of the routine, so that if we had not been holding hands, we'd still have crossed the same quiet back-streets at the same points and the same pace.

The traffic was busier when we came in sight of the railings and the down-curved emasculatory steel spikes that guard the corner walls of St John's. Where the street narrowed, we were jostled by gowned undergraduates in twos and threes. A tooting Morgan sports-car tried to back into a parking-space that would hardly have taken a scooter. I was enjoying a diatribe.

'...And here's another instance. Back home, at the front of the house, we had a row of railings and a railed gate I used to swing on. Then one day when I was small, a bit of printed paper came through the letter-box, saying iron was urgently needed to help the Allied War Effort, to make tanks and big guns; that was the idea...' 'Mmm.' 'Next minute, a gang of men with oxy-acetylene cutters arrived and sliced off the gate and those railings as if they were dandelions and slung 'em on their clattery lorry.' 'Mmm.' 'Now what I'm asking you is, why didn't they cut off the railings round St John's College, then, or round the stately homes of England, or fucking Buckingham Palace?' 'Mmm.' 'Same with rationing. It stopped us getting foreign fruit and chocolate all right, but it didn't stop Churchill getting his brandy and cigars. He didn't even know what the bloody ration *was.*'

'*Mind* that car. Oh, do look where you're going. I think Churchill deserved every drop of brandy and every cigar. Anyway, without those railings, private gardens turned into public parks. And, can we please have a drink in the Blue Boar now?'

'If you want; yeah. Why *there*?'

'Because it's just across the road, and it's got a luxurious lavatory, and I'm about to burst, that's why.'

'And thank you, Marghanita Laski, for your contribution to this week's Brains Trust programme. I nearly rupture all my mental muscles for years, trying to win a place in this world-famed intellectual ghetto, so I can dine beneath the portrait of Edmund Spenser and enrich my soul with the precious life-blood of the world's choicest master-spirits, and all you can think of is a free and luxurious piss-house.'

She half-turned and pressed her forehead to my shoulder: she was shaking against my side with suppressed giggles while the specks of dandruff glinted in her dull-brown hair. 'Didn't you see them? That man and his wife? She just gave you a disgusted look.'

'What have I done?'

'It's what you *said*. I have to keep telling you: half the time you mumble, and then when you get warmed up talking about something, you almost shout. You've just told half the street that all I can think of is a free loo.'

'Not "loo",' I said, steering her through the revolving door of the Blue Boar, 'Piss-house!', I concluded, emerging to confront an old gent who was departing. A contemptuous glare animated his face; then we were past him, the thick carpet almost stickily soft underfoot, and on into the crowded bar.

As it was a middle-class stronghold with draught bitter at a tanner a pint more than I'd have paid at the Mill, I didn't expect to see anyone I knew; but, after Jan had returned, Piggott hailed us from a corner table and bought us a round. 'Jan, this is Dr Piggott, no relation to the famous jump-jockey, alas. – Michael, this is Jan, a petrol-pump attendant', I said with socialistic pride; and he took immediate interest in her, asking about the job, whether she was in a trades' union, whether she lived by herself, then what had brought her and Jenny from Portsmouth to Cambridge. (Answer: Jenny had passed the interview for the teaching job, and Jan, a loyal friend, had come with her to help care for Patrick.) I guessed Piggott was playing that social game of genial polite interest in passing acquaintances that comes as easily to Cambridge academics as self-pity does to me. And Jan replied quietly and good-humouredly, so that I was pleased she was acquitting herself so well, and annoyed that she wouldn't see how Piggott was just making the habitual moves of a social game (an interview posing as conversation, again). I was annoyed too, that as he asked her about her parents at Cosham (pronounced *Coss*-um, he knew), her schooling, and her friendship with Jenny, he was learning more, factually, about her than I had found out, or bothered to find out, in seven months. He even inferred from a blush-making rumble of her stomach that she was famished, and bought her a round of ham sandwiches adorned by a golden twirl of mustard on the plate-rim. (Yes, people generally liked her.).

As Piggott laughed with Jan, and his thick lenses created the illusion that he had beady-bright twinkling eyes, I leaned forward with elbows on the table and stared at my pint; a posture which, I hoped, would suggest nonchalant relaxation to Jan and a meditative intelligence to Piggott. (Blame Sterne.) In the first week of National Service, when the new conscripts had to assemble in the barracks' cinema for the Commanding Officer's regular pep-talk, we'd actually been ordered to 'sit to attention'; and row upon row of us, a whole weary cinema-full smelling of sweat and disinfectant from cleaning the Victoria Barracks' heads (from 'bulkheads' – latrines), had had to mime erect servility; and 'your beer?', Piggott was asking, to 'Eh?' from me.

'There's nothing wrong with your beer?', he repeated.

'Oh no, it's fine', I said, realising that Piggott and Jan were giving me the tolerantly patient smiles that the alert give to interrupted day-dreamers, parents to toy-absorbed infants, or the sober to the semi-drunk. To catch my mumbled answer he'd shifted forward into a tutorial posture that belied the smile, and 'Look, Jan, quick: he's doing it now', I said to her.

The thumbs stopped as she turned to look, but he didn't understand. 'I told Jan once that when you're giving a supervision, and you're trying to listen to what someone's saying, while at the same time you're thinking out what to say next, you've got a habit of clasping your hands on your lap, very properly, but at the same time prodding repeatedly at the sides of your crotch with your thumbs.'

He was disconcerted, but only for a moment. 'I suppose I should thank you for not pointing this out during the supervision, where the effect might have been a little disruptive... I suppose I do, now you mention it. The first principle of comedy, of course: you show man as a mechanism, with compulsive tics, repetitive mannerisms. Hobby-horses in Sterne, catch-phrases in Dickens...' And he proceeded to quote (first in French, then mercifully in translation) Bergson's definition of comedy: 'the postures, gestures and movements of the human body are risible precisely to the extent that this body makes us

51

think of a simple mechanism.' I nodded knowingly, having entered Bergson's definition in my notebook the first time, two and a half years ago, that Piggott had commended it. They'd been so impressively erudite, those early supervisions from him; but as it became clear that on every occasion when comedy was discussed, he would, by reflexive association, utter that same definition, as if he himself were Bergson's man-automaton, my deference had dwindled. It happened often, at Cambridge, in those days. You'd go to a lecture and think it impressive; go again, a year later, and the same lecturer is using the same script, perhaps with identical asides and 'impromptus'. Contrast Charlie Parker: Parker was never a university graduate, but on the variorum records (in the 'Immortal Charlie Parker' set of posthumous LPs) you can hear him play in rapid succession – duff takes and master – an exuberant series of improvisations on 'Billie's Bounce'; and they're all different and all vivid – But before I'd got this argument out, Piggott was apologising to Jan for our 'talking shop', and asked her if she'd seen the new Antonioni film (of course she hadn't), and said that it was a hoax, 'because anyone can film the human face against a vast background of a stone wall, or a mountain-side, but that proves nothing about alienation. Look at us, now: we'd ruin his film. We're managing to communicate rather well, don't you think?'

'Relatively', I said, taking care with the pronunciation, the word seeming oddly bulky in the mouth.

'And that's all that matters', he beamed. 'Why, even relativism's only relative, after all. I'd back Johnson against Berkeley any day. Ah, you, ah, know how Dr Johnson refuted Bishop Berkeley?'

'Do teach me', murmured Jan.

And he then gave her a miniature supervision about Johnson kicking the stone to refute solipsism, and about why Johnson carried orange-peel in his pocket; and he proceeded in his best Augustan voice to quote some of Johnson's dicta. '"Sir", boomed Johnson – imagine the crushing authority behind that "Sir" –"Sir", he boomed across the water, "Your wife, under pretence of keeping a bawdy-house, is a receiver of stolen goods!".' Then, by easy stages, Piggott introduced some mildly bawdy but witty jokes I'd heard from him before. E.g.: Academic to his wife at breakfast: 'Tell me, my dear:

52

be honest: were you faking it last night?' – 'Certainly *not*: I really *was* asleep!' Jan told him the gag about the atheist and the grizzly bear (being a militant atheist, Piggott laughed long and loud). That's the one where the atheist, having been cornered by the hungry bear and having cried 'Oh my God', says to God (who, stopping time, has promptly appeared and offered him Heaven), 'I'm no turncoat: I'll remain an atheist. But while you're there, Lord, please, please, convert that bear to Christianity.' There's a flash of light, time resumes, and the grizzly bear piously intones: 'For what we are about to receive, may the Lord make us truly thankful.'

In Piggott's mind, the bear bred pigs, for then he asked Jan what she thought of last month's Bay of Pigs fiasco. She said, 'Perhaps it's just as well it was a fiasco. Otherwise – is this right? – the Russians might have sent troops and rockets to help Castro, and World War Three could have started.' He said that though it had blundered at the Bay, the CIA was so powerful and pervasive that it not only propped up a lot of unsavoury dictators in South and Central America, it even secretly subsidised British magazines and publishers: he mentioned *Encounter* and Eyre & Spottiswoode. I suggested that Moscow subsidised the *Daily Worker* and Gollancz. He said that a dangerous cold-war development was the secret construction of 'Regional Seats of Government': locally, the big construction-site on Brooklands Avenue was creating one of them. If leading members of the ruling class believed that they could survive nuclear warfare in these bunkers, that would make those rulers more likely to approve the warfare. But they'd emerge into the ultimate waste land, totally devastated, and poisoned by radioactivity for a thousand years. So Samuel Beckett's *End Game* was the *King Lear* for our era. (I quoted Premier Khrushchoff's threat: '*Mi vas pokhronim!*': 'We will bury you!'.)

Jan said that her aunt who lived in Cumberland had told her that there had been a disaster at the Windscale power-station in 1957. The place produced material for atomic bombs. Apparently it had caught fire in October 1957 and spewed radioactive smoke and steam into the atmosphere. Thousands of gallons of polluted local milk had been taken away in tanker-lorries and dumped in the Irish Sea. Everyone involved had been sworn to secrecy, and no newspaper had ever mentioned the disaster. Piggott judged this tale to be entirely plausible, and said that a future nuclear mishap was bound to happen, given the race to build nuclear power-stations and the inevitability of human error. Jan said that the Bikini Atoll hydrogen bomb was supposedly a thousand times more powerful than the bomb that destroyed Hiroshima. He agreed, adding that a 'neutron bomb' was being developed: it would kill people but preserve property. All this, he concluded, proved the wisdom of Mary Shelley's *Frankenstein*, a novel far-sighted in its warning that that science would generate uncontrollable monsters.

I tried to deflect my thoughts from imagery of Doomsday, reflecting that when I was at school, I'd have been partly scared and largely exultant at the prospect of sharing beer and gossip with a Cambridge University lecturer whose name was on the spines of hardbacks, whose photo was on paperbacks, and who had even appeared as a pundit on television; and yet now, sometimes, he seems human, all too human, as he prods at his crotch with nervous thumbs; but perhaps the true self can live only in the printed pages which last.

Polished shoes went by, glossy against the dark matt green of the carpet. Waxy gloss of newish shoes. Not the twinkly, hard shine of old leather, not the shine my father forced into his shoes almost every evening for the next day at the shop, the dewdrop trembling at the end of his nose as he brushed and brushed the Cherry Blossom polish into the long-glazed ridges and corrugations. He'd give a month's wages just to see me talking to a real Doctor of Philosophy here, a real Lecturer of the University of Cambridge, and a Fellow of Pembroke... He'd call Piggott 'Sir', and 'Doctor' too, reverentially.

Piggott meanwhile was being warmly affable to Jan, asking about her O-levels and urging her to seek a better job than working in a garage. Once or twice he started to prod himself but checked the tic. Then he said he had to go to collect his wife from a harpsichord recital at King's: a better bet than Antonioni: 'At least Purcell isn't sentimental. And by the way, Peter, since I've now mentioned one type of self-indulgence, did you re-write your research application before you submitted it?'

'No.' (I thought I heard a familiar voice, and glanced over my shoulder, but there was no sign of Arabella.)

'That's a pity; but never mind. It's just that some members of the

54

Research Board are – let me put it this way: it can obviously be argued that research in English should be dispassionate and scholarly rather than polemically critical or contentious. However, as you will. Work hard. – And good night, Jan; I enjoyed our talk. I know you'll pardon my neurotic little mannerism, just as you forgive a person... as you would forgive a person who rubs his toe-caps innocuously, furtively but innocuously, against his trouser-legs.' And with this inconsequential observation, he went. I was puzzled. I'd never seen him rub his toe-caps like that.

With Piggott, at least, it was just conceivable that I'd gain more prestige by being seen with Jan than with Arabella. He'd been a Marxist in the 1930s, and he, as the main interviewer and marker, had been responsible for admitting Jack, Casey and me to the College.

I bought two more beers (pint for me, half for her), and we inhaled the delicious smoke of a couple of Senior Service fags. My shoes settled themselves against the crossbar of the table, and the arm-chair became more comfortable. Inside my head, alcohol started to wash away words and worry, so that objects glowed richly. The suds on the beer glinted and twinkled, almost hypnotically. But Jan sneezed.

'What did you think of him?', I asked.

'Do you really want to know?'

'I asked, di'n't I?'

'Well... Well, all right. I was thinking he'd be fun in bed.'

I straightened up swiftly. 'You must be out of your tiny mind. He'd sit on the edge of the bed all night telling you about Dr Johnson's embarrassment at the white bosoms of actresses. You're joking.'

'It's just something about him. About the way he was asking me questions. Nosing away as if he wanted to... well, get under my skin, somehow. Feeling jealous?'

'I'll sue him for attempted nasal rape. You need an analyst. They call it an Electra complex. Or more like, it's class prejudice. Humble bird like you thinks smooth accent means hidden virility. The sexual equivalent of the deferential working-class Tory voter. It's warped, thinking like that...'

'I was only thinking. You *did* ask. Don't go on about it, Pete, eh?

She gave me an ingratiating nudge. After a while, we left and had more beer at the Still & Sugarloaf under the cinema on the market-place: the wide Still & Sugarloaf basement, bright with chromium and mirrors, where the usual pair of old queers saluted us ironically from their corner; and we looked in at the Angel in Hobson's Passage, where Spike Thorpe's gang of sporting ex-National-Service-men, bellowing dirty songs in the smoke-fog, resembled a tableau from Hogarth; and out into the crowded streets at closing-time. Then up the stairs to the long room over Miller's music-and-record shop, where some Saturdays, like this one, they had modern jazz, and let people in free after pub-closing-time, for the last few minutes of the session. The shocked shades of Marlowe, Spenser, Milton, Dryden and Marvell would have deemed the place an outpost of Pandemonium, I smugly imagined.

The quintet was in full cry – no, 'cry' is inadequate: Graham Bond's alto-sax was wailing and squealing like a tortured titan, and beside him, Dick Heckstall-Smith's tenor was honking exclamatory riffs, sometimes in *chords*. Yes, he could achieve the incredible: imperious riffs in chords on a tenor-sax. Soaring over the pounding drums, the throbbing bass and the staccato piano prompting, the saxmen were urging each other in a passionately aggressive modern-jazz number with a twelve-bar-blues structure: it might have begun as 'Route 66'. Fans were yelling, joyful. Once before, at a Miller's session with the same quintet erupting boppy jazz that inclined to r-and-b, I'd said to Jack: 'How's that for a paradigm of Utopia? No written score, no boss, no Bible; just five different selves being fully expressive; and the more they seem to compete, the more in fact they're collaborating in expressiveness. Maximum individuality with maximum co-operation. Christ, a Utopia with no laws except the chord-sequence and the four-times table.' But he'd said: 'The only instrument you can play is the genital organ; you can't tell an A flat from a C sharp. And how many other people enjoy this stuff? How d'you convert chords into customs? In your Utopia, who are the counterparts to the paying customers here? And how long do you think Graham Bond can afford to play as well as this? You've been reading too much Ginsberg and Kerouac.'

So tonight I said to Jan, hopefully, pointing to the quintet, 'How's that for a model of Utopia?'

'Can't – hear you – for the glorious noise', she bleated back in my ear.

I led her to the far end of the room, where we joined bopping couples. Jan and I bopped in the fashionable restrained style. Not for us the extrovert skipping and prancing of fans who at the Corn Exchange jived to trad jazz, the followers of Chris Barber, Kenny Ball (his 'Samantha' a hit this year), Acker Bilk and their ilk. We ignored the two couples in the corner who were doing the Twist, shaking their hips in a monotonous routine even simpler than the Creep of the 1950s. We assumed the appropriate blank expressions, and, shuffling in time to the beat, I led with a hand-push at waist-level or hand-twirl rising from the shoulder, right-hand catch, left-hand catch, while she gyrated neatly to and fro, deftly recoiling, rotating undulantly back again; both of us imitating rhythm-powered automata. The more strident the music, the more effortless the movements. Admittedly, I stumbled once or twice; but her fluent turns formed an incarnate quotation: 'How can we know the dancer from the dance?'. W. B. Yeats fancied Louie Fuller, the exotic whirler; but Jan, lithely rotating, with pink glistening face, her lips parted, might have converted even Yeats to an appreciation of jazz.

Later, we walked through the mild back-streets, away gradually from the city's hubbub; and on to the common for the long, easy, beer-powered, zigzagging, arms-round-waists stroll by the black river, with the breezes cool and clean, but not chilling the benediction of booze in the bloodstream. We stopped from time to time to press together, lurching a little, mouth to mouth. And when at last the alcohol's bliss began to fade, and a pressure of urine started to nag my guts, and our feet started to remember that walking is a matter of effort and not just a weightless by-product of boppy blues numbers humming in the head, then at that moment we're crossing the foot-bridge over the sham-dead swans below, and Jan's flat is just round the corner. That's where we win the competition against thousands of frustrated undergraduates who are tossing in lonely beds all over the city.

In Jan's room, coffee, a smoke, and bed. I slurringly recited and sluggishly enacted Donne: 'Licence my roaving hands, and let them go / Behind, before, above, between, below.' Sprawling, we thus played with each other, mindlessly sensual, and enjoyed our usual relaxed, sweaty, grunty blending; and sleep overtook us before we'd even completed the slow-motion rolling-away-from-each-other aftermath.

In short, one idyll for two: by courtesy of: Tolly, Worthington, Greene King, Bass, Messrs W. D. and H. O. Wills (manufacturers of the 'Wild Woodbine' tipped cigarette), Messrs Gallagher ('Senior Service' untipped), Miller and Co., Esso petroleum, Adolphe Sax, Cambridge City Council Parks and Gardens Department, the fighter pilots (especially the Poles) of the Battle of Britain, the 1944 Butler Education Act, the London Rubber Company, Hardy's Jude, the Rochdale Pioneers, and the British taxpayer; among countless others: the causal sequences spread and multiply back into time like infinitely-deepening tree-roots.

What makes idylls idyllic is that they don't last. If you look for the Angel pub now, in 1969, you won't find it. (In its place is a Barratt shoe-shop.) But those who heard Spike Thorpe's raucous choir there, bellowing 'The Sexual Desires of the Camel' or 'Four-and-Twenty Virgins', are unlikely to complain. Nevertheless, various people we'd glimpsed in those days have seemed to flourish. Graham Bond, after taking up the Hammond organ, has led a group called 'The Graham Bond Organisation', with Ginger Baker on drums and Jack Bruce on bass. Dick Heckstall-Smith, from Sidney Sussex College, has joined a successful rock band, 'Colosseum' (vocals by Chris Farlowe, drumming by Jon Hiseman), in which he sometimes plays urgent blues choruses on two saxes *simultaneously*.

# Chapter 6

Tuesday, 23 May 1961, 9 – 12.30

CRITICISM AND COMPOSITION

...2. Discuss the peculiarities of the following poem, giving your critical opinion of it, and make, for comparison or contrast, such references (if any occur to you) to other poems as you may find to the point:

> Ah, Sun-flower! weary of time,
> Who countest the steps of the sun;
> Seeking after that sweet golden clime,
> Where the traveller's journey is done;
>
> Where the Youth pined away with desire,
> And the pale Virgin shrouded in snow,
> Arise from their graves, and aspire
> Where my Sun-flower wishes to go.

———

Chink-clink go the empties and clunk, dull clunk, go two full bottles replacing them on the sill, a few inches from my sore eyes, on the other side of the shabby curtain and the sash-window's grimy pane.

Above my throbbing head, a scarlet-jacketed bullfighter-puppet, souvenir of Spain – Jan calls him 'Escamillo' – hangs by the neck against the drab grey-yellow wallpaper. It might have been cream once, that wallpaper, a generation ago in the 1940s; but years of dust and cigarette-smoke and damp, the exhalations of beds and bodies and wardrobes, have weathered the paper to this grey-yellow. ('Escamillo'? Ha! *Carmen*.)

The jingling whirr of the electric milk-van diminishes away and out of the street, and Sunday morning's stillness reasserts itself, as though the density of the sleep and the dozing in a hundred flats and bed-sitters around were a dynamic principle, dynamic sleep-inertia billowing like an unseen fog from the curtained windows and filling the carless street. The occasional clatter, or a distant door slamming, was like a propitiation rather than an interruption; that unseen fog of slumber, sloth and stupor merely digested and absorbed the clatter, and lay the more nourished, the more resiliently dense. No, 'resiliently' is too active; try 'repletely'.

I'd slept on the inside of the single bed, nearest the wall, as was my defensive custom; so, to see my watch on the table, I had to lean over her strong white back. She grunted like a sow as I pressed on her; half the sheets and blankets were on the floor, and she lay largely bare and flaccid; together we exuded a dried-sweat aroma. Through veils of headache and myopia, shutting my blurry left eye, I looked for the time. 'So far, so good,' said the Ingersoll watch. 'I'm still intact. Remember, I am a loan from one Henry Green of Hewlett Road, Cheltenham, first hand of the gents' outfitting department, Co-operative Retail Society, High Street, Cheltenham, and am to be returned to him when – if ever – you are in regular employment, you parasite. P.S.: It is now 8.30. P.P.S.: Eight days to Finals.'

Eight days to go. And within them, a hundred texts to be leafed through, forty old essays to be reduced to their elements, a hundred memorised quotations to be exhumed and burnished, a score of definitions and epigrams to be devised or recalled. My hand rested on her warm thigh. I allocated yet again the authors to hours and the centuries to days... Don't spend longer than ten hours today on Tragedy; you've got the Greeks sorted out... This week, the Special Period needs a full day of revision, and it'll take a couple of days to summarise the material for the English Moralists...

My tool was still hotly bloated because of (a) the internal pressure of relics of last night's ale, now kidney-filtered to urine in the bladder, and (b) the external pressure of the 'electronically tested' Durex contraceptive, clinging like an optimistic leech. This ribbed sheath I tugged off – ouch! – and knotted; and I held the dangling latex in the air like a transparent pendulum above me, the creamy glob of imprisoned semen swinging to and fro... 'Most ignorant of what he's most assured – his glassy essence'... That's easy, *Measure for Measure*. 'A liquid prisoner pent in walls of glass': same play? Or a sonnet? Early sonnet. Talking about...spring? No. Summer? Better. 'Summer's distillation': that's it. 'Liquid prisoner' is magical phrasing: an assonantal oxymoron, delightful to utter. Meanwhile, shove this knotted Johnny under the pillow, and remember not to leave it there. Outraged tooth-fairies wouldn't give a tanner for it, nor would Jan.

A sterile outcome. Barren. ...And yet 'sterile' became a pro-word, favourable and not pejorative, for Pater and Huysmans and Wilde. And they're all post-Darwinian. 'Nature, red in tooth and claw'... Somewhere in that, there's a ploy for the 'Special Period' paper. A link between popularised Darwinism and the Aesthetic cult of sterility, the Aesthete reacting against Darwin... If Nature looks nasty, ugly and fertile, some people in the late nineteenth century will be attracted to the unnatural, beautiful and sterile. Therefore: Darwinism generates antithetical Aestheticism. An orang-utan fathered beautiful Bosie. Ache, ache, ache: my poor aching head.

'Where've you gone?', said Jan; and, without opening her eyes, she rolled over onto me, trailing her dangling dugs on my chest. We fondled each other for a while, lethargically; and at 9 she got up to make coffee (breakfast: coffee and a cigarette), and we had our bath. Jan sat as usual at the curved end, and I sat by the taps; and we splashed about and groped under each other for the elusive soap, while blaming each other for the greyness of the water; and I was mentally comparing Arabella's taut, lithe beauty with Jan's wrinkled chubbiness: Jan's pear-shaped breasts, rolling loosely about her chest as she laughed; the pale pink down-pointing nipples; the waxy skin-bulges; the smile-crows'-feet at her eye-edges: suddenly it was like sharing a bath with a grinning *memento mori*. I got out quickly and dried myself and pulled on my warm scruffy clothes, the thin black jeans, the dark blue shirt and the worn black cord jacket.

We arranged to meet next Saturday, and I cycled off. Round the corner, I pushed the bike wearily up the ramp of the foot-bridge. Webs of analysis wove between my ears, intermittently obscuring the concrete path. What good's a moral preference for Jan if at times like now she can seem so lardy and flaccid? What sort of revenge on Arabella if now I feel knackered? Suppose she'd been studying while I'd been boozing? Yesterday evening I could have learnt, say, six four-line quotes – and what if I fail in Finals for want of just those six quotations? How does *that* fit a moral pattern? And when I sleep with Jan, who's winning, anyway? Am I defeating her, or is she defeating me? 'You get on with your studying', said my mother's grim lined face, 'and don't you go bothering your head with bits of girls. You'll have time enough for gallivanting when you're a man earning money. You've got chances now that your parents never had, and don't you forget it. Don't go throwing them away!'

Below were two swans on a glassy drift reflecting the luminous haze of the sky; a tamed river with cemented banks, its course geometrical, its flow sluggish. The swans must think they own it. This river doesn't 'glide at its own sweet will': that's Wordsworth, 'Westminster Bridge', 1802; he wanted houses to seem asleep: rendering the animate inanimate, and vice versa, that's Wordsworth's obsession. Blake's 'London' was truer: he saw 'chartered streets' and even a 'chartered Thames': subject to maps, laws and property-ownership.

Behind me lies the dingy rectangular geometry of repetitive red-brick terrace streets with martial and imperial names: Trafalgar Street, Pretoria Road, Kimberley Road, Haig Road; built around 1900, Boer War aftermath. Ahead, there's the grey-green common leading to the treed lawns and patterned towers of a college called Jesus, the beginning of gownland. Cambridge: it's a both-and-neither city, with each part reproaching the other. Jan gets ready to spend a Sunday afternoon pumping petrol into this Austin and that Morris and this Vauxhall; and ahead, someone with ivy entangling his mullioned window high above a moat may be putting neat ticks in the margin against Dickens's description of Coketown or Blake's lines about mind-forg'd manacles. On the map, the centre of Cambridge has plenty of green rectangles, guarded by walls. (Looking at a spider, who'd think that its brain conceived that glistening delicate symmetrical mesh?)

The swans drifted aimlessly on the glaze, 'like you now, day-dreaming on this bridge', said my work-self, 'like a shagged-out extra in need of a director'; and it dawned on me that it was *my* habit and not Piggott's to rub toecaps against trouser-calves. Director: director of studies. Ha! That's the link.

In my room, I locked the door and took a can of beans from the bottom of the wardrobe; opened it and ate with a desert-spoon. (Crosse and Blackwell's beans, with black specks of spice in the tomato sauce, so they taste spicier than the redder Heinz's, richer than the paler Co-op's.) Early lunch, because I needed the cigarette which, according to my rationing system, I'd time-tabled to follow it. The sooner the lunch is consumed, a red carpet to welcome the fag-smoke, the sooner I light up and inhale hard. (Brief image flickers: Agamemnon's boots treading purple carpet.) Austere lunches like this saved the money I could later spend on fags and beer. I recalled (i) a Max Miller maxim: 'Half my money I spend on women and booze; the rest I waste foolishly'; and (ii) graffito in the Fort St. George: 'Please do not drop your cigarette-ends in the urinal. It makes them almost unsmokable.'

I chammed the beans while revising Tragedy. On Friday night and Sunday morning, by making drastic summaries of old weekly essays and long notes, I'd done the basic work of condensing plays by Aeschylus, Sophocles, Euripides, Racine and Ibsen onto note-pages which were then reduced to smaller pages with diagrams and key-words.

Check those sheets, now, Pete, while you're not carrying a handicap. Tool and balls, light and emptied. Even if today's hazy warm weather continues, it'll be three or four days before the pulses and vibrations of sexual need start to become a nuisance. I knew from bitter experience that masturbation was not only no substitute for a woman, it was demoralising: it was an admission – by emission – of failure in the competition for a female; and the conditioned guilt that followed could mar days of revision. All that insistent conditioning by teachers, preachers, boys' magazines and playground jokes: they teach you that masturbation is the sin of Onan, self-abuse, self-pollution, filthy betrayal of manhood, perverse spilling of seed, stunts your growth, makes bristles grow on the palm of your hand – ha, caught you looking! – and could make you go blind.

The Aeschylus stuff still seemed good. For *The Oresteia*: general themes: evolution of justice and the state; particular details: imagery of night, snake and net (justice as revenge, talion, female principle, Furies) giving way to imagery of light (democratic justice, courts of law, civilisation, male principle, Furies tamed as Eumenides). My gimmick, what the others won't have seen: the grumbling nurse. Orestes' nurse in *Agamemnon*, grumbling that babies shit un-

63

predictably. Not just a comic turn anticipating the nurse in *Romeo and Juliet* by nearly two thousand years, but a thematic prolepsis: she grumbles about pollution that is washable: you can clean the kid's nappies; so she anticipates what'll happen two plays later in that trilogy, when the pollution incurred by the adult Orestes in vengefully slaying his mum can be washed away by a visit to the shrine and by submission to the newly established court of the Areopagus. It's all part of the cultural shift in the definition of guilt. Sophocles' *Oedipus Rex* and *Oedipus at Colonus* centre on this. Primitive definition: guilt can be incurred involuntarily and fatally, when a bad deed entails pollution. Modern definition: guilt should be incurred only when a bad deed is voluntary. Intermediate stage: guilt as pollution, but pollution that can be expunged by rites and a jury's verdict. That stuff about the nurse's thematic significance was my idea, not the critics'; Piggott had said so.

But my Euripides ploy on *Hippolytus* and *Bacchae* looks more vulnerable now than it had looked on Friday night. I ought to check it by reading some of the earlier Euripides plays, but there isn't time. Better ask Jack at College dinner tonight what he thinks of it: he won't be able to stop himself attacking it if there's something wrong with the idea. But if it's right, he might well use it himself. And certainly I shouldn't tell him my Ibsen ploy. As far as I could see, after riffling through recent commentaries on Ibsen's dramas (in Heffer's bookshop), no commentator had realised that *The Wild Duck* ends with two suicides, not one: not only with the death of Hedvig but also, unnoticed behind the doors at the back of the stage, the death of Old Ekdal. (That's why his last words are: 'The forests avenge themselves; but I'm not afraid, all the same'. This time he *will* commit suicide; he'd funked it previously.) *Covert plotting*: I claim the patent for the phrase. Thematically it turns the play into a both-and-neither play: two-faced, like Janus: yes, 'janiform', Jack's term. The suicide of Hedvig implicitly criticises the idealistic philosophy of Gregers – that's obvious, that's what the commentators generally see; but the hitherto-unnoticed suicide of Old Ekdal criticises the cynical philosophy of Relling; so the play becomes a great symmetrical moral paradox; and that's my new angle; and there's nothing in the text to refute it, I reckon.

If it hasn't been noticed before, does that mean that Ibsen has blundered by hiding it too well? No, it proves one of the play's points: self-centred people don't perceive a tragedy even when it's happening just a short distance away from them. The moral myopia the play warns us against has been shared by the play's commentators, who, by their inadequate commentaries, have unwittingly vindicated Ibsen's insights. That would do. Snag: I didn't know Norwegian; best I could do was compare two translations to make sure that the bits of textual evidence I needed were there in both, and therefore could be assumed to be in the Norwegian. And I'd done that for the essay.

Jack says covert plotting is a great new area for lit crit: there's a book to be written on it.

A bigger snag. From past exam-papers in the College library (what a salutary discovery that was, those bound volumes of previous question-papers!) – from those papers I knew that students taking the Tragedy exam never have to tackle more than four questions; so, with Aeschylus, Euripides, Racine and Ibsen sorted out, I should have enough stuff, in theory. But I need an insurance policy: first, because sometimes in the past the Ibsen question has yoked him to Strindberg, and I've no time to add to my sole Strindberg text, *Miss Julie*; and, secondly, I'm not confident about Racine. I've plodded through the French texts of *Adromaque* and *Phèdre*, I've memorised a sufficient assortment of quotations, and I've learnt enough contextual stuff to make my answer (assuming there'll be the stock springboard type of question) look more flexible and knowledgeable than most of those written by students whose knowledge of French is as limited as mine. Trouble is, those students are in a minority. At school, I had to choose between doing O-level French and O-level German, and I'd picked German.

To get into Cambridge to read English, I'd had to take the College entrance exam, and in it I'd had to undertake a translation paper, selecting two languages. One had to be classical language, Greek or Latin: I only had Latin (standard: O-level pass at second try). The other had to be a modern language, from a choice that included German as well as French, Italian and Spanish. Of course, I'd picked German, as (although I'd been taught French as well) for O-level we were told to select just one modern language, and I'd selected German 'with oral component'. And I'd been lucky to pass at all in that language: I'd scored just 44 and two-thirds per cent, which the examiners then rounded up to the pass-mark, 45 per cent. Lucky? In the event, I'd been led (to use one of my dad's phrases) up the garden path.

At the start of this, my final year, when studying old question-papers, I realised with dismay and a sudden clenching of the guts that although you could use German to qualify for getting *into* Cambridge to read English, you couldn't use German to get *out* with a degree in English: the languages provided in the Final Exam translation paper did *not* include German. I said to Piggott, 'This is grossly unfair. If it's legitimate to use German to enter the University, you should be able to use German to exit at the end of the three years. My O level is in German, not French; so all the lads who've got French O level have an unfair advantage on me: the class of my degree in English may be dragged down by my lack of skill in a foreign language. It's unfair and illogical.' Piggott reflected for a while; then he chuckled. 'Good Lord, you're right. It's a gross anomaly. And it's been going on for years. The Exam Board must have assumed that everyone was qualified in some modern language other than German. But you're right, if there's German at one end, there should be German at the other.' 'So?', I said: 'Can the paper be changed, so that by the time I take it, German appears?' He chuckled again. 'The Exam Board takes years, even decades, to make a change like that. No, I'll pass the word up the line, and eventually something may be done; but far too late for you.' 'So what do I *do*?' 'Learn some French quickly. We're now in October; you've got seven months to mug it up. You must have done *some* French at school'. 'Yes, but not to O level.' 'Well, then, brush it up. Good for the soul. The language of love, banquets and scepticism. *Bon appétit, et bonne chance.*'

I reckoned that most of my competitors in the prospective exam would have done French at O or A level; and, because most of them were relatively well-to-do, they'd have spent weeks or months holidaying in France, as against my two hitch-hikes across the Channel. Victimised again by the world-conspiracy. The educational system loads the dice in favour of the bourgeoisie all the way from birth. Even in infancy, before school, the Farthingales and Eastbournes of this world are hearing parental conversations which are more abstract, theoretical and conceptual, and are better informed about the world and its cultures, than any that the average infant would hear at home...

Back to the Tragedy paper. What would a first-class answer on Racine look like? Probably it would be larded well with French quotations and would discuss some actual French stage-productions... I'd lacked the privilege of sitting through a theatrical evening of that vacuous never-never-land neoclassical rhetoric, only intermittently relieved by the hexameters of violence that everybody quotes – typically *'C'est Vénus tout entière a sa proie attachée'*, with an emphatic caesura after *'entière'*. My Racine notes, I reflected, are copious enough, and I'd done an alpha essay on him; but that alpha might have been the apologetic concessionary mark of a tutor diffident with Racine. Piggott had speculated that neoclassical drama was boosted when the fashion for real tennis ended, as the drama then adapted to indoor theatres, the former tennis-courts, eliciting audiences more select than you'd get in the Elizabethan open-air theatre. But then he'd apparently run out of ideas, as had Farthingale and I, and the discussion of *Phèdre* had modulated into a time-killing chat about whether President de Gaulle could fairly be called a dictator.

My essay had advocated the centrality of the labyrinth image in *Phèdre*, but Jack had told me afterwards that Turnell's *The Classical Moment* (*'Moment'*? Daft title for an account spanning decades) had exploited that already; and my ensuing inspection of the well-thumbed grimy pages on *Phèdre* in the Library's copies of Turnell's book made evident that in the exam, scores of students would be churning out stuff cribbed from there on labyrinths in Racine. Some of them would have found their way to the conclusion I'd reached in my essay: in Racine's hands, French neoclassical conventions became, in effect, the Cretan labyrinth: a formal trap with the monstrous at its heart, the monstrous being the brutally murderous passions of the over-civilised aristocrats. Then, inevitably, they'd spout about Racine's Jansenism, citing not the impious Hank but the devout Cornelius Jansen; or about the ruthless competition for places at the court of Louis XIV. When the Sun King had asked some obsequious courtier what the time was, the sycophantic buffoon had replied: 'Whatever time your Majesty desires.' No; I needed a

67

different man: a writer who had at least a three-to-one chance of appearing in the question-paper and who wouldn't put me at a linguistic disadvantage...

I lifted the heavy little alloy-framed picture of Rochester (in which the seventeenth-century aristocrat insolently makes his monkey a laureate), the picture that served as a paperweight and talisman, and leafed through my stack of old Tragedy essays. Best bet? Chekhov. Fewer students would write on him than on Racine, because he's a trickier and subtler writer than Racine. That reduces the competition. And most of those who will write on him will be tempted into waffling discussions using musical analogies; it's the standard line; and Farthingale, my public-school partner at those Tragedy supervisions, had read out that week some puke-making spiel about Chekhov's art aspiring to the condition of music. My advantage here was that during National Service I'd taken that forces' Russian course. Naturally it had been mainly parts-of-a-rifle military Russian, and not a tenth of that remained in my memory; but I would be able to pepper my exam answer with enough Russian terms to make it look as though, when I did quote the Penguin translation, I was merely doing the examiners a courteous favour. When I consulted the relevant weekly essay from my stack, I found that I'd treated Chekhov as a both-and-neither man: janiformity again. I'd used some Cyrillic script but transliterated it too:

'..."*Skuka*", "*skuchny*": the words echo and re-echo throughout Chekhov's pages, and their force eludes the reader who, dependent on the translation, sees only the familiar and relatively forceless words "boredom" and "boring". "*Skuka*" has connotations of anguish which are absent from the English counterpart: for Chekhov, it's the name of the central limbo, virtually despair, which threatens the Chekhovian superfluous man...The key to the polarities of conduct of the "superfluous men" in his plays, those heroes who oscillate constantly between being paralysed Hamlets and febrile Quixotes, is provided by Turgenev's essay, "Hamlet and Don Quixote". Chekhov had read that essay with interest, as we know from his early letters. In the essay, Turgenev claims that the two eponymous figures represent "the two ends of the axle" of the personality of civilised modern man. Hamlet is envisaged (or melodramatised) by Turgenev as the perceptive man whose very powers of perception, by revealing to him the hollowness or illusoriness of the goals of activity, inhibit action; while Don Quixote, on the other hand, can act dynamically, but at the cost of rationality: his actions are futile, his giants are windmills. A depressing dichotomy, but cogent in the vast oppressiveness of late-nineteenth-century Tsarist Russia. In his first major play, Chekhov deployed this dichotomy all too schematically and explicitly in the person of Ivanov, who himself veers constantly between extremes; but in the later plays the process of assimilation has –'

'And our fielding was *hope*lessly bad! All *o*ver the place! Four dropped catches, and –'

'Well, yes, yes, but Hamilton had a damn' fine innings, don't you think? Hmm?'

'Oh, Hamilton of *course*, but one expects that of him; one knows the batsmen are competent. But the fielding, there's simply no *team*-work –'

And the door shut after them: Eastbourne, whose room in this lodging-house was next to mine, with an ex-Harrovian lad. I tried to muster a fart by way of comment on their prattle but found that the arrangement of crap in my gut didn't permit the retort. 'Our fielding was *hope*lessly bad': they actually talked like that, in what sounded to me like mimicry of an upper-class accent; but for them it wasn't mimicry. 'Our' became 'ah', 'over' became 'eh-*oo*-vah', and 'bad' became 'bed'. Sometimes it hurt my ears like chalk squeaking on a blackboard. Many of them evaded National Service. And their fathers own the country, and can dodge taxation by endowing colleges.

Work. Beat them in Finals.

By 6, I'd completed the job that Chekhov's tuberculosis had started, draining the life out of the man. I'd shrunk him to a single sheet of file-paper bearing plots reduced to diagrams and name-clusters, accompanied by some dates and quotations, and a few statistics on economic tensions in late 19th-century Russia, to prop the 'superfluous man' argument. As a final salvo, I'd give the examiner one of the Russian proverbs we'd been taught at J.S.S.L.: in literal translation, it was 'When it rains, one does not re-roof the cottage, and the roof is not leaking when it does not rain' (which fitted *The Cherry Orchard*'s passive gentry well enough): but the examiner would get the Cyrillic version and no translation. Plenty of Cambridge lecturers fire Latin and Greek at the undergraduates without translating; so what's sauce for the goose... Or the dodos. On Mauritius, the dodo became so used to the easy life, finding food on the ground, that its wings became stunted and useless; so, when men with guns arrived, the dodo couldn't fly away, was a sitting target, and became extinct. Chekhov's gentry resemble the dodos, glimpsing their nemesis but lacking the ability to avert it. That's usable.

I Sellotaped the sheet to the wall beside my bed, in readiness for a memorising session later that evening. I stared at the Sellotape for a minute or two, recalling the Senior Tutor's injunction. A few days into my first term at the College, the Senior Tutor had made a speech in Hall to the assembled new undergraduates. Most of it had been predictable genial platitudes: he hoped we'd enjoy our stay, work hard and play hard, appreciate the wonderful opportunities, admire the chaste Wren chapel if not the Waterhouse Gothic library, and you play ball with me and I'll play ball with you, et cetera; but, as a peroration, the distinguished old gent warned us of the perils of 'adhesive papers and plastics, as, for example, popular proprietary brands such as "Sellotape".' He reckoned there was no harm in our putting maps and art-reproductions on the walls of our rooms, provided that we didn't stick them on with adhesive stuff, because the adhesive left unsightly and enduring marks on the walls. We should, he said, fix the pictures with drawing-pins. Casey had whispered to me that even here, little things please little minds; so much for citadels of learning; and Jack said afterwards the bloke had probably been reading *L'Etre et le Néant* and had become infected by Sartre's morbid fear of the viscous. At least we didn't have to sit at attention.

So here I was, two and a half years later, in a college lodging-house where the notice over the gas ring says 'Gentlemen are Requested to Refrain from the Use of Frying Pans, Owing to the Mess and Smell which are Inevitably Occasioned', stopped by a flicker of guilt because I hadn't taken a minute to find some drawing-pins. Yet if I hadn't spent the night before with Jan, probably the pleasure of hammering home the pins with a shoe-heel would have prevailed. Little things... Ignis fatuus.

Chekhov had foreseen the Russian revolution: *The Cherry Orchard* makes that clear. Lopahin buys the estate where his father and grandfather were serfs; and the chopping down of the cherry orchard (an orchard picturesque but unproductive) itself portends the brutal end of the line of Tsars. Now Chekhov hung, taped on the bare yellow wall by the bed; just as the 'Buddies and Comrades' picture had once hung over

70

the table at Alan's house. Alan Wills had been in my class at primary school; I often went round to his house to play; and one morning – near the end of the war, it must have been late April 1945 – over the kitchen table was a picture that his mother had stuck up with sticky paper, the brown sticky paper that in war-time the people put across the windows in Union Jack patterns to reduce the shattering if bombs fell nearby. She'd cut the picture out of a tabloid paper, the *Daily Mirror* probably. It showed a bridge on the Elbe in Germany on which the vanguard of American troops from the west had just linked up with Ukrainians from the advancing Red Army. They were grinning, all friends. The caption was 'Buddies and Comrades – at last the Big Link-Up', or something like that. I felt mild envy at the muddly cabbagy-smelling informality of Alan's house, in which such liberties could be taken with newspapers and walls, in contrast to the shabby austerity of my own home, where my mother battled daily against dust, soot and cobwebs.

Buddies and Comrades, and then the Cold War, and the Korean War, and now Armageddon impending. Collaborators overnight become competitors.

And how d'you make a fully co-operative, therefore classless (therefore necessarily cashless) society in one country, let alone in Europe? If you try to build it by compulsion, repression breeds a repressive resentful society. If you try to build it by persuasion and education, you find that the educational system reflects and instils élitism and competition. The most affectionate human beings are not the best educated or most intelligent; sometimes, indeed, they are people with congenitally marred intelligence. And if the economy becomes cashless, it becomes insular, operating at a primitively low level; back to the Dark Ages. As Piggott mischievously pointed out, William Morris cheated: his English Utopia in *News from Nowhere* is radiant with sunshine, and somehow maintains an import trade: Tokay wine, Latakia tobacco. (What's the international currency, then: carrots?) Nevertheless, part of me still relishes Wilde's aphorism: 'A map of the world that does not contain Utopia is not worth having.'

But that stuff would keep for the ' English Moralists' paper. What happened to Alan? Haven't seen him since I was ten and passed the exam to win a place at Grammar School. Back to Chekhov. Memorise. His dates, 1860-1904; *Ivanov*, 1887. Work to ward off the recurrent tremors of exam-fear...

71

# Chapter 7

ENGLISH TRIPOS, PART II

Wednesday, 24 May 1961, 1.30 – 4.30

SPECIAL PERIOD OF ENGLISH LITERATURE FROM 1880
TO 1910

...8. 'Then, as now, critics were anxious that "Life" should not be
impoverished in favour of "Art". But then, as now, the "life"
that matters to literature was less endangered by Art, however arty, than by Ideas.'

Discuss with reference to ONE OR TWO authors of
the period. ...


Thursday, 25 May 1961, 9 – 12

THE ENGLISH MORALISTS

...15. How far has your understanding of any ONE of the
following pairs been enriched by your reading of English
literature? You may confine your answer to ONE author if
you wish:
(a) Nature and Grace.          (d) The Right and the Good.
(b) Love and the Law.          (e) Agape and Eros.
(c) Virtue and Merit.

———

It was the short grace again. '*Benedictus benedicat*', proclaimed a
fruity voice from the high table; and the hall at once reverberated to
the thunderous clumping of hundreds of shoes as the rows of students
clambered over the long oak benches and sat to eat.

Jack assailed his food as usual like a starving cannibal. He'd finished his soup before I was half-way through mine, and while Casey on his other side was still blowing diffidently at his first spoonful.

'You and Casey are doing your best to construct a bedroom farce', said Jack cheerfully, ripping his bread-roll in half so that brittle crumbs confettied the polished black oak of the table.

'Go on.'

'Tell him, Casey', he said.

'The negotiations are at a delicate stage', murmured Casey, sipping fastidiously.

'*What* negotiations?'

Sip. Sip.

'Friend Casey, intrepid as ever, entered Newnham this afternoon on the hunt for Miss Arabella.'

I tried to keep my face inexpressive but felt it redden. 'What was his ploy? "I'm your new master, the second Nietzsche, whip in hand: now drop 'em"?'

'Enlightened altruism', said Casey, sipping.

'Friend Casey', Jack continued through a mouthful of half-chewed bread, as though he were an interpreter between two foreigners, 'as far as I can make out from his veiled comments, calls on Miss Arabella and, at her doorway, says to her: "I understand that comrade Green of Gloucestershire (known, unfortunately, to us both) is not taking you to the May Ball. I, madam, by merest chance, possess double ticket to said May Ball; and I have long been a devoted admirer of your parts, madam, from afar, ever since fate first entwined our eyebeams at Piggott's party, and" – for fuck's sake, you finish the story, Casey; I want to eat.'

'And with that', said Casey, 'a man inside laughs, stands up, and says he's her... fiancé. Her fiancé! A frame-up. You craftily kept quiet about him, I notice. No wonder... No wonder you stopped seeing her yesterday. A six-foot-two polo-playing financier fiancé.'

'Oh, great! What a scene! I'd have given quids to see it. I've outployed the master, and I'm the one who's supposed to be the chief victim in the conspiracy.'

'And to complete Casey's mortification – wait for it – the two of them then took him for a so-called spin in the fiancé's MG, MGA to be precise, and dropped him off at the College like Good

Samaritans.'

'He's garbled the story', said Casey, shaking his soup-spoon at me across Jack's plate. 'Hopelessly. I didn't say anything about... mortification. I admit that matters are... a little trickier than you first gave me to suppose, but in the long run... or protracted lope ... there should be no difficulties.'

'Face it', I said. 'You're on an impossible pitch. The fiancé'll be taking her to the May Ball anyway; so you've had it.' I felt genial towards little Casey, now the object of patronising consideration by Jack and me; perhaps I'd over-rated him. While I'd been compiling my Chekhov notes, he'd been humiliated in a wild goose chase after my cast-off.

For once, Casey seemed to acquiesce in the patronising. 'I might have been killed', he grumbled. 'Those green sports-cars only have seats for two. The folding roof was down. I had to perch on... a sort of luggage rack behind, over the petrol tank. The man drove like a dandified cretin: at last I understand Marx's attitude to Lassalle. Every time we came to a corner, I had to lace my arms and legs through the bars on the rack –' *'And legs*? Pull the other one', I interjected – 'or I'd have been thrown into the air. Most of the time I was clinging flat... with my eyes shut. Stupid goats. *Untermenschen.* When my *Putsch* prevails, they're on the black-list.' Then he turned back to his soup, and found that his bowl had been deftly removed by the young waiter, the spotty one with the Tony Curtis hair-style (the D.A. it was called, 'Duck's Anatomy', or more familiarly 'Duck's Arse').

I felt so genial that, after a brief hesitation, I confided to Casey that I hadn't known a visit from Lionel was imminent. Casey, responding with unusual magnanimity, offered the theory that Arabella had been so distraught after I'd left her that she'd phoned Lionel and begged him to drive down to console her. So, by way of celebration, I promptly presented to Casey and Jack the ploy on Euripides that I'd planned to conceal from them.

The basis of it was this recurrent problem: The naturalistic view of Euripides' gods seems to be contradicted by the atheistic view, so that critical interpretations are commonly either consistent but inadequate (they maintain one view or the other) or else adequate but self-contradictory (since they claim that the gods are, for

74

Euripides, both real internal psychic forces and unreal external immoral deities). The way to resolve the conceptual problem is to imagine something like this: 'Euripides is saying: "I'll dramatise the gods as though they were external, autonomous, anthropomorphic beings, and you'll see that as such they are morally contemptible, not worth belief (being jealous and vindictive). That'll show the folly of your primitive anthropomorphic conception of the gods. But the plot-structure will also say it's no good walking down the street and avoiding all the temples, because Aphrodite-feelings and Artemis-feelings are, in humans, real, important and potentially destructive.""

'But that's just the naturalistic interpretation', said Casey.

'No: that would say that Euripides says we should ignore the temples, or chuck stones at them. But what he says is that we should go down the street and go into each temple we come to. Get it? At the Aphrodite temple we pour a libation, splash, in a pious-enough but not credulous way. We say: "Aphrodite, I know bloody well you don't exist as an autonomous anthropomorphic being with a human-type moral nature. But I pour this libation to remind myself of the need to respect and come to terms with the Aphrodite-impulse in myself and others. Thank you, kind man who put up this temple, because without it I might have got hubristic or forgetful about my Aphrodite-impulse, which I should intermittently serve. In short, I'll have a good poke now and again." And in your personal life, you shouldn't do a golden mean, steering a middle course, sort of caper, because that'd be like going down the middle of the street without entering the sodding temples. You got to be fully but intermittently an Aphrodite-man, an Artemis-man (athletic-austere), and so on. Okay?'

Jack was wolfing down the roast potatoes of the second course. 'What about Apollo, then?', he growled without looking up, spitting gravy from the 'p' of 'Apollo'.

'He's a bit tricky. You go into the temples of deities that have a psychic and physical aspect – sexuality with Aphrodite, chaste athleticism with Artemis. But in *Electra* Euripides seems to say that when gods don't have that sort of aspect, then you can thumb your nose at them as primitive morally-unsatisfactory figments of men's imagination. So Apollo is just a sort of word-god who talks crap, a sort of Hellenic Farthingale.' 'You're all right with *Hippolytus* and *Bacchae*', said Jack, 'but you're in big trouble with *Alcestis*, brother.'

'Don't know it.'

'Are you leaving those two spuds? Because I'll have 'em, if you are. There. – *Alcestis* gives you a benevolent humane Apollo, and not the duff Apollo you've got in *Electra*. Roast spuds, I love you.' ('Spoods', he pronounced it: he deliberately exaggerated his Geordie accent when he was gloating over food.) 'Look', he mumbled, tonguing potato into a corner of his mouth, 'It'll do, but if you use it in the exam, you'll have to do it like this: Offer it as an interp of *Hippolytus*; say that *Bacchae* confirms it; and add that the principle of the interp doesn't apply to early – say "relatively immature", or something like that – works like *Alcestis*. That's your cover. If you don't do it that way, you could be up shit creek unpaddled. Waste not, want not', he added, scooping the brown gravy with the flat of his knife and licking it off. 'Come on, Casey. Comment, man. *Think*.'

Casey cleared his throat and murmured words to Jack that I couldn't hear through the general din of clattering cutlery and jabbered conversations all round. Jack then explained to me that Casey had said: (1) He couldn't hear half what we'd been saying, because of the disgusting noises of communal eating; (2) He would be inclined to endorse Nietzsche's view of Euripides (in *The Birth of Tragedy*); (3) He hadn't yet read sufficient Euripides, having preferred during the course to meditate at length over *The Oresteia*; and (4) He had come to the anti-Dionysiac conclusion that Miss Arabella was psychologically – and probably physically – a virgin.

When Jack leaned over to relay all this to me, I could smell the exhalations of sweat and heat coming from him, breathing out through his shabby and too-tight corduroy jacket. The enjoyment of eating or the excitement of working on other people's ideas would each have made Jack sweaty; when both combined, the wafts from his fleshy mass were pungent. Jack after an argument smelt like I did after fornication. I tried to memorise what he'd said about Euripides, but jostling the words in my head was the notion that Jack's aloofness from sexual pursuits over the years was perhaps achieved through an ability to translate sexual energies into mental ones and into simpler appetites, for food, for beer.

76

'Talking of virginity', I said to him, before I could stop myself, 'how have you managed to hang on to yours all these years?'

'Give us a kiss and I'll tell ya', he snarled in my ear. I flinched. The aged waiter took our plates; Jack and I both said 'Thanks' to him, by reflex, and got a blank stare in return.

After the meal, Casey and Jack proceeded to the Mill for bar-billiards, but I found the courage to say I was going back to my lodgings to work. As I cycled along Trumpington Street past King's College, I reflected that Casey had vindicated my decision about Arabella, Jack had validated most of the Euripides ploy, and their joint reassurances had given me the confidence to leave them for now. Sometimes it seemed that what passed for friendship between us was just an intermittent buttressing of our various kinds of isolation. It was good, for now, to cycle away from them, from Casey's quiet spideriness and Jack's sweaty voracity. 'Thank God I'm normal', I thought, recalling Jack's retort; and isn't 'Thank God I'm normal' a quotation from a play?

King's College Chapel was proudly reminding the passing traffic of itself, a vast stone ark that had voyaged through time from the 15th century to run aground, intact, arrogantly sublime and soaringly stupendous, on level lawns opposite the chemist's shop where I sometimes reconciled Aphrodite and Artemis by purchasing Durex Gossamers, half-a-crown for a packet of three.

In the window of Bowes and Bowes' bookshop, Lady Chatterley, exonerated at the Old Bailey six months ago, was now on open sale: the adulterous lady, in her hour of peril betrayed by heterosexual Leavis (who wouldn't testify on her behalf) but befriended by homosexual Forster (who bravely did bear witness). The prosecutor had rashly said to the jurors: 'Is this a novel that you would wish your wife or your servants to read?'

# Chapter 8

ESSAY

Write an essay on ONE of the following subjects:

...6. 'Comedy is necessarily cruel.'
 7. 'Loyalties are the enemies of principles.'
 8. 'Contemporary – what is contemporaneity?'...

———

The track seemed to be a dried-up river-course, winding up a long hillside under the glaring sun. The other two travellers seemed to be only one, sometimes. We were rivals in a race, and I wanted to rest. But when we got out of the open gritty desert into the jungle where the river-course became more rocky and precipitous, where the polluted sky was screened by the mesh of grey waxy leaves, then we sensed that we were being watched and might be attacked; the wind that never reached us called sniggers out of the creepers and trunks; and defensively, as the fear grew, we banded closer together, and actually began to help each other, now with pushing and heaving, now with pulling and dragging, up over the dusty rock-falls in the bed of the long-dry rapids where black crabs scurried sideways. The sharp grit stung knees and hands. As our fear of the hidden watchers grew, so in proportion grew our readiness to help each other up the boulder-falls; sometimes, when there was a brief avalanche of shingle and stone from under our feet, we rolled back together in a tangled Laocoön of arms and legs, but our curses resembled cheers. Yet when we reached the top, out of the muddle of jungle and into bare open desert again, the attackers had faded away into the landscape or perhaps had never existed, and the three of us gradually straggled away from each other, snarling to ourselves. A pebble hit the back of my leg, stinging; I picked up a heavy stone and hurled it towards them; other stones pattered in a shower on the shingle of trampled sun-glasses in front of me. I threw more back, and was hit on the ear;

I started to fall, but a heavier stone hit me there again, and I heard my skull crack like glass; with a last effort I forced myself to sit up out of the desert and into white sheets and a sliding-away blanket; but the landlady went on tapping at the outside of the door and calling 'Eight o'clock, Mister Green! You asked for a call at eight! Eight o'clock!'

'Thank you. All right. Thank you.' Born again, trembling, into cold air. But, on with the stress-harness: 'Chekhov: dates, 1860 to 1904', I muttered, dressing; '*Ivanov*, 1887; Ivanov and Anna; Sasha; Jeesus, it's cold; Dr Lvov; Zanaeda, moneylender; quote, Ivanov to Lvov, "Build your whole life according to a commonplace pattern." Shit. "Build your whole life according to an ordinary, commonplace pattern... Don't go fighting with windmills." End quote. The link with Turgenev.'

Seven days to go. Trembling.

# Chapter 9

## THE ENGLISH MORALISTS

...16. 'By far the most valuable things, which we know or can imagine, are certain states of consciousness, which may be roughly described as the pleasures of human intercourse and the enjoyment of beautiful objects.' (G. E. Moore).
What effects has this observation had on English literature?

———

Farthingale was reading in his best 'poetry' voice: a surge of melodious sanctimony, the syllables quivering with enacted emotions:

"'While I stand on the road*way*, or on the pavements *grey*,
I hear it in the dee-eep – heart's – *core*.'"

('Stand' became 'stend', 'hear' became 'he-ah'.) He continued to read his essay: "'It was when he was true to those haunting voices in 'the deep heart's core', not to the clamour of politics, or the quaintness of occultism, that William Butler Yeats speaks most truly – and" – and – mourningly? No, I'm dreadfully sorry, I can't for the moment read my own handwriting here. How silly. Just a moment. "Movingly"! I'll do that last bit again. ... "that Yeats speaks most truly and movingly to us: in such memorable poems as 'Ephemera', 'The Song of the Happy Shepherd', and, of course, the immortal 'Lake Isle of Innisfree'."'

He bowed his head as though in prayer for a moment over that last paragraph of his weekly essay. His after-shave lotion scented the air.

Piggott, hands clasped in his lap, prodded at himself with his thumbs and gazed wearily towards the window. A gardener was pushing a heavy roller over the weedless turf of the Fellows' Garden, striding in strange slow-motion against the roller's weight.

It's going to be a weak supervision, I thought. One third of the hour's gone already, wasted and more than wasted while Farthingale recited his essay. Daylight robbery. Piggott is paid (from our fees) to give us an hour of his wisdom every Wednesday, but invariably he begins by getting one or the other of us to read out an essay. He ought to pay *us* for those first twenty minutes. The worst of it was that Farthingale seemed to believe his own waffle: his personality harboured some kind of alchemist's stone that could transmute his facile romanticism into judgements he really seemed to cherish. The essay-title set by Piggott had been: 'By means of an analysis of a few poems, discuss Yeats's development.' I guessed from Farthingale's selection of examples that he hadn't read beyond the first fifty pages in *Collected Poems*: yet to listen to his tremulous delivery, you'd think he believed every word he wrote; and by now, probably, he did. Piggott reluctantly retracted his gaze from the man with the heavy roller, and stubbed his cigarette.

'Ah... Thank you, Richard. Ah... Peter: have you any comments to make on this – certainly eloquent – paper?'

'Lucid', I said. A reference from Piggott would be backing my research application. So: 'Narrow range', I added; 'and I think the essay over-praises the early work.'

'Narrow range, yes. But I see that *your* essay looks rather short.'

'It's only a short one, because I don't reckon I'll be writing on Yeats in the exam.'

'And why not?'

'Well, tactics. The good poems have been worked over very thoroughly by critics; and, given Yeats's range and diversity, it's hard to find short cuts, ploys that'd fit nicely into the less-than-forty minutes we've got for each question.'

'"Ploys"! I've warned you before not to use that reductive jargon. This is a university, not a ping-pong club; we're discussing poetry, not shove-ha'penny; and the Tripos, though essential, is not the *raison d'être* of the curriculum. So: Yeats offered you little scope for... gambits. Which poems *did* you condescend to write about?'

'I used "The Two Trees" to show some weaknesses of the earlier verse, and "The Second Coming" and "Crazy Jane Talks with the Bishop" to show the strengths of the post-Pound material.'

'"The Second Coming"? Well, perhaps we might look more

closely at it now. (Thank you again, Richard, by the way. I'll add some written comments to your essay later.)'

He reached for the volume on his coffee-table, and he didn't have to look up the page-number in the list of contents or the index, he just scooped at the edge of that book with the tip of his middle finger, and it flopped open, as it must have done in a hundred supervisions previously, precisely at the much-annotated and dog-eared pair of facing pages that bore 'The Second Coming'. He then did a fluent Ellmann-type analysis of it, giving the analysis an air of spontaneity by occasionally strolling to his bookcase to take down a relevant book – *A Vision*, once, and later *Thus Spake Zarathustra* to cite a parallel between a passage in Nietzsche and the desert description in the poem. Farthingale was scribbling notes, like a reporter, but Piggott interrupted and gently persuaded him to define some of the ironies and ambiguities, and Farthingale then praised the evocative aptness of the verb 'slouches' in the concluding 'slouches towards Bethlehem to be born', claiming that 'slouches' (in contrast to, say, 'strides' or 'strolls') suggests arrogantly weighty and loutish self-assurance. He gave me an oddly critical glance as he said it.

Once, Piggott was galvanised into energetic life by the ringing of the black telephone on his desk. Evidently an old colleague of his was coming to Cambridge on a brief visit, and for a few moments Piggott joked and laughed as though we weren't there. Then he put the 'phone down, and very slowly walked back to his arm-chair; he looked at the pages for a while without seeing them; then, with a deep breath, he resumed that gentle, droning tone of exposition. Precisely at the end of his discussion of that poem, the ivy-muffled bell in the red-brick Waterhouse library-tower struck twelve. Piggott wished us luck in Finals, and the next pair of undergraduates walked into the smoke-vapoured room for *their* supervision on Yeats. Mentioning Finals made me feel the weight of exam stress like a throbbing leaden crown on the brain, and a faint trembling briefly vibrated in my hands and knees.

Outside, the sky was overcast; but the lawn of the Fellows' Garden shone in alternating silver-green and grey-green stripes where the heavy roller had come and gone systematically from side to side during the hour. For centuries, undergraduates had been forbidden to walk on the lawn, so that the Fellows, strolling on it in conversation, could relish privilege.

In Piggott's room, Eastbourne began to read aloud an essay on Yeats's development.

# Chapter 10

Wednesday, 24 May 1961, 9 – 12

FRENCH AND ITALIAN SET BOOKS AND UNSEEN
TRANSLATION

...4. (i)                           *La Musique*

La musique souvent me prend comme une mer!
            Vers ma pâle étoile,
Sous un plafond de brume ou dans un vaste éther,
            Je mets à la voile;

La poitrine en avant et les poumons gonflés
            Comme de la toile,
J'escalade le dos des flots amoncelés
            Que la nuit me voile;

Je sens vibrer en moi toutes les passions
            D'un vaisseau qui souffre...

———

20 May 1961.

            'Ah swear, ah swear, mah honey,
                        Bah all the stars up above,
            Ah'd give every cent of mah money,
                        If ah only won –'

The bluish circular glow appeared, zigzagged in the dark like a will-
o'-the-wisp, and disappeared.

                        'If ah only won –'
                              84

The glow of the watch-dial hovered and zigzagged. To notice the banality of the lyric, that's only a Class II.ii or III response.

'If ah only won – yo' – lo-o-ove!'

To see the ironic counterpoint of the lyric with what we're doing, that's more like II.i. And the Class I response might be to think that life is imitating a cliché of 20th-century literature. Eliot and his Shakespeherian Rag, Aldous Huxley, Graham Greene – they've all used this type of facile juxtaposition: popular lyrics, supposedly representing modern vulgarity and decadence, juxtaposed with activities amatory, sexual or poignant. The mere passage of time, however, often renders the vulgar valuable, just as it sometimes converts junk into antiques. (There's hope for me yet.)

I halted the glow in its orbit, my hand cupping her loosely-flopping breast. Horace Batchelor interrupted the pop-chart-assailing celebrations of Aphrodite to offer all listeners to Radio Luxemburg his amazing Infra-Draw method. Thousands of pounds have been won on the pools by the amazing Infra-Draw method. Just write to Mister Horace Batchelor, Keynsham, spelt K.E.Y.N.S.H.A.M., Keynsham...

Eleven p.m.

'I've got to go now', I whispered; and in the dark I felt Jan's shoulder shrug against my chest. But I kissed her in a manner I deemed gentle, forgiving and understanding.

She'd been oddly withdrawn and intermittently resentful during that Saturday evening. I'd arrived late; Jenny had already gone out to meet her boy-friend; and we had to stay in and baby-sit. Staying in suited my plans quite well, not merely by being cheap but also because it meant I'd be sober when I returned to my lodgings at 11 to revise. Jan wasn't going to see much of me: we had only two hours together; and I could understand her mood. It was flattering: I could read it as an almost naïve indication of her need for me. But, of course, as retaliation for my late arrival, she'd had to raise the matter of the May Ball yet again.

The May Ball takes place, with curious Cambridge logic, in June; but the tickets are on sale before Finals. Jan said she could get hold of a double ticket at cut price and would pay her share.

'We had this argument three weeks ago', I'd said. 'It isn't the *price*, it's the *principle*. The May Balls are the bacchanalia of the bourgeoisie. They go prancing around the streets and colleges in their penguin outfits and ball gowns for everyone else to gape at. Ah, be reasonable, Jan: I'm prepared to sell out, up to a point, but the May Ball's where I draw the line. It means hiring a dinner suit, which is a badge of privilege and ostentation, yeah, and it means a bloody boring night mixing with all the debs and stockbrokers' sons and Eastbournes and Farthingales and budding capitalists in the university. I've heard all about it, I trust my instincts, and my instincts throw up at the idea. And you ought to know better. Where's your sense of class gone? I can understand *Jenny* wanting to dress up as an aristocratic scrubber, but I thought *you*'d be above it –'

'Oh, you're talking *cock*!', she interjected. 'It's nothing to do with politics. It's fun, and I fancy some of it, and I don't see why you shouldn't. They let you eat as much as you want, and there's free champagne; and they have jazz bands too. The Caius Ball's got Alex Welsh this –'

'Trad, Dixieland –'

'I know he's trad, but you said he was good.'

'Even if it was Dizzy Gillespie, I still wouldn't dress up in a penguin suit for him or anyone else.' I didn't point out that, principles aside, going to the ball entailed staying on at Cambridge after the end of term, when it was a darn sight cheaper to get home quick.

She tried again. 'Just this *once* couldn't you do it, to please me? Go on. It won't do any harm.'

'When the exam's over, we'll go to any film, any theatre, any dance-hall you fancy; but I'm not going to sell out to the sodding snobs.'

'But *you're* being the snob, Pete, not *them*: you don't sell your soul by hiring a dinner jacket. You'll be doing it on degree day. You're blind sometimes. And I said I'd pay my half; I can borrow the money.'

'I tell you it isn't the bloody money. All right, so I'm stupid. You can like it or lump it, but that's the way I feel and I'm not shifting. Now talk about something else, eh? Have another fag.'

She started to say something – 'If you don't' – but cut it short. 'Have another fag and forget it', I repeated. We were sitting on the

86

bed, and a spring squealed like a squeezed fart as I leaned towards her. It was then she'd switched on Radio Lux as a way of showing defiance (but not so loudly as to waken the infant). 'Ah'm in love', mooed Elvis; 'Ah'm all shook up'. I considered explaining to her the symbolic force of the gamble I'd made, the risk I'd taken, by still coming out to spend two hours with her, so close to Finals. (And I was a day behind schedule, in spite of having saved time by jettisoning Arabella and by dodging several bar-billiard sessions.) But what was the need? She'd surely understand that.

I stroked and fingernailed two flecks of dandruff from her hair. 'Quarrelling doesn't suit us, Jan. Let's turn off the light and go to bed while there's still time. Come on.'

'Aren't you really going to stay the night?'

I explained gently that it was in her interests as well as mine for me to get back early to revise. If I did well in Finals, then I'd be accepted for research; and then I'd be in Cambridge – and with her, of course – for three more years. It was, perhaps, flatteringly romantic that she seemed to prefer a full night now to a hypothetical three years in the future; I could see that from her point of view, a bird in the hand was worth two in the bush; yet the thought of my goal's status becoming that of the 'two in the bush' made me all the more determined to leave promptly.

In bed she was tense, her entry dry and tight, so that the friction, while making me sore, made her wince repeatedly. (I didn't have a Durex; saved ten pence.)

'I yearn for your kiss, / A heaven of bliss', howled a crooner on Radio Lux.

'Ow – ow – *ouch*!', said Jan, wincing. In compassion, no doubt, I stabbed harder and quicker; and prudently I pulled the stabber out at the well-timed last moment and it spurted jissom over her chest. I sank back and let caresses send my wrist-watch in vagrant orbits above her breasts, the bluish glow of its luminous numbers and hands flickering out of sight and reappearing like an ignis fatuus. Pedantic phrasing formulated itself: 'such intercourse is the stabbing that confirms the male's victory in the competition intrinsic to the relationship'; phrasing mocked by the crooner:

'Ah swear, ah swear, mah honey,

Bah all the stars up above...'

But a little later, as I climbed on to my bike to pedal away, she dashed across the pavement to hug me and wish me luck.

'I'll be off the rack by noon on Thursday', I said, 'and then I'll have time to prove I'm human.'

'You don't need to prove anything to me.' Her cheek seemed wet. I sensed in her tone the embarrassing emotion, and retreated from it as if it were taboo. ('Woe to the man whose heart...')

From the radio, through the open doorway, Cliff Richard and the Shadows serenaded my departure with 'You are My Theme for a Dream', but quietly, to let the infant Patrick sleep on. To shut out the memory of Jan's tears, her tone, and the echoes of such sentimental pop music, I envisaged an improvement to the lyrics of 'I Got Rhythm': namely, 'I Got Jissom', sung and danced by a leering priapic Gene Kelly, exuberantly accompanied on violin by Stéphane Grappelli, volatile virtuoso; and I hummed it as I cycled away.

# Chapter 11

## CRITICISM AND COMPOSITION

...1. Assign approximate dates to FIVE of the following passages, giving your reasons:

(a)     But then the thrushes sang,
  And shook my pulses and the elms' new leaves:
  At which I turned, and held my finger up,
  And bade him mark that, howsoe'er the world
  Went ill, as he related, certainly
  The thrushes still sang in it.
       ...'See,' I said,
  'And see! is God not with us on the earth?
  And shall we put him down by aught we do?
  Who says there's nothing for the poor and vile
  Save poverty and wickedness? Behold!'...

———

Early on Sunday afternoon, a big foamy wave of panic rose out of the general sea of worry to batter my plan. In the morning, following belatedly the schedule, I'd been revising in a fog of cigarette-smoke for the French translation-paper which was due on the 24th, learning my vocabulary sheets. Sunday afternoon should also, in theory, have been spent on French, *Les Fleurs du Mal* in particular, leaving the evening free for final preparation of the next day's papers.

Then, just after 2, I thought: 'This time tomorrow, you'll have finished the Essay paper and you'll be thirty minutes into Tragedy.' My armpits prickled and oozed like a woman coming wet in sex: under the left arm the drops mixed and ran in a trickly driblet over my ribs. I dropped the files of French notes on the floor, and took out, from beneath the Rochester paperweight, the ash-dusty wad of paper bearing my scribbled permutations of three-hour essay topics, the dry fruits of several sessions in the College library where I'd analysed previous years' question-papers.

They say that the three-hour general essay paper is the one you can't cram for, the one that tests your gradual accumulation of knowledge over the years; but that's balls. If the perennial topics are vast and elastic ones, like the state of the arts at the present time, the nature of the ideal university, censorship of lit, et cetera, they still hinge on definitions you can deliberately prepare before you get into the exam-room. Accordingly, I'd prepared and memorised an assortment: for instance: 'Intelligence: the art of seeing or making connections between apparently unconnected entities'; and 'Addressing God is prayer; hearing His reply is schizophrenia'. I also wanted to exploit my range and give the answer a philosophical cutting-edge that the examiner wouldn't find in the average Eng. Lit. student's answer. Defining the real, or defining how we define the real: that could be crucial to various discussions. I spent half an hour revising my notes on Ayer's *Foundations of Empirical Knowledge.* Certainly a minority of students might cite Ayer, but they'd bore the examiner by using the much-too-familiar *Language, Truth and Logic.* Learning a couple of quotations from *Foundations* took longer than I'd expected: I'd forgotten that the more lucid and functional the prose style, the more slippery it is to glue in memory, particularly a lethargic memory. (Ha: words melt into Ayer, into thin Ayer.)

Another item you can prepare in advance is the quotation that heads the essay, the epigraph. Casey didn't accept this: he said he'd wait until he'd thought out the answer, and then an appropriate epigraph would emerge. I said that the trick was to catch the examiner's attention by deploying the unexpected: so I'd memorised some adaptable examples. One was '"The world is pooped out" (Henry Miller)', a citation of *Tropic of Cancer* – banned novel – for any essay with an element of pessimism. Another was: '"Aesop saw his master pissing as he walked. 'What!', cried Aesop, 'Should we then shit as we run?'" (Montaigne).' Montaigne is often cited, but not the obscene Montaigne, and the obscenities would wake the exam-marker up; and the quotation would be passably relevant to any essay about custom, conventional morality, efficiency, or censorship. Jack, like me, held that epigrams could be learnt in advance, and he, too, favoured the unexpected; but his preference (exploiting his range and magnetic memory) was not for the mildly shocking but for the delphic and arcane – e.g.: '"Orage remarked on the 'recession of power'" (Pound, *Canto LXXIX*)' – which his discussion would nevertheless vindicate.

At dinner in Hall, Casey looked worried and preoccupied. Jack was eager to trade ideas. 'Here's one for you, brother', he said to me. '*Bacchae.* Link it to *Death in Venice.* Euripides' *Bacchae* gave Mann the inner plot, the hidden plot, of *Death in Venice.* Puritanical Aschenbach the new Hippolytus.' 'Dionysus, where?' 'Everywhere. Britten's opera proves it. Same singer, different roles: the gondolier, the barber –' 'The traveller at the cemetery with the staff. Thyrsus. Hey, it's covert plotting again.' 'Yes. Okay. Another trade?' Well, I relented and gave him the 'Old Ekdal's hidden suicide' ploy: it fitted this idea of hidden plots so well. Casey, taking notice at last, cleared his throat and offered us, for the 'covert plots' collection, Abdulla's successful stratagem in Conrad's *Almayer's Folly.* Far from being a minor character, as critics think, Abdulla schemes successfully to destroy Almayer, his trade rival: the Muslim is shrewder than the supposed Christian who scorns him. The seemingly marginalised character is really central, if you piece together the clues to his scheming. Jack promptly trumped that with Golding's *Pincher Martin*, explaining that the rocky tooth-shaped island is merely part of Pincher's willed dream of survival as he drowns: the tongue presses the tooth: hence the topography. 'Yeah', I agreed. 'That ... works', added Casey after a reflective pause. Jack, grinning, snapped his thumb and middle finger under our noses: 'We'll show the bastards!'

After dinner, even Jack and Casey went away to revise instead of playing billiards, so I came promptly back to my lodgings, stoked with the useful class-resentment that the meal in Hall usually gave me (those ubiquitous public-school accents grate), lit the twentieth fag of the day after breaking a couple of matches, and started on the final skimming of the Tragedy notes and memorising-sheets. Then, about 9.30, when I happened to be picking my nose absentmindedly over an account of Agamemnon's hubris (walking the purple-dyed carpet, entering Clytemnestra's web, soon donning the lethal net-like bath-robe: links with the imagery of fisherman's net and serpents, implying entanglements in the law of talion), there was a knock at the door, and, surprised, unthinking, I said 'Come in', unlocking it.

'Salutations', said Alex Eastbourne in his melodious public-school voice; and, before I could work out how to stop him, he'd walked in, smiling nervously, gripping a book, and sat down in the only chair that wasn't heaped with papers, the one I'd been sitting in.

'This is an unexpected pleasure', I said bitterly. 'What are you after?'

'I have this problem about Finals', he said at last.

'Jesus! Who hasn't? And my problem is, getting on with the work you're interrupting. Okay. I'll give you three minutes. Just three minutes. Fire away.'

'You see? That's the problem. You're the sixth person I've called on since dinner, and they're all cramming desperately, like you. Even the one or two who usually ask me in for coffee. It doesn't make sense, when you think about it.' He tugged at his angelic curly locks with a trembling hand.

'It's perfect sense. What d'you think we come to this place for? Gourmets' soirées?'

'I meant... I meant that I felt... Going along from room to room, it seemed to me that all of you, swotting, were just cancelling each other out. It's the wrong way of going about things, it seems to me. It *must* be.'

'We *don't* cancel each other out at all. The weakest go to the wall, and the others get ahead. It's Social Darwinism.'

'But we're reading English Literature, not Darwinism. Surely reading English is supposed to be learning to understand – to understand understanding. I mean, being more sensitive, and that sort of thing. So, at the end of the course, it seems somehow perverse for everyone to be swotting away behind locked doors. This really worries me, truly.' He frowned at his book.

'Sentimentality.' I glanced at my watch. 'Sentimentality. You're just bloody lonely, that's what it boils down to. And now, if you don't mind –'

'I'm going', he said, fumbling at the pages of his book as he stood up. 'But just listen to this one bit first. It isn't only me, you see: this man – Hoggart, Richard Hoggart – says it too, but better. Here we are.' Eastbourne stood in an old-fashioned orator's pose, with his forefinger in the air (like Corporal Trim). '"He" – that's the scholarship boy he's talking about – "He tends to overstress the

92

importance of examinations... He begins to see life as a ladder, as a permanent examination... He becomes an expert imbiber and doler-out..." Now, this is the part: "He rarely feels the reality of knowledge, of other men's thoughts and imaginings, on his own pulses –"'

'All right', I said, gripping his elbow to lever him out through the doorway. 'Thanks for the sermon. All right. Good night. My pulses say "piss off".'

'I thought that you, at least...', he started, his mouth puckering and trembling oddly. He was almost crying.

'*Piss off!*', I shouted, and he turned and stumbled away at last.

I wasn't sure whether I was irritated because I hadn't been able to get rid of him sooner, or whether I hadn't been able to get rid of him sooner because I was irritated. His father, a director of several companies, was a Tory grandee. Perhaps Eastbourne Senior had advised Eastbourrne Junior to go round nobbling the other runners on the eve of Finals. The visit had cost me five minutes, and it was quarter of an hour or more before I'd restored my mental focus on Agamemnon, doomed to be desecrated by liquid siftings, and on the web of talion that enmeshed him.

# Chapter 12

CRITICISM AND COMPOSITION

...1. Assign approximate dates to FIVE of the following passages, giving your reasons:

...(b)  A secret fury ravisheth my soul,
Lifting my mind above her human bounds;
And as the eagle rousèd from her stand
With violent hunger towering in the air...
So Solomon, mounted on the burning wings
Of zeal divine, lets fall his mortal food,
And cheers his senses with celestial air,
Treads in the golden starry labyrinth
And holds his eyes fixed on Jehovah's brows...

———

'Now nine years' vengeance crowd into a minute', *Revenger's Tragedy*. Where are my socks? 'Build your whole life according to an ordinary, commonplace pattern, and don't go fighting with windmills', *Ivanov*...

The getting-up routine was outwardly the ordinary, commonplace pattern: crap, wash, shave, brush teeth, finish dressing, boil water for coffee, eat one slice of Wonderloaf lubricated with Anchor butter and thin Golliwog marmalade; but everything was awry, and I felt trembly and nervy-feverish. The me on one dimension seemed to be manipulating the me on another dimension into a simulacrum of normal routine. It was like one of those science films where a nervous scientist manoeuvres a radioactive object that's on the other side of a glass screen by moving a duplicate object on his side of it. The fever recalled the fear-fever that accompanied O level and A level and entrance exam days, and forces' Russian exams, and Prelims and Part I of Tripos, but now intensified by the sense that this time it was the ultimate exam, the Everest climb after the foothills.

Sometimes that morning's routine was entangled in tentacles of quotes and recapitulations, and I'd find, for example, that I'd been leaning over the wash-basin without raising my trembling lathered hands to my face, while lines of Ayer, Shakespeare and Aeschylus had been meshing on the inside of my eyes, and I'd hurry the washing to keep to the schedule of normality; and when I started to dry my face (*Oresteia*, net imagery, 'Thraldom her deep dragnet trolled'), I found it had already been dried by an automatic insentient rub with the towel. Then, as I sat eating the sandwich while reading a sheet of Shakespeare-notes propped against the Robertson's marmalade jar ('And appetite, an universal wolf, / So doubly seconded with will and power...'), I found that when I'd read to the end of the sheet, my mouth still contained the first bite of bread, which had been rotating there unable to absorb sufficient saliva to be swallowable. I had to sluice each chewed gobbet of that sandwich down with coffee.

Next, the weapon-check. I tested the three cheap ball-point pens I was carrying, to make sure they wrote smoothly and had full ink-tubes. I fingered my pocket where the cigarette-packet and matchbox nestled. Then: the additional visit to the bog that was a crucial part of the pre-examination ritual. Squatting on the pan, Ayer notes perched on the bog-roll holder, urinating with a stinging pain, deeply inhaling the smoke from the first cigarette of the day, I reflected that my consciousness was trapped in a ludicrously primitive and sadly conventional body, an atavistic biological fear-system: hands trembling slightly, sticky areas under arm-pits, dry mouth, skin hot but shivery, and now – yuck! – bowels voiding a sudden spatter of diarrhoea. Ayer, meanwhile, assured me that 'the ascription of "reality" depends on the predictive value of the sense-data on which the predictions are based'; and I tried to recall his examples. There was a tapping at the bolted door and an urgent posh-voiced enquiry: 'I say, whoever you are, are you going to be in there very much longer?'.

Mrs Channing had zealously woken all the students in the boarding-house at 7.45: all of us had Finals today. Her zeal (tap-tap-tap, 'Time to rise!') reminded me of Petty Officer Feasey, striding down the mess-room at Victoria Barracks, Portsmouth, banging on the steel bunk-ends with his swagger-stick and yelling 'Hands off cocks – Put on socks!'. By the time I'd emerged from the smoky bog, three lads were standing in a fidgety impatient queue. Public-school lads: I knew them by sight but not by name.

At 8.45 I parked my bike at Casey's digs. He was already standing on the doorstep: his normally pallid face looked grey and ill. He talked with predictable contempt about the indignity of having to parade for assessment: 'It's like the National Service medical all over again', he said; 'but at least they didn't pretend to be... assessors of your mental and moral health. In the fourth century B.C., the examiners murdered Socrates, and... they still haven't learnt the lesson.'

'Some small differences. In your case, you *have* corrupted the morals of the young.'

'Corrupted them? I... educated them. Before they met me, half those girls had nothing in them worth corrupting anyway.' But he continued to grumble about having to parade for the rack at the premature hour of 9 a.m. (as he usually arose at 10), and he admitted he hadn't slept much last night. He didn't need reminding that he had to wear his gown to the exam. 'It's ridiculous', he grumbled. 'On the writings we make in the exam-room depends... the class-mark that brands us for the rest of our lives. It defines our future jobs, our careers or lack of them; our incomes, our leisure, houses, friends, wives.' 'But it's revenge time too', I said: 'Time to elbow down some middle-class lads.' He cleared his clear throat. 'Exams tend to corrupt, and final exams corrupt finally. What quality of thought emerges from... from a three-hour stand-and-deliver against the clock?' 'Well, the bloody system got us our Exhibitions', I said. 'The conspiracy isn't foolproof.' 'The conspiracy...is trying to incorporate us,' he said; 'and, over the decades, the exam system will gradually make capitalism seem... natural and normal and inevitable. Your libertarian anarchism... particularly your Cheltenham Spa variety... will look increasingly cranky, and then... perish.' 'The system's contradictions will tear capitalism apart', I insisted. He merely groaned.

In College, Jack's door on O staircase of New Court was wide open, and the whole corridor was deafeningly filled with the grim choral finale of Stravinsky's *Oedipus* from his record-player: psychological warfare, and I guessed that Stravinsky would soon be cited in one of his Tragedy answers. Jack made us sit and wait while he lumbered about the room, buttoning a red-check shirt tightly over his fur-blackened chest, combing his hair at the mirror beneath a big Modigliani nude that he had hung upside-down, and bawling questions over the noise. He resembled a bloodshot-eyed bull in a china shop or a crazed bridegroom late for a wedding as he blundered around. 'Who was it said: "By education most have been misled?"' He knew; we didn't. Or 'Performing dogs never carry their tails'? He knew, we didn't. Ergo, though he naturally hoped (he said) we'd all get Firsts, in our cases it would take some luck, whereas in his case it would be mere justice.

At seven minutes to the hour, in spite of our anxious nagging, he made us wait for the first few bars of his old Clifford Brown LP ('Delilah', with deftly varied drumming by Max Roach), which he put on immediately after the Stravinsky; and, with Brown's sprightly bop phrases continuing to soar and cascade between our ears, we scurried across the road to the soot-grimed building in Pembroke Street where the examiners would rack us into confession.

The exam-room door wasn't open yet. Scores of students were herding on the steps, in the hallway, and on the street. Apprehension gave the chatter a curious general tone and rhythm: an excitable jabbering at-rather-than-with, rapid modulations from crescendo to diminuendo and back; and even on the fringe of that crowd, in the street with cars cautiously going past, you could smell wafts of a sharp, sour, soap-veiled pre-exam perspiration. So much nervous electricity about: a light-bulb in a paper bag might have switched itself on. I lit my second cigarette of the morning and inhaled hard and repeatedly till the brain buzzed: no more fags for three hours.

Through a gap in the crowd, I glimpsed Arabella: she saw me and made a brief ambiguous grimace, a half-pout; I shrugged. Casey went wriggling through the crowd to talk to her; after a while I saw her inclining her head to listen (she was about three inches taller than he was). Farthingale had arrived with half a dozen of his ex-Harrovian friends, and they started a dirge of 'Why are we waiting?'. There was even a hint of the upper-class 'Hw–' sound at the start of 'Why?'. 'Cunts', I said to Jack. 'Pricks', he replied, staring at the inner panelled door. Vengeful anger, apprehension, impatience, the lust to vent our long-amassed material: our emotional rapport seemed to surge.

Then the door opened, I took a final deep inhalation of smoke, and dropped the cigarette-end (almost an inch long, I'd wasted some); and Jack pushed ahead, elbowing his way through the surging crowd to find the right desk – there were numerous desks arranged in rows, with names on them; and, in his wake, I found mine almost at once, so that while Farthingale and his friends were still zigzagging about, hunting their places, I'd read the list of topics on the paper, the Essay paper, and was already eliminating the less promising options.

The room became quiet and tense. The invigilator said: 'You may begin to write: *now.*'

The topics were:

1. 'Great art is never merely personal.'
2. Tact and candour.
3. The uses of distortion.
4. The idea of a university.
5. 'It is one of our illusions...that education...can create nobleness and beauty.' (Yeats.)
6. 'Comedy is necessarily cruel.'
7. 'Loyalties are the enemies of principles.'
8. 'Contemporary – what is contemporaneity?'
9. 'It is desperately hard these days for an average child to grow up into a man. Our society does not want men.'
10. 'The intolerable wrestle with words and meanings.' (T. S. Eliot.)
11. 'The corruption of a poet is the generation of a critic.'

After ten minutes I'd reduced the alternatives to title 3 or title 5. I spent another five minutes sketching on rough paper an outline for an answer to 5, on illusions of education. I could follow the Yeats title with a quotation from 'Among School Children': 'Labour is blossoming or dancing where / The body is not bruised to pleasure soul.... / Nor blear-eyed wisdom out of midnight oil': then the chestnut tree and 'How can we know the dancer from the dance?'. One of Yeats's formulations of an ideal education. Seldom realised. Well-educated Nazis. Conrad on Singleton: 'Would you seriously, of malice prepense cultivate in that unconscious man the power to think? Then he would become conscious – and much smaller – and very unhappy.'... I had plenty of material on anti-rational primitivism, nostalgia for some Eden prior to the fall into knowledge. Genesis,

Gilgamesh, Wordsworth, Butler, Lawrence. So often, the criticisms of education come from the well-educated. Many students would be answering this one with reference to *Mill on Bentham and Coleridge*, ed. Leavis (widely recommended) and to *Hard Times* (warmly commended by Leavis). Main difficulty for me was that I didn't know the precise context of the quotation about education; and, in the eyes of an examiner marking rapidly and impressionistically, being over-influenced by first impressions, that initial sogginess might put me in the second-class league.

With title 3 I didn't have that handicap; there was more scope for diversity of material; and with a bit of ingenuity, some of the material that the Yeats quotation had summoned up could be accommodated under that heading 'distortion'.

I looked along the rows of students. Some chewed their pens, some looked disconsolate, some were already scribbling impetuously, and one or two displayed neurotic little stress-symptoms, mouthing words or muttering to themselves, or fingering their ears and noses. Most of them would choose the safer, obviously literary titles, like 6, where they could bullshit about the sunny geniality of Chaucer and conclude predictably that sometimes comedy is cruel but often it isn't. Title 1 would be popular, too: they could use Leavis's criticism of gushing Shelley, and cite Eliot on how the great artist is continually trying to extinguish personality: 'The more perfect the artist, the more completely separate in him will be the man who suffers and the mind which creates'. (So said the man who admitted that *The Waste Land* was his 'rhythmical grumbling'.) Wilde, too: 'All bad art is sincere.' But the Eliot title-quote is from his *TIT*, *Traditional and the Individual Talent*; and that's a set text for the students who have taken the Literary Theory course, which I haven't. That would be too well trodden, that path. And 11, too, about the corruption of a poet being the generation of a critic: a lot of candidates would inform the examiner that Dryden, Johnson, Arnold and Eliot were, surprise, surprise, good poets *and* good critics.

What would a safe and commonplace approach to topic 3 be? Probably a discussion of entertaining grotesques in literature. Ben Jonson's satiric characterisations and 'humours'. Dickens' use of caricature. More vigour in Fagin and Sykes than in Oliver or Brownlow. Pope and Swift: satiric exaggeration, supposedly for

99

moral ends. I could deploy ten-minutes'-worth of that stuff, as an insurance, but not till half-way through my answer. I could range outwards by invoking the principles of pictorial caricature (citing some particular cartoon by Vicky, perhaps): cartoonist may aim for a combination of maximum identifiability, minimum of delineation, and maximum of moral loading. Then to the kinds of distortion you find in El Greco (elongated saints) or Michelangelo (smallish heads on weightily muscular bodies), and their implications. (Use some of Gombrich's examples but don't mention Gombrich, because his *Story of Art* is a popular best-seller to be found in all good school libraries; let the examiner think I may have seen the originals).

I gazed at the rows of predominantly well-fed-looking students. I guessed that a high proportion of them, if tackling 6, would have a central weakness in their answers. They would harbour confidently generous and capacious ideas of the un-distorted, the normal. They might even use the word 'real' without giving it at least temporary sceptical quotation-marks. I could cite extreme cases of sceptical relativism using the argument from illusion to solipsism (bent stick in water; our senses delude us some of the time; they could delude us all the time); then would follow the art-history material and the suggestion that the prime criterion of the real is normative, not empirical; then, as an apparent *coup-de-grace*, the pseudo-conclusion, I could use the arguments of Ayer against solipsism, the arguments of *Foundations of Empirical Knowledge*. Predictions based on the assumption the world is as phantasmagoric as solipsism suggests are *not* borne out; predictions based on the assumption the world is much as common sense suggests *are* borne out. Define a coin as round: useful, you can find it if you drop it. Define it as a slim rectangle: also true, but useless if you're looking for it. Finally, a complicating true conclusion undermining Ayer, thus going further than the examiner would expect.

I sketched a labyrinth on the rough paper, trying to get the sequence and that conclusion clearly visualised. The first forty-eight minutes had passed and I hadn't written an examinable word. Practically everyone in the room now seemed to be writing diligently. I needed a smoke, but the exam-system naturally victimises ex-National Servicemen corrupted by duty-free fags. The sentences of the conclusion began to shape, but cloudily: they

100

could be about the ultimate criteria of the real and the sane, about how they were necessarily connected and economically influenced; but now, the more I tried to fix the phrasing, the more my awareness of all the scribbling hands in the hall, of all their Babeling minds, seemed to jam my own thinking, as if radio signals from my past to my present were being jammed by a hundred twittering incomprehensible foreign stations. The fulcrum of the transition from the pseudo-conclusion to the real conclusion could be the passage from Ayer about reality being dependent... being dependent on specifying optimum predictive conditions: not exact; but there was a quotation on those lines hovering between my ears if I could but shut out the jamming.

Some sort of disturbance at the door. The invigilator, a withered, sour-looking don with a patched gown, was rebuking in penetrating *sotto voce* someone I couldn't see, someone whose murmured apologies and explanation had a melodious and almost patronising tone. Then the invigilator stepped impatiently aside, and Alex Eastbourne strolled quietly in to take the only vacant desk. By the clock, Eastbourne was almost an hour late. I reckoned the calculating bastard had timed his entry on purpose to disrupt the planning of the rest of us in general and me in particular. But, on the sheets that counted, the sheets to be handed in, I'd got no more to show than he had. I felt some waves of panic, the first surges of mental nausea. So, to suppress them, abandoning the hunt for the elusive finale, I wrote the question-number 3 at the top of the sheet, and quoted Blake: 'A fool sees not the same tree that a wise man sees.' Then out tumbled a second quotation: '"When the sun rises, do you not see a round disk of fire somewhat like a Guinea?" "O no, no, I see an Innumerable company of the Heavenly host crying, "Holy, Holy, Holy..."'.

Next, middle of the lines beneath, a big bold cartoon of Hitler, in the manner of Vicky. In school-days I'd drawn it often enough. It was a passable caricatural likeness: lick of hair over forehead, nose exaggerated, chin receding, angry eyes. Then: explanation of the cartoon, legitimate distortion for moral ends; then to discussion of El Greco's elongations, and of surrealism and its justifications; and, via Dalí's 'Apparition of Face and Fruit-Dish on a Beach', to the satiric exaggeration in Dryden's 'MacFlecknoe', where, I argued, the satire wasn't just a matter of reducing the target (Shadwell) by jestingly juxtaposing him with the great; no, the pleasure lay in the fantasy, the surrealism, that mock-heroic generates. Shadwell, if vacuous, becomes gigantic: 'Thoughtless as Monarch Oaks that shade the plain, / And, spread in solemn state, supinely reign.' Later, when satirising Timon's villa, Alexander Pope writes 'Here gladiators fight, and die, in flowers.' And what do you see? Not, initially, statues of gladiators foolishly located, illustrating the owner's bad taste (as the commentators claim), but, bizarrely and delightfully, real gladiators fighting incongruously in flower-beds: Dalíesque surrealism. They call the Augustan Age the Age of Reason. In its satire, it's the age of exuberant fantasy. Madness by the back door. Timon is satirised by Pope for distorting the relationship between man and nature; but Pope then magnifies Timon's distortion to create the exuberantly and wonderfully crazy: distortion as mental holiday from the regulated.

Then: on to attempts to define the undistorted. How the empirical attempt leads paradoxically to solipsism. (Evidence of the senses depends on fallible senses; sense-datum sure, its source unsure.) So by 10.30 I had completed the Intro and was well into the main part of the argument, crossing off scribbled headings on the rough paper, and my pace of writing was accelerating, with sentences coming *ad lib* and not mentally rehearsed. I became too embroiled in the literary illustrative part of the middle section; and then with Ian Watt's *Rise of the Novel* and its claim that the realistic novel rises with the bourgeoisie: so realism is a stylisation that influential people, as capitalism burgeons, wish to regard as a reflection of the real, the reflected being what profits them to regard as the real. But while the surface of my mind was engaged there, another submerged part must have been toiling to find the way to a conclusion, because the Ayer quotation popped up like a slice from a toaster, and I saw how I could tie the last knot of argument. The definition of reality, according to Ayer, is a matter of 'specifying the conditions in which it is to be said that a perception is veridical'; and of course he proposed predictive utility as the basis of those conditions.

The invigilator's sepulchral voice jolted me: 'Fifteen minutes remain. Fifteen minutes remain.' The voice demolished the perilously-balanced wraith-structure of my unwritten conclusion, and for a full minute I had to put my pen down to reconstruct it, proposition by proposition, quotation by quotation; but then at last it was rebuilt, and I scribbled its form and texture onto the last page.

Ayer's criterion of utility is itself normative. A society which had different values could establish different realities, different criteria of the 'undistorted'. Marx: 'Your very ideas are but the outgrowth of your bourgeois means of production.' (But does that include Marx's ideas? If so, are they invalid? Including that one?) In Orwell's *1984*, 2+2=5. But not if you are building the Ministry of Truth and don't want it to fall down. Even 'sanity' is dependent on a set of historically-generated conventions: *Erewhon, Brave New World* and *1984* suggest that; and proof is offered by the Inquisition, witchcraft trials, and now the USSR, in which dissidents are treated as insane in clinic-prisons. Good novels suggest that the study of literature is the recognition of social inscription. In realistic fiction, the better the author, the more independent seem the characters. In the book of life, the more skilful the authority, the more the people may have the illusion of sufficient independence. Great novels like *Nostromo* remind us that for centuries, society has inscribed women with submissive characterisation, and inscribed men with aggressive characterisation. Is an 'undistorted' view of the world possible? The world is real and not *in* the mind, for it can break our bones; but it can only be *of* the mind. The universe known to science is a map of the human mind: we see only what our senses permit us to see; different beings would see a different universe. 'Objective reality' is the product of grand anthropomorphism, of anthropocentric im-perialism. Blake:

> 'If the doors of perception were cleansed, every thing would
> appear to man as it is, infinite.
> For man has closed himself up, till he sees all things thro'
> narrow chinks of his cavern.'

Then cite Wordsworth on Blake: 'There is no doubt that the poor fellow is mad.' And for the last two lines, to complete the janiformity of the answer:

> As Omar Khayyám says:
> 'Who is the potter, pray, and who the pot?'

Those final words, as I scribbled them, coincided with the invigilator's cry, 'Please stop writing *now*. Stop writing. Make sure that you've joined the sheets together and entered your place-number and the question-number on the cover-sheet. Leave the scripts on your desks. Stop writing *now*. Thank you.' He gave a big yawn: there was a bulky wedding-ring on the hand he raised to his mouth: the ring seemed by its colour to be lead. I stood up slowly, feeling blankly empty as a spent salmon.

After lunch in College, the three of us for half an hour sprawled on the weedy grass outside the Mill, down by the river. The sky was overcast, and the mild breeze blew the scattered sheets of a newspaper, *Daily Telegraph*, to and fro over the scrubby turf. The paper chattered at us: 'Eichmann Blocked Emigration of Jews, Court Told... More U.S. Defence Aid to Vietnam... Soviet Threat over Nuclear Tests: Resumption if France Does Not Stop... Four More New Universities Planned...' For a while, we lay quietly, mentally spent; scarcely aware of the place or each other, our brains stunned following the ordeal of the morning's enforced thinking but unable to relax because at 1.30 another three hours of the rack awaited us. I exhaled lung-filtered smoke into the jungle of dusty grass an inch from my nose. Jack belched.

'We'd better move', he said after a while. 'They might let us in early.'

'Yeah. We might get two minutes' advantage over the others.'

'They won't let you start writing before 1.30', said Casey.

'So what?', I said. 'We might still get a couple of minutes for reading the questions before the others have all arrived.'

As we walked back up Pembroke Street between the high soot-streaked walls, Casey grumbled: 'This isn't an exam; it's a *via crucis*. Daiches says his Poetry course is designed to develop sensitivity and discrimination; but the assessment-method is designed... to brutalise... or induce a slave-mentality.'

'"What is truth? Confine your answer to three major writers and forty-five minutes flat",' said Jack in a posh voice ('Con-fain', 'may-jah', 'flet'). 'All right: so it's a farce. All they want you to do is muster a more intelligent farce in three hours than the next man. While you two were sucking your pens this morning, I filled twenty foolscap sides. Joyce at one end and Creeley at the other. In the middle, Pound's creative translations. My raid on the inarticulate with shabby equipment. Beat that, brothers.' He'd tackled the Eliot topic about words and meanings.

104

'Thirteen sides, I did,' I said.

'*Ach, meine arme Kinder*', responded Casey. 'Counting sides! Using 2, "Tact and candour", as a pretext, I gave the examiners a tactless but candid reprimand... for presuming to think that anyone working in a battery-hen situation... could say anything well-meditated on the topic.'

'Battery hens lay fast and don't sit there whining', I said.

'And they end up in plastic bags... with their intestines tied in a little bundle stuffed up their backsides', replied Casey.

'You haven't got the message,' I objected. 'Look. Competitive capitalistic economy needs young blood, right? Examiners assess your ability to fit the economy. They don't really want your ideas on Art and Truth and Tact and Candour; that's just a means to an end. Now: what they *do* want to find out is whether you can stay cool, calm, collected, sane, and thinking like a salesman, under stress conditions. That's why we do a marathon of three-hour papers instead of being assessed on our week-by-week course-work. Because: the men who survive this sort of marathon are men capable of selling fridges to Eskimos or toasters to Zulus –'

'And with their integrity tied in another bundle stuffed up their backsides, as I tried to point out... just now.'

Jack stopped to adjust his right shoe. The rubber patch (from a John Bull cycle-repair-kit) that held the upper to the sole was coming adrift. 'Even as cynics you're – inefficient – hicks. Who are the markers for this morning's paper? You didn't think to find out, did you? It's McConville and Blane. I, brothers, don't just wank my spiel off the top of my head. I do a chairmanly act, relating my stuff to the nightmares and preoccupations of Messrs McConville and Blane, as implied in their critical tomes. That isn't capitalism; that's high civilisation.'

'You bleedin' Machiavel', I responded. 'You never told us.'

'If I'd known', said Casey, 'I couldn't have written even one sheet. Isn't Blane... a notorious Christian?'

'"Aye, and a virgin too, that grieves me most"', responded Jack. 'Source?'

———

The Tragedy paper required a technique very different from the

105

Essay paper's. Different format, different personality. Later in the week I planned to criticise Eliot's 'dissociation of sensibility' theory – but if anything could have induced a dissociation of sensibility, it would have been that exam system.

I was writing within twelve minutes of the start, having scanned the questions and picked the four that would let me display range and variety of approach. At first I thought I'd made a blunder in preparation, because there was no question specifically on *The Oresteia* – I nearly crapped myself with fright (an apt irony, in the circumstances) when I glanced through the paper and didn't see it mentioned. But the first question still turned out to be a good springboard which enabled me to combine the stuff I'd prepared on *Oresteia* with material about Sophocles and Euripides. Another feature that attracted me to the question was that it used the term *Weltanschauung*, as I reckoned that some students, particularly those who hadn't taken O-level German, would be deterred by that noun. Another crafty detail: this questioner wanted to hear about two or even three of the three great Greek tragedians. I had the range; I knew from my talks with Farthingale, Eastbourne, Arabella and others that most students wouldn't have it. Here's that question:

1. 'Greek tragedies were, it is true, written for performance on an occasion that was both civic and religious, but the great tragic poets were "intellectuals" and creative writers, each expressing, not an orthodoxy or a state religion, but his individual *Weltanschauung*.' How far do you find it possible to confirm that contention by comparing work by **two** (or if you prefer, all **three**) of the tragic poets?

Down into the answer went, inevitably, Kitto, but laced with Bertrand Russell and (Jack's recommendation) Dodds' *The Greeks and the Irrational*. (Dodds wasn't in paperback those days, so he lent more gravitas to an answer than he would later.) My prole side interrupted to point out to me that my answer was becoming too abstract and polysyllabic, so, to make it more concrete, I used Lattimore's discussion of *Oresteia*'s imagery, and unburdened my memory of a quartet of quotes. I used the grumbling nurse and her proleptic imagery of excrement (she can wash nappies; Orestes'

106

pollution can be washed away). *The Oresteia*'s story of the evolution from the chthonian to the rational, from the barbaric to the civilised, was paralleled by Tragedy's evolution from the communal and ritualistic to the relatively realistic and character-centred; but the evolution culminated, in Euripides' *Bacchae*, in a magnificent reconciliation of the realistic and sceptical with the communal and ritualistic.

I'd taken a liking to the Greek dramatists, partly because of the availability of handy cheap lucid Penguin translations: Vellacott's *Oresteia*, with all its helpful commentary and notes, for 3/6 (price of a packet of 20 fags), Watling's Sophocles' *Theban Plays* for two shillings (price of a pint). Then there had been the joy of discovering that, far from seeming ancient, those plays seemed modernistic: verse-drama, chorus, interlacing of realism and stylisation, and a use of imagery and symbolism that invited 20th-century analytic techniques. In fact, the finale of *Oresteia* was modernistic on a spectacular scale surpassing any 20th-century modernist work, with the chorus of Furies, now Kindly Ones (Eumenides), being encompassed by a procession of older and younger women and children, the drama blending with the people of the city-state of that day, the ancient becoming the contemporaneous – and the old women are wearing purple, a benign echo of the ominous purple of *Agamemnon*, the grim opening of the trilogy. (It made Eliot's *Family Reunion* look quaintly old-fashioned.) Then *Oedipus Rex* was not only Freudian (he blinds himself for sexual transgression, balls of the eyes being a symbolic substitute for balls between the legs) but preter-Freudian, almost mocking Freud ('Nor let this mother-marrying worry you: many a man has dreamt as much', says his mother). And *Bacchae* proved that Euripides was amply Freudian in showing how repressed desires become destructive. Of course, on the basis of the surviving plays, you could indeed argue that Aeschylus, Sophocles and Euripides had distinctive creative identities, as scepticism grew, and as the notion of involuntary guilt, guilt as pollution, was eroded by the notion that guilt should follow only a voluntary deed. You could see the chorus becoming marginalised as you advanced chronologically from Aeschylus through Sophocles to Euripides. But then, in a glorious conclusion to the sequence, *The Bacchae*, probably Euripides' last tragedy, reinstates the chorus as powerful and integral with the action. The Bacchantes, the wild followers of Dionysus, were not only necessary as characters but also logical as noisy chorus: I found myself using Jack's reference to Mann, citing *Der Tod in Venedig*, and suggesting that its Aesthetic pre-occupation made it less radical than the Euripidean original. (For Mann, the problem lay in the artist's nature; for Euripides, the problem lay in human nature at large.) Fleeting reference to the Mingus band's dionysiac cacophonies, the tension between abandonment and control. Then the dramatists' varying treatments of Electra showed their different predilections.

The majority of Eng. Lit. students wouldn't have read any Aristophanes (not on the list of authors for the course), so I deployed *Frogs*, (a) to prove that the modern view of Aeschylus as relatively conservative and Euripides as relatively subversive is no anachron-istic reading but was one current in the 4th century B.C.; and (b) to show that though the tragic drama might well have developed from the worship of Dionysus, the dying and rising god of wine and ecstasy, and though Dionysus makes a triumphant and horrifying return in *Bacchae*, when Dionysus features in *Frogs* he's a comic turn, a cowardly buffoon. Yet, if Kitto was right, the high priest of Dionysus would be sitting in the middle of the front row during the performance. I squeezed in a reference to the mocking of philosophy in Aristophanes' *Clouds*. (A sentimentally private recollection had made that reference spurt. While stationed at J.S.S.L., I'd been the second drummer, the jazz drummer, in a free adaptation of *The Clouds* at St Andrews' Town Hall. One of our tutors, Dmitri Makaroff, alias 'The Muse of Fire'; directed it; and the production enabled the frustrated recruits at Crail to fraternise with the rather wary young ladies – no Bacchantes – of St Andrews' University.)

I'd been writing rapidly and fluently, and what gave me extra confidence was the sight of Eastbourne's empty chair. He hadn't arrived at all. One of the things to be said for this corrupt system: psychologically it does sort out the men from the boys. Almost too much confidence that empty chair gave me, because I tacked on to that first answer a ploy that was risky. I said that although there's a strong recent critical tradition of suggesting that Tragedy is paradoxically consolatory, arguably the prime consolation of Tragedy is fraudulent. Whereas, in actuality, sufferings and painful deaths are

108

often gratuitous, senseless, ludicrous, chancy or just plain incomprehensible, in Tragedy the climactic suffering, however unjust, *is* climactic, *is* a comprehensible focus in a coherent pattern. In *Hippolytus*, admittedly, Euripides comes close to challenging any notion of tragedy as consolatory by stressing the arrogant wilfulness of the gods. But even there, he offers gods you can at least shake your fist at; which is marginally consolatory.

And that's how, with the sweat prickling constantly in my armpits, I spent twice as long as I should have done on that first question, and therefore had to cram into the last ninety minutes my answers on Shakespeare, Chekhov and Ibsen. Fortunately those questions were as accommodating as a row of whores, and three more times I spurted my load of prepared verbiage. Sometimes the headlong fluency might have risked resembling Lucky's word-salad in *Waiting for Godot*; but nevertheless I was almost beginning to feel at home in that exam room. And given that from the year I was ten, my parents had ceased to understand my homework, what better mental home could I expect? Stretched, I was adapting to the rack, and confessing glibly, like a co-operatively treacherous coward.

There followed several nights of preparation and days of regurgitation. At night my head digested and memorised material, and by day my head regurgitated it onto the pages. Outside the exam room I largely insulated myself from news, people and social life, so that inside the exam room I could on paper demonstrate (as I fondly imagined) responsiveness, tolerance, sensitivity, altruism, discrimination, socialistic-anarchistic idealism, humane agnosticism, and the god Janus. Another deity I worshipped was the clock; for the rack had a clockwork engine; and, to the accompaniment of its ticking, up there on the wall in front of me, I freely confessed such allegiances, unaware of the omitted words, mis-spellings and mixed metaphors which inevitably characterise precipitate volubility, unaware that to impatient examiners (unused to my scrawl) my 'creative' might be read as 'creature', 'iconic' as 'ironic', or 'tense' as 'terse'.

Tuesday's 'Criticism and Composition' paper (three-and-a-half hours) was the one where much depends on the ability to identify unascribed passages. The compulsory first question obliges the candidate to seek to identify several passages from a range. The later questions, requiring criticism of literary pieces, are obviously easier if you recognise the piece to be analysed and assessed. You need to have a wide range of reference (and both Grammar School and National Service had helped me there), but also a particularly good memory for dates. I had tried to compensate for the slothful unreliability of my memory by the systematic learning of dates of authors and main texts, but bouts of amnesia could still assail me under exam conditions. I envied Jack's magnetic memory and ease of recall, his facile proficiency.

This question-paper was nine close-printed pages. Yes, *nine.* So perusal of it, then deciding on the best options, took thirty-five minutes. You had to tackle question 1, and two or three others, from a total of 7. After 1, I'd attempt three others, exploiting my range and increasing speed. I recognised some of the passages but not enough to feel safe, not enough to feel near the class-1 limit. I had to make the best of what I did know, acting like a sergeant who puts his strongest men at the beginning and end of the column and his weaklings in the middle. So, at the end went a discussion of an unattributed poem, 'Ah! Sun-flower', which of course was by William Blake. Most of the candidates would have seen it as Blake's. There the gimmick of the discussion was my claim that poems like this from *Songs of Innocence and of Experience* (1794) resist orthodox 'close reading' techniques (of the kind favoured in America by the 'New Critics' and in Britain by followers of Empson and Leavis), because the symbolic-semantic associations are defined cumulatively through the contextual sequence of which the poem is part, rather than being fleshed out in the individual poem. In other words, if you know the other poems in the sequence (notably 'The Garden of Love' and 'The Sick Rose') and a modicum about Blake, you can see that this one is part of Blake's yearning for a revolution which is, among other things, a sexual revolution: sexual liberation is linked to, perhaps is key to, the general social and political revolution; freed love inaugurates New Jerusalem. *Then* the poem is replete; but taken in isolation, it is meagre. Here, the necessity of knowing the context not only calls in question the procedures of many present-day 'close reading' critics; it also, to perhaps cynical eyes (I ventured to suggest), calls in question the merits of exam papers like this, where apparently isolated items must

110

be interpreted and evaluated.

My main piece of luck concerned one of the passages for identification in the first question. This was uncanny: it was as if my wicked hero, Rochester (abetted by his monkey), had been practising voodoo on my behalf. Luck of the devil. One of those unattributed passages was an extract from my favourite satire, Rochester's 'Satyr against Mankind', where Rochester attacks 'Reason, an ignis fatuus of the mind / That leaves the light of Nature, Sense, behind'. According to the poet, the follower of reason (rather than instinct) may devote his whole life to useless 'Bladders of Philosophy', until

> ... Old Age, and Experience, hand in hand,
> Lead him to Death, and make him understand,
> After a Search so painful, and so long,
> That all his Life he has been in the wrong...

Glowing with the joy of recognition, I began my script with a eulogy of Rochester in general and this satire (of 1675, yes, I'd memorised that date too) in particular; indeed, I even criticised the examiner for having curtailed the extract immediately before the best couplet Rochester ever wrote, namely:

> Huddled in dirt, the reas'ning Engine lies,
> Who was so proud, so witty, and so wise.

(The strangely-insensitive examiner had ended the quotation at 'in the wrong...'. I guessed, and ventured to speculate in my comments, that he'd been using the incomplete text in *The Oxford Book of Seventeenth Century Verse*, ed. Grierson and Bullough, which abridges the poem by a crass cut there. That *Oxford Book* was a 'set text' that year.) The full associative context of the poem, I argued, should include the grinning monkey, who, in the portrait attributed to Jacob Huysmans, proffers a page he's ripped from a pile of tomes, offering it to the poet, as if to say 'You can wipe your arse with this', while long-haired Rochester, in his lavish robes, holds the laurel wreath, the reward of poets, over the monkey's head, and looks at the viewer as if to say, 'Observe: the monkey is wiser than you or I.'

A photo-reproduction of that painting was one of the three paper pin-ups stuck to the side of my portable bookcase at my digs. The uppermost picture showed Dizzy Gillespie, bullfrog-cheeked, blowing that special trumpet with the uniquely erect barrel; beneath it, Shakespeare, looking sly, with a ring in his left ear; and, last, Rochester, posing allegorically with his monkey, in the insolent portrait. I liked that perhaps-Huysmans portrait of Rochester so much that a smaller copy of it, in a heavy alloy frame, had served as a desk-ornament and paperweight for years. My hunch was that if you could read the hand-writing on the torn sheet held by the monkey, it would be the opening of the 'Satyr against Mankind'.

I suspected that I might be the only person to recognise so fully that passage in the exam paper; and my suspicion was confirmed when Jack, in the street later, said he was confident the passage was from Alexander Pope, though he couldn't identify the precise poem. 'Jack', I crowed, 'You're about half a century out: it's John Wilmot, Earl of Rochester.' He frowned in annoyance, swearing under his breath. 'Besides,' I added smugly, to rub Cerebos into the sore, 'Wilmot's couplets don't have the slick euphonious smoothness of Pope's: that should have guided you, surely.' 'Don't push your luck, Mr Green', he said angrily, wagging an admonitory dirty-nailed finger under my nose. An alarmed fly fled from my oily quiff. So Jack could get things wrong; therefore notions I'd derived from him looked vulnerable.

Wednesday morning's French translation paper (featuring Ronsard, Stendhal, Baudelaire and other big stars) seemed straightforward, apart from a few terms that eluded me completely; but Jack showed me afterwards – rather complacently I felt – that I'd made some puerile blunders with tenses and idioms. That was worrying enough.

However, the breaking-strain came in the afternoon, with the paper called 'Special Period of English Literature, 1880 to 1910'. Encouraged by Jack to do so, I'd made the mistake of having for lunch not a sandwich but a pint of beer, to accompany the usual couple of cigarettes. The question-paper, sophisticated and generally formidable, raised complicated tactical problems. Question 1 was compulsory: gobbets for commentary. For the next two answers, I planned to write on Hopkins and Butler. For the fourth and final answer, I couldn't work out whether to deploy my Conrad stuff or my Pater stuff. I couldn't start promptly, because what went into the first answer depended on which man I was excluding from the last; and the difficulty increased because of the elastic nature of some of the questions. For example, question 3 (inviting discussion of a writer illuminated by the history of ideas) was an ideal springboard for my Butler material, but that would entail deploying the Pater material elsewhere, under a more demanding and less hospitable title. But if I wanted to conclude strongly with Conrad instead of Pater, the ideal question for Conrad would be 3 – to which I'd first allocated Butler. So I went round and round that question-sheet like a dog chasing his tail, juggling permutations of questions and answers.

After fifty minutes I'd written nothing. I looked up at the big clock, and around at the rows of scribblers; and, for the first time since the exams had started, I leaned back in my chair, and found that its curved wood was surprisingly comfortable; I relaxed slowly into it. All down my back, from my shoulders to my buttocks, tensed muscles abandoned their tension and sagged into ease. The room was soothingly stuffy, as though every soft lungful I ingested had first been warmed in the lungs of the hundred scribblers around. They sweated under the incubus of the exam paper, while I stretched luxuriously, the only autonomous self in a hall of slaves. My eyes shut for a moment, and the houses of cards behind them, the cards inscribed with kaleidoscopic themes and facts, names and dates, sank into an innocuous paper snowdrift, and the drift pulsed lazily to and fro; white scum washed to and fro on an oily tide the length of the beach... Words and scum soaked and faded into the damp grey sand where crabs roamed. But the sand spoke: it sounded bored but sinister: '—have two hours left.' 'I repeat', said the bored invigilator, 'The time is 2.30, and you have two hours left.'

I looked round the room, dazed, struggling to make it real again. A fly buzzed away from my ear. Over there was an empty place: Eastbourne's. To the right, Arabella stroked back with one hand her long splendour of coppery hair, shaking it back over her gown; and with that black gown offsetting a virginally-white crisp blouse, she looked so cool that I could imagine that, even now, her armpits would still smell only of mild roseate scent. Living hypocrisy: I've groped the bulges under that blouse, the hairy stickinesses under that

113

skirt; but today I've no stir of sex, with the tick of the clock and the scraping of pens like a bromide in the brain, an icepack on the gut...

Behind me, Jack's desk creaked as he cumbrously shifted his elbow on it. His shirt-sleeves were rolled up, and the massiveness of his dark hairy forearms made the desk look like a flimsy toy, something he could have exploded into splinters with his fist. His writing hand moved ceaselessly in a vibrating slither from side to side of the foolscap sheet. Casey, further along, was studying the ceiling with contempt; carefully and deliberately he wrote one word on his paper; contemplated the ceiling again; and, as deliberately, with two neat flicks of the pen, crossed out the word he'd just written. Farthingale had the expression of a spaniel on heat, his tongue lolling out, his head bobbing a little as though he were panting after a run. Eastbourne's desk was still empty: perhaps he'd had a breakdown, or perhaps he'd simply realised that if you have a wealthy father, you can still find a cushy job regardless of whether you get a First or a fail or a bare pass or an expulsion with ignominy. (He'd evaded National Service, as had plenty of the public-school lads.) A sniff at my side: I was being watched, in turn, by a character at the next desk who looked like a well-groomed stoat, sporting that middle-class fashion of a silk neckerchief tucked inside an open-necked shirt. He looked down at my feet, than up at my stare, sniffed in a theatrical this-is-an-opinion-and-not-a-cold manner, and turned his back. Perhaps he could smell my feet, which were congealed to my Indestructible brand socks and the insides of the cheap Tuff shoes. He flicked ink aside from his pen: arrow clip, hooded nib... An advert came to mind: 'This Christmas, Sir Oswald Crud is giving his wife a Parker 51'...: and that did it. At last, malice and self-pity sent the adrenalin coursing afresh through me, and I was writing on the Shaw gobbet: it came from the preface to *Man and Superman*, I realised. Two hours later, I had completed a flow of commentary on the cluster of gobbets and on Hopkins, Butler and Conrad; and I'd managed to interweave with my discussion of Conrad and Hopkins a good fifteen-minutes-worth of my Pater material.

On the final day, I did John Stuart Mill in twenty minutes.

There are many ways of beating the bones of the buried. (Armado.) I could have saved time by excluding from that final answer half of my patiently-learned quotations, but that would have

114

given my 'English Moralists' script as a whole the appearance of tailing away into sketchiness; and I managed to get the quotes out and analysed, and the analysis concisely concluded, as the balding invigilator gave the minute-by-minute countdown and bawled with melodramatic vigour: 'Please *stop* writing now. *Stop* writing, everyone.' The final exam had finally ended.

On her way out, while I was still sorting my stack of sheets, Arabella turned to give me a distinctly ironic smile, almost a smirk. It could have meant anything from 'In those spectacles you look like an owl' to 'I've stabbed you in the back, but you don't know it yet.' Whatever the meaning was, it couldn't penetrate a skull still echoing with Plato, Hume, Mill and *On Liberty* and Packe's biography and Popper's praise of the Open Society. But I noticed that even the desiccated invigilator glanced sidelong at her legs as she went out, and then, as if to punish everyone else for his own little lapse, he shouted in a harsher voice than before: 'You should all by now have completed the binding of your scripts. Leave as soon as you have done that. Anyone whom I see writing now will be – ah – penalised!'

Outside in the sun, 'So much for "The English Moralists"', said Casey, weakly. 'Two thousand five hundred years of philosophy, most of it not English, some of it not moral, subjected to... three hours' opinionating by cretins who can't even *spell* "Nietzsche", let alone understand him.' Casey was too tired to look evil; more like a little old man shrivelled by malnutrition. And Jack had purplish bags under his eyes. 'The drinks are on me', Jack said.

So, as though nothing had been broken, we walked slowly, like somnambulists, away from the rack and towards the Mill. '"Eyeless in Gaza, at the mill with slaves"', murmured Casey, quoting a Cambridge alumnus.

# Chapter 13

CRITICISM AND COMPOSITION

...1. Assign approximate dates...

    (a)      ...And he bore with me
                In melancholy patience, not unkind,
                While breaking into voluble ecstasy
                I flattered all the beauteous country round,
                As poets use, the skies, the clouds, the fields,
                The happy violets hiding from the roads...

----

At the Oakley Farm site in Cheltenham, the foreman was sitting on an overturned bucket in a shed that smelt of clay, tea, smoke and sweat. Around the shed, what once had been pasture now resembled a muddy battleground. G.C.H.Q. (Government Communications Head-quarters), the technical hub of Britain's espionage, the national centre for international monitoring, was being extended over many acres.

I said: 'I'm looking for a temporary job. I wondered if you had a vacancy.'

His blue eyes circled lazily over me. I squared my shoulders, knowing that again, though in an unfamiliar way, I was being examined and assessed as a working-machine. Surprisingly, he stood up, extending a grimy hand.

'O'Connell', he said. 'And what would your name be?'

I told him, thinking that perhaps something in my phrasing had commanded this gesture of apparent respect from him; but the handshake was painful: like a nutmeg-grater his palm scoured mine. At first I thought I might pass the test, because from my mother and a grandfather (station porter) and a line of agricultural labourers I'd inherited a broad-shouldered build, though the shoulders had done little to work for their keep; but after a moment the foreman explained in a round-about way, and with a courtesy that might have been mockery, that there weren't now, in spite of the advert in last week's *Echo*, any 'vacancies' for unskilled labourers. It was true they needed a tea-boy, quite important a tea-boy; but, to be sure, much as they'd like to do otherwise, a tea-boy, never mind how strong the tea, could only be paid at boy's rate, 'which wouldn't be no use to a grown man like yerself, now, would it?'.

I thanked him and walked back towards the road, hopping over cables and tubes. I didn't mind, even if I *had* wasted a walk out to the site. The disappointment at knowing I'd have to continue to seek temporary work (to keep myself in fags and beer: at home, bed and board cost, as always, nothing) was counterbalanced by the ease of conscience that comes from knowing I had at least made a genuine effort. I could enjoy sloth for another day yet, having demonstrated that I wasn't really slothful. (I never thought of claiming the dole; in those days, students generally didn't; ten years later, they would regularly be doing it.)

In the past I'd affirmed subtly, in weekly essays, my (qualified) solidarity with the working man (not the *Lumpenproletariat*, of course); but for all that, it wasn't until Graduation Day that I grasped the foreman's logic.

On my way out of the site, I jumped a deep trench like a long grave and was stopped by a sudden shattering blatta-tatta-tatta as the drill resumed. A workman on the road ahead of me was drilling asphalt: with slow emphasis he leaned down on the drill, and it vibrated there, a heavy bright phallus banging at the blank surface: but as he pressed his weight down on the handles, the blade sank smoothly through the splitting crust of the road so that the metallic edge of the noise was partly muffled. He bore down harder, tilting it sharply; a slab of road-top broke free and slid glinting up the vibrating blade; he switched the drill off.

'Like shagging, ennit?', said the earth behind me. 'Except he can do it all day long in broad daylight.' The voice came from a face at ground-level, the face of a man who was standing neck-deep in the trench, leaning on his pick. I'd never seen the man before, yet I seemed to know his face.

'You're Peter Green, aren't ya?', said the tanned face. 'You won't remember me, though. Oh no.'

I didn't suppose I would; I'm bad at remembering people,

particularly when challenged suddenly. But something happened that was like the recognition I'd made when criticising the passage from *Lord of the Flies* in the 'Criticism and Composition' paper: the recognition that, trapped in Golding's narrative were the schoolboys of Ballantyne's *Coral Island.* I didn't know this navvy, but trapped beneath his truculent weather-leathered face was a face I *did* know, with the same slant of mouth, the same jut of ears. In memory a grinning boy with softer skin danced out for a moment from this stolid burly shape.

'Hey, you're Alan: Alan Wills. We used to go and play at your house after school. Junior School.'

'Ah', he replied. (It was the Gloucestershire 'Ah' that meant 'Yes'.) 'We arsed about in them days, didn't us?'

'You had Dick Tracy comics. I was jealous of those. Proper Yankee comics, full of colour. Sometimes, then, American comics were printed in black and white and not coloured.'

He lit the butt of a cigarette. 'I don't remember no Dick Tracy comics. I remember the bloody cane, though. That headmistress was a cruel sod. Miss MacDonald. Remember the hand inspections? Clean hands, you're all right. Dirty hands, and she'd try and cane 'em off your arms. You were a jammy bastard, weren't ya? Before she got down the line of kids to you, you'd have a crafty spit on your hands and wipe 'em down your shorts. It were mine that were always shitty because she'd come straight to me first, and then after prayers she'd call me up to the platform for the stick. Christ, she loved her bit of stick, didn't she?'

When he'd returned from the platform and shown us his hands, the welts across the fingers and palms were criss-crossing indentations, turning blue-black as we looked. Then we had to sing 'All things bright and beautiful', with the infamous quatrain,

> The rich man in his castle,
> The poor man at his gate:
> God made them, high or lowly,
> And ordered their estate.

'Ah. You were a jammy bastard,' he went on, inspecting me critically. 'The Grammar, you went to. You don't want a job *here*, do ya? A holiday job, is it, then?'

'That's right. Temp'ary.' I'd consciously colloquialised 'temp-orary'. Once, in 1945, he and I had found a stretched used gaping condom in the rain-puddles on an air-raid shelter's steps, and he had confided to me that it was what the Yankee soldiers piss into when they're taken short.

He sucked reflectively at the cigarette-butt. 'Don't you do it. Know how much I take home? Fifteen pounds a week. That's with overtime. And how much would they pay you? Ten. Eleven if you're lucky. See, you wouldn't get no overtime. If you're tempary, you can't expect none. For another thing, you'd be done up after eight hours of this. Nah, you don't want it.'

He spat the dog-end into the trench and rubbed a muddy boot over it; then, swinging up the pick smoothly, he brought the blade down hilt-deep into the mixture of limestone and blue-grey clay. Don't worry, Alan, I thought; I'm not competing with you for overtime. In life's lottery, I seem to have won.

'See you', I said.

'Yeah', he replied out of the corner of his mouth, sceptically, like Dick Tracy.

# Chapter 14

ENGLISH TRIPOS, PART II

Monday, 22 May 1961, 1.30-4.30

TRAGEDY

Answer FOUR questions in all, at least ONE and not more than TWO on Greek tragedy.

...11. 'Even the excessive sensibility which ruins the *Tragédie bourgeoise* has its positive functions. In it we should see not only a subterfuge and a falsification but a fresh, though fumbling, grapple with the passions which Reason was seeking to make taboo. The achievement of this genre was the discovery of a new tragedy, the tragedy of common life.'
EITHER develop or demolish this justification; OR trace the evolution of the tragedy of common life...

———

'Isn't there a *cleaner* sort of job you could try for anywhere?', my mother asked when I returned home. She was peeling the potatoes in the narrow scullery with its shallow stone sink.

I didn't reply. I tugged the deck-chair out of the coal-shed, wiped it, and (after a little difficulty) set it in the corner of our back yard which, towards mid-day, usually caught a rectangle of sunlight. After 2.30 the yard would be enshadowed by the surrounding walls and rooftops and chimney-stacks. With my feet propped on a leaking earth-box of nasturtiums and geraniums, I read the *Guardian* at leisure. When I was away, my dad took the *News Chronicle*; when I was at home, he took the *Guardian* because I preferred it for tactical reasons (e.g., it published book-reviews by Piggott). He ordered papers not from the nearby newsagent but from one half a mile away, so that neighbours could not infer his political views. A few flies buzzed avidly round my grease-glued quiff.

In those days since Finals, I was enjoying the most stress-free and worry-free time I could recall. It seemed that ever since I'd entered school, there had been tests and exams, tests and exams; and at last I'd emerged into the peaceful land beyond them. Even infants' school had offered its ordeals.

Highbury infants' school, Grosvenor Street. My mother had taken me the first morning, but thereafter I went and returned alone. That first day, she had been embarrassed. The other mums were, on average, twenty years younger than she; one had commented on the fact that the 'little grandson' was wearing specs. In the classroom, halfway through the long strange morning, the teacher had carried around milk-crates, and had set on each desk a small bottle – a third of a pint – of milk. I realised that we children were expected to open the bottles ourselves. I'd never done such a thing before. The girl next to me held the bottle in her left hand, and pressed her right thumb to the perforated disc in the centre of the cardboard cap; the disc gave, and she deftly lifted the cap out, and drank. When I applied my thumb, the cardboard resolutely resisted it; I pressed ever harder; and eventually, shockingly, the cap plunged down, and milk sprayed up, over my spectacles blindingly, over my face, my jacket, and my immaculate glossy-brown gas-mask case; dismayed, I let go of the bottle, which tipped over and, rolling on the desktop before dropping to the floorboards, discharged the rest of its milk on to my short trousers. 'Clumsy clumsy boy!', said Miss Lazenby, trying to rub the milk off my jacket with a chalky blackboard-cloth.

A later embarrassment at infants' school was the 'the' matter. One afternoon, Miss Lazenby wrote 'THE' in capitals on the blackboard and asked the lad next to me (Alan perhaps) what the letters spelt. 'Tell me', he whispered to me. I thought: 'H' and 'E' spell 'he', so 'T' plus 'HE' spell – why, 'tea'. 'Tea', I told him. 'Tea, Miss', he said. 'No, no, no', she replied; 'It's "the".' Red-faced, I cringed. But that embarrassment eventually proved useful. Imprinted in me was the sequence: 1, enigma; 2, false decoding; 3, true decoding. So, much later, I found that that same sequence could explain the engaging vividness of numerous literary works. In *Heart of Darkness*, Marlow sees white objects on Kurtz's fence. That's the enigma. False decoding: they're carved ivory balls. True decoding, after a delay: they're the skulls of Kurtz's victims. 'Delayed decoding': Ian Watt, in a guest lecture at Cambridge, used that term. I saw that if you extend the principle on a large scale, you find covert plotting. (Watt, incidentally, had survived brutal treatment in a Japanese prison-camp. He'd had to decipher shouted commands. It all fits.)

Now, on the other side of the corrugated-iron fence, someone pulled the chain and coughed and spat as he emerged from the outside lavatory, so I didn't hear the knock at our front door. After a while, my mother leaned out of the kitchen window: she sounded frightened. 'There's this telegram just come. It's for you.'

I thought: 'It's Arabella. She's killed herself. My mother'll want to know'; and I held the telegram close to my chest as I opened it so that she couldn't look over my shoulder and see.

The telegram said: 'Congratulations on first. Piggott.'

I read it three times, to make sure there was no mistake. At the third reading, I exhaled, as the meaning soaked in. There's a superstitious rule that what you would most like to happen never *does* happen: which suggested that the message was a malicious hoax by Jack or Casey or one of the Angel gang. The Cambridge postmark didn't refute this theory: they could have been in Cambridge on a visit. Stylistically, the note seemed genuine, though. Piggott's comments on essays were usually curt scrawls, just one or two words; whereas a hoaxer, trying to be both ironic and donnish in style, would have put something like 'Congratulations on your brilliant first, am stricken with admiration'. The clincher was the time on the date-stamp: '0920'. Rather early for a hoaxer: a hoax telegram would more likely have been sent after pub opening hours. I concluded that it was genuine; and Piggott, experienced man who liked scholarly precision, was highly unlikely to make a blunder, to misread a list. The *Guardian* was due to publish the results in the next few days; Piggott had kindly sent early notice.

I put the telegram in my shirt pocket and resumed looking at the *Guardian*, though sometimes the print went blank as I stared, dazed.

When my father came home from the shop for lunch ('dinner' to him), I showed them the telegram then, at the table, over the pork sausages and spuds and cabbage. My father wiped his hands first on

122

his handkerchief, and held the telegram fastidiously with his finger-tips. He read every word and number, beginning with the address side, turning it over, and finally turning it over again to re-read the address. Then he passed it to my mother without saying anything.

'I suppose you'll think we're daft,' she said, 'But you'd better tell us what it's all about. It sounds very nice, but what does this "first" mean? The first of what? Does it mean you've passed your exams, or is it about something else?'

I explained, with a patience I'd mentally rehearsed earlier behind the *Guardian*, what it meant.

My father stood up and said, 'Ah, well now. Well done. Congratulations, well done', and shook my hand energetically and at length. He pulled his white handkerchief out of his sleeve again and blew his nose, and shook my hand again. His eyes were glistening, brimming.

'That *is* good, then,' she said. 'Don't let your potatoes get cold. Yes, that *does* seem good. Don't fuss over the boy so much, Harry: you've shaken his hand twice now. – That must be just what you've wanted, touch wood.'

I then made the modest speech I'd prepared during the previous half-hour, saying that university lectures were trivial; what really mattered had been deeds like, e.g., my father sending five bob of his pay to *John Bull* magazine when I was fourteen to buy their 'Bargain Offer – Odhams' *Complete Works of William Shakespeare* in Sturdy Binding'; and his motto 'We're here to help each other'; and, e.g., my mother always being willing to read stories to me when I was four or five (Hans Andersen, Brothers Grimm), and her motto 'Never rely on other people; they will always let you down'. I experienced eye-prickling self-gratification at my well-calculated act of patronising gratitude.

Of course, my father marred the effect when he was getting ready to cycle back to work. He asked me, in a protracted way, if I could just let him take the telegram back to the shop with him – he only wanted to borrow it for an hour or so, he said, and he'd look after it very carefully and wouldn't lose it. I tried hard to stifle my irritation, but inevitably his style triggered it.

'What the *hell* you want to take it back to work for?', I asked.

'I'll bring it back at tea-time. It won't get lost', he repeated.

'What d'you want it *for*?', I said. 'Give me a straight answer. It's no use to anyone else.'

'Leave it alone', said my mother. 'The boy's right. It won't mean anything to anyone at the shop, no more than it did to you. Heaven knows, he's just had to explain it to *us*.'

'Well, but I can tell them now. And Mr Lee would understand. His boy went to Bristol University.'

'You put that telegram back on the table', I said. 'I'm not having you going all over the Co-op from the Women's Underwear to the Hardware bragging on my behalf.'

'Bragging hasn't got – *has* got nothing to do with it. Look. I don't suppose you'll remember Mr Lee, but he's often asked after you. He'd be interested, that's all. I know he'd be interested. And Mr Pink, and Mrs Hardy, they've both asked after you.'

'Put.. it ... down.'

'Ah, put it down, like he says, Harry. Can't we have *one* day without arguments in this house?'

'All right', he said, going out. But at the kitchen door that opened on to the side passage, he hesitated and looked back at us. 'It wouldn't have done any harm.'

I crumpled the paper and slapped it into his hand. 'Oh, *take* the bloody thing. Frame it if you want. Go on.'

He didn't take his bike straight out of the passage into the street; and, when I looked out of the kitchen door, I could see him standing there, intently trying to smooth the creases out of the telegram. A tuft of white handkerchief showed at the cuff of his suit jacket. Why did he keep his handkerchief up his *sleeve*?

124

# Chapter 15

CRITICISM AND COMPOSITION

1. Assign approximate dates...

(*f*) 'Gratified ambition, or irreparable calamity, may produce transient sensations of pleasure or distress. Those storms may discompose in proportion as they are strong or the mind is pliant to their impression. But the soul, though at first lifted up by the event, is every day operated upon with diminished influence, and at length subsides into the level of its usual tranquillity.'

———

Next day, the full Cambridge English results were in the paper.

I sat in the deck-chair with the *Guardian* spread over the dustbin lid, and had a gratifying read. There were columns of names allocated to degree-classes, the names being followed by the abbreviated educational pedigree of the candidates, saying what school had provided their secondary education and which college they'd entered. Not the richest of prose. But those columns yielded an hour of pleasure keener than Shakespeare or Lawrence could yield.

The 'Class I' paragraph of the honours lists was perhaps a little larger than I would have wished, with 14 entrants, but it was still satisfyingly exclusive, and very small compared with those for the following classes. There I was, in black impregnable type, unfortunately connoting soup ('Green P.') but still preserved from misprint by a mercifully accurate compositor (for the *Guardian*'s compositorial inaccuracy was already notorious). Jack, of course, was listed in that paragraph; and twelve other names that meant nothing to me. I counted every name in the other classes, and the totals were: Class II.i: 75 students; Class II.ii: 76 students; Class III: 39; and 'declared to have deserved the Ordinary B.A. degree' (bare pass, no honours): four. Failures were, discreetly, not listed. Out of more than

208, I was in the top 14. Or, as a percentage, the top 7%. Or, if the whole list was a ladder with just 14 rungs, the top rung. I gloated, smug as the drunken Caliban.

It was an altruistic pleasure to see Jack's name by mine. But I couldn't resist the slightly malicious pleasure at seeing that he hadn't won the *starred* First he'd wanted. The only starred First I could see was someone from Newnham. On paper, on immortal record, in the eyes of the examiners, irrevocably I was his equal, but I'd learnt more from him than he from me. In one respect the system was anti-intellectual, because the three to three-and-a-half hour limit on answer-papers clearly favoured rapid regurgitators and penalised meditative truth-seekers. The examiners' motto seemed to be '*Ars longa, vita brevis*', delivered with cynical leers.

Casey's name appeared in the II.i paragraph. I felt sympathy, but also, again, a certain amount of malicious pleasure. There might have been only the thinness of a coat of paint between the marks for our papers, but Casey was now irredeemably, for all history, where Cambridge University was concerned, my inferior. I couldn't resist some reflections of this kind: 'That'll take the wind out of his sails; that'll weaken his sneer; that might even curb his right-wing fantasies.'

Another malicious pleasure was generated by Arabella's II.ii, which relegated her to the below-average of finalists, for all her beauty and inbred grace. Was it perhaps my doing – might she have fared better if I hadn't unsettled her by deserting her? Well, that's still her fault, vicariously: *her* class made this system, not mine. Gratifications four and five coming up. No sign of Eastbourne's name: ergo, a total flop. And Farthingale had been branded with the Third he so condignly deserved: the wages of romantic waffle are a lousy III.

Two bright wasps hovered over the page, and finally found a gap under the dustbin-lid and vanished down inside the bin. With every result, the justice was pleasing. Where they'd marked down people I disliked, I was prepared to concede that the examiners might include men of discernment, unwitting allies; and where they had dealt with me, they were enemies and rack-masters that I had outwitted, gulled and defeated. At first, most of the names seemed faceless: when I'd picked out a dozen or so that I knew, there remained two hundred

126

names without faces. But faces, admittedly comic-strip stereotypes, appeared when I studied those abbreviated educational pedigrees in the list. There was a grotesquely undemocratic preponderance of public-school boys. 'Hapgood, K. S., Harrow and Peterhouse; Harsnett, L. J. V., Winchester and King's; Hasselton-Reeve, P. L., Stowe and Trinity; Inchman, H. J. A. R., Eton...'. It didn't take much imagination to see faces that, whether finely-boned and fastidious or pudgy and complacent, would speak with the accents of wealth and privilege, the privilege to draw ample teachers (as garbage draws foraging wasps), so that schools like mine were consequently under-staffed (quite often), under-equipped (generally) and over-crowded: my shabby Grammar School, on its High Street site between the brewery and the Black and White bus station, had needed renovation since the 1930s.

A familiar greeny-yellow aroma of cabbage-water rose from the steaming drain while the list of names and provenances continued to turn itself into gratifying reflections. One reflection was that by deploying critically the contradictions in my nature I'd beaten the competitors in their élitist competition while remaining centrally uncontaminated. I could survey with a feeling verging on benevolence the fifteen foot by ten foot cracked concrete rectangle of this back yard, its corrugated iron fencing, high brick walls and rotting wooden coal-shed and wash-house; and, above them, the sooty monotony of red brick walls and dark grey slate roofs; and the curious variety of chimney-pots, variously crenellated, unadorned, fluted, or occasionally helmeted in grey vaned swivelling cowls. This yard, this bleak claustrophobic eye-sore, which my mother sought to mitigate by pots of geraniums and tubs of nasturtiums, must have toughened my mental muscles from infancy: books offered travel, space, wide horizons, sun; but I wouldn't be fooled by them. Perhaps my decision to pursue research on D. H. Lawrence (critical research, certainly) proved that my mental growth was a protective carapace rather than a corrupting incubus. No: 'rather than a corrupting *narcissistic* incubus': a more resonant rhythm and assonance... The first-class degree surely guaranteed that my research application would be accepted; and there would ensue three years of state-funded research, during which period, while I was dissecting Lawrence, in my spare time there I could complete the novel I

127

hoped to write (realistically digressive and ironically plotless). Five thousand words of it had served as my submission in the optional 'creative writing' component of the exams, Casey and Jack having submitted poetry.

'Mind, *mind*, the dust-cart's coming', said my mother, moving the newspaper and grunting as she lifted the laden dustbin to carry it down the side passage to the street.

'Blackleg labour, that's what you are', I grumbled, trying to find the 'results' page again. 'Let the dustmen come out the back for the bin, for once. It's *their* job, not yours.' The wasps whined out of the bin, spiralled round her muscular forearms, and fled.

'I should think you want – your head felt', she said, heaving at the bin. 'D'you think I want them tramping – their dirt all down the passage, when – on wet days – clean washing hangs there?'

She carried the crammed bin not steadily but in a strained series of jerks and swings, letting it grate dully on the concrete between heaves. I glimpsed a possible scientific law: the tendency of a dustbin to grate rather than clatter is in direct ratio to the weight of its contents. I was irritated at her for making me experience – yet again – guilt at her labour; but we'd both have been embarrassed if I'd offered to help. Her bin-shifting ritual was a dozen years older than I was. If I'd offered, she'd have said something like: 'I've been doing this for forty years, and I dare say I can do it a few more years yet'. And if I'd insisted, wouldn't that have made her feel less independent, an object of charity, all the more keenly a sixty-four-year-old? Indeed, the lines had to be drawn: the lines between altruism and sentimentality, between common sense and insensitive gallantry, between blood-consciousness and mentally-willed benevolence.

Two flies circled my Brylcreemed head as I turned back to the columns of the *Guardian*'s class system.

128

# Chapter 16

CRITICISM AND COMPOSITION

...3. Compare the two following poems, defining any essential differences of quality, kind, or interest which you may find between them, and establishing your preference, if you have one:

(a)     Why art thou silent? Is thy love a plant
        Of such weak fibre that the treacherous air
        Of absence withers what was once so fair?
        Is there no debt to pay, no boon to grant?
        Yet have my thoughts for thee been vigilant –
        Bound to thy service with unceasing care,
        The mind's least generous wish a mendicant
        For naught but what thy happiness could spare.
        Speak – though this soft warm heart, once free to
                                                    hold
        A thousand tender pleasures, thine and mine,
        Be left more desolate, more dreary cold
        Than a forsaken bird's-nest fill'd with snow
        'Mid its own bush of leafless eglantine –
        Speak, that my torturing doubts their end may know!
                                                    WORDSWORTH.

(b)     There's not a nook within this solemn Pass
        But were an apt confessional for one
        Taught by his summer spent, his autumn gone,
        That life is but a tale of morning grass
        Wither'd at eve...

        ———

Jan sent a telegram of congratulation, which, though inexpensively brief, had the effect of reminding me that I hadn't written to her since I'd come home. So I wrote to her saying that the degree ceremony was on June 22nd but I'd arrive in Cambridge before then and looked forward to a private celebration. To make the innuendo clear, I explained in a postscript that in spite of the hot weather I'd remained chaste since last seeing her – which was true, but more through bad luck than fidelity. I didn't tell her exactly when I would return: perhaps to keep her on tenterhooks; perhaps because of that convention in Western films for the travel-stained hero to arrive unexpectedly, to be embraced by the surprised, delighted and avid heroine. I examined this banal motivation but let it pass on grounds of innocence; and, in any case, Finals had made me wary of clock-time deadlines.

I hitch-hiked back on the 20th. My father had been allowed two days off work, Thursday and Friday, so that he and my mother could travel to the degree-giving. Therefore, by travelling back on the Wednesday, I'd be able to avoid a coach-journey with them, and in theory I might thus manage twenty-four hours' unimpeded celebration with Jan and Jack and Casey. I'd told my parents that Jan would 'find me accommodation at her place'. (Yes, 'accommodation', 'c' twice and 'm' twice, favoured word in spelling tests at primary school.) They looked at each other with a questioning expression, the question perhaps being 'Will you ask him exactly what that means or shall I?', but, to their credit, made no awkward enquiry. I told them I'd be travelling by Black and White coach, but I said that only to save myself from their catalogue of warnings about the social indignity of hitch-hiking ('It's just a form of begging') and its manifest perils ('The driver could be *any*body; cars crash').

As usual, the hitch-hike to Cambridge wasn't much quicker than the coach: there are too many small towns on the Cheltenham-to-Cambridge cross-country route avoiding London, and so you get too many short local lifts. A long lift in a slow lorry makes a quicker journey than a score of lifts in Jags and Vauxhalls and Sunbeam Talbots: it's the walking to each new pitch that wastes the time. The final lift was in a big BRS truck (that's 'British Road Services', the nationalised carrier) from Bedford. It was particularly tedious because the driver was one of those opinionative characters who think that as they've given you a ride, you're obliged to repay them in conversational currency; and, in the cab of a twenty-ton lorry, conversation can be onerous. The engine roared under its steel cowling between us, accompanied by metallic vibrations and jangles from every part of the cab, and most of the time I caught only fragments of his sentences. But he still insisted on being repaid in replies. 'Don't you reckon?', he'd bawl at the end of a howled argument about the government or the roads; or 'Ent that right?' or 'What d'you say to that, then?', after some stuff about immigration I hadn't deciphered. 'Dead right', I'd howl back in proley tones over the grinding of gears; 'Stands to reason', while mentally I stripped Jan for the twentieth time; 'Dead right', as the lorry thundered along the Cambridge road.

At last he stopped at the Common, and I jumped down.

'Thanks, mate', I yelled. Above the place where I'd been sitting was a notice that said 'Drivers are strictly forbidden to carry unauthorised personnel'.

'Don't thank me, brother', he shouted back. 'It's what I been saying, we whites are 'ere to 'elp each other, ent we?' ('Whites'? What have I been endorsing?) The cab stank of dark hot oil and eggy farts. I reached on tiptoe and slammed the high door.

The Common's customary serene stillness had been invaded by the vanguard of a travelling fair. Caravans and a generator-lorry lined the footpath, and among the evening shadows of the trees some hands – 'hands': metonymy? No, synecdoche – were assembling the frameworks of stalls and side-shows. In the middle of the green, they were hammering and bolting the struts of the Big Wheel, rapid cacophonous hammering with no rhythm. I didn't pause on the foot-bridge to spit at the swans below: lust-powered, I hurried on, almost trotting, to Jan's.

And there was no response.

The first minute after I'd rung the bell passed easily enough. I was mentally selecting the most engaging sort of greeting, and took some time before settling for the modest flattering banality of 'Well, it's good to be home again', accompanied by a tired but affectionate grin. I still wore the rehearsal-grin on my face when the possibility at last crossed my mind that she might be out: there wasn't a sound. Yet the bell hadn't made that chilly, echoey noise a bell seems to make when a flat's empty. She would have returned from work at least an hour and a half ago. Downstairs, a yard or so from the front door, the curtains were drawn shut in her bedroom window that faced the

131

street, but that was normal; she often left them unopened all day. I thought: She's guessed it's you at the door, she's excited, and she's hunting for a pair of unladdered stockings or struggling to pull on her best bright flowery dress. Try again.

No answer. No Jan.

Now, this is becoming curious. Because if she's out, then Jenny must be in, looking after baby Patrick: so why doesn't Jenny answer? I put down my travelling-bag and jabbed the bell-push repeatedly for a full minute. This time there was a response from inside, the muffled wail of a wakened baby; somebody moved; after a few breathless yelps, the baby fell silent. Nobody came to the door. Jan was evidently out; Patrick was evidently in; someone had lulled Patrick back to sleep; therefore, Jenny was in; but, for some reason, she hadn't answered the door. That much seemed clear, and it was enough to make my tool and balls shrivel and cool with bitter annoyance. Momentarily I recalled, with (for the first time) fellow-feeling, that loony hero of Sartre's *La Nausée* who, when his mistress is absent, says 'I felt a sharp disappointment in my prick'.

I went to the nearest pub (Fort St George) to drink and wait for Jan to come back, and, after two meditative pints, I saw an obvious reason why Jenny hadn't dared to come to the door. Jan's out, so Jenny's boy-friend comes in, so Jenny and boy-friend seize the opportunity for copulation; and in the very middle of it – life has these ironic consolations – in the very middle of it, what perhaps seems to them like some spectral conscience or a finger rebuking Jenny's hypocritical prudishness comes and rings the bell till they tremble, rings the bell till the brat's awake, and, having thus vetoed their back-room blisses, vanishes. Serve Jenny right, the hypocritical goat (goatess? Nanny?). I could gratifyingly envisage her frightened face.

I had a couple more pints. Twice I returned to Jan's, and each time there was no answer; Patrick didn't stir. After a final attempt at 10.15, I pushed a note under the door, to say when I'd return the next evening, and walked into gownland. I felt tired, bored, blurred, frustrated and angry; but I planned to make the best of a bad job by boozing with Casey and Jack before the pubs closed.

But Casey evidently hadn't returned from Leeds yet: his landlady said he'd gone away two weeks ago, and she had no idea when or whether he'd be back. Mrs Fletcher spoke with some bitterness. Though middle-aged, she was passably attractive, I thought, as I retreated.

In College, no Jack. But at least his door was ajar, and, by the muddle inside – big hold-all open on the bed, spilling clothes; brush and comb on a chair – he wasn't far away. I couldn't find him in any of the nearby pubs, though: not in the Mill, not in the Anchor or the Bun Shop. The evening was resembling a one-man itinerant performance of *Waiting for Godot*. At closing time, I lurched back into the silent college, down 18th-century passages smelling of Nescafé and occasionally of urinals, back to Jack's empty room where the inverted Modigliani nude kept watch, her rosy buttocks in the air. I rolled myself up in the duffel coat he used as a door-stop and draught-excluder, and settled to sleep on the carpet.

After meditations on the world-conspiracy that treated me as both victim and agent, I addressed myself with a scrupulous and deliberate simulacrum of sobriety. Roughly as follows. 'You cunt. You poor cunt. Your life has no Hollywood director. Jan is no mind-reader. All you had to do was to say in the letter from home exactly when you'd be calling for her. You're looking a gift horse in the mouth. You rebelled against clock-time but you merely frustrated nature-time. While you and your Dark Phallic Principle have been traipsing the streets, Jan's probably been hurrying in anguish and on heat between Drummer Street and the British Railways station to wait for the bus from Cheltenham and the trains from Liverpool Street and King's Cross. And all the time, half the beds of the world have been bouncing with copulation, billions of spermy runners jumping neck-and-neck in the human race.'

Steeple-chase. The distant bells of the Catholic Church played their mechanical four-bar intro and rang midnight, fading and swelling as the wind veered, and during the next five minutes the hour echoed at different pitches and keys and paces from clock-towers and spires all over the still town. They'd echoed as coldly and lengthily as that when I'd travelled up from home to take the Entrance Examination six years before; and I'd damned the bells at twelve and one for interrupting my quote-learning, at two and three for wrecking the sleep that I needed before undertaking the exam papers. They'd echoed as coldly and desolately when, after the Navy and the East End Service Station, I'd first arrived as an under-graduate, a new recruit in seductively historic barracks.

Moonlight, cold on Jack's bed and on his long rows of stolen books. Once the Research Board had approved my application, there'd be three more years of books, three more years of Cambridge's clock-time; but sanctuary with Jan, on Jan, in Jan... ('Sanctuary' evoked, first, Charles Laughton in *The Hunchback*, and, secondly, the shelter called a Morrison, delivered to my home in 1944, replacing the wooden kitchen table. In the day-time, its steel surface had to function as a table-top, and meals would be served on it; and at night, while the searchlights crisscrossed the skies, we'd all three huddle, like trapped animals, inside the cage it made with its bolted steel uprights and side-mesh...) Jan would be in bed by now, footsore. In bed with her arms folded over her squashed-pear breasts, a crusader's wife on a tomb. Pair of breasts I've squashed. Crusader's wife locks her legs round crusader's undulating back; the Roman Catholic church echoes to the slop and slap of their reunion, and the Verger nervously shoos away the procession of touring parents; and the slop and slap is also the noise of waves where the tomb floats, the waves where Burt Lancaster and Deborah Kerr writhe... in the film *From Here to Eternity*...

And I woke fast then with my hand still on my tool, and thought: *From Here to Eternity*? Even your id uses third-rate Hollywood scenarios! Why not have a wank and at least milk two seconds' relief from the evening? No, of course not: that's failure and shame. Save it for Jan tomorrow: enjoy revenge and altruism combined. Verb 'milk' evoked Petty Officer Feasey's vindication of Holy Matrimony: 'Why pay for pints of milk, when you can keep a cow in the back yard?'

The floor-boards hardened against my hip-bone through the carpet, the duffel coat and my jeans. If this is liberty, said my aching hip, it feels much like the rack: you might as well marry Jan and enjoy an honourable draw in the sexual contest. An honourable discharge (ha!) from competition. A withdrawal with honours. Crusader and wife, fast interlocked on Dunlopilloed tomb: marriage: yes; even an owlish Philip Larkin seemed to be advising it, making an almost-instinct almost true. Why wait for better, when the politicians were locked in their competitive dementia? Their nuclear arms-race seemed bound to culminate, by accident or design, in a vast swift Armageddon, brighter than a thousand suns.

I woke once more that night. The book-spines glistened under the moon. Jack snored again from the bed, and ground his teeth with a squeaking sound. The duffel coat seemed warmer and fringed: there was a blanket on it: he must have thrown a blanket over me after he'd come in. He snored again, teeth squeaking softly. Had it been friendship or patronising contempt when he'd dropped the blanket on my huddled sleep?

All over the city, in the cold air, clocks struck three, for five minutes.

———

We got up at eleven, comparing hangovers, and for breakfast went to the espresso bar on Free School Lane, where Jack expected to meet Casey.

'I'll grant – you – this much', Jack was saying while licking the second cup's foam from his lips, 'For sheer parasitic intelligence you probably deserved it. But if you deserved *that*, then by rights I should have got a *starred* First, even from Christian fellow-travellers like McConville and Blane. I'll prove it: have you started any lines of research to get your Lawrence thesis properly under way yet?'

'Fuck all, yet. What d'you expect? Jesus, man, we've only just jumped through the last lot of hoops.'

'See? What did I tell you? You've done nowt, while I've started getting the manuscripts rolling in, copies of them. Last night, brother, I called on Piggott and picked his brains about Carpenter. Drank half his Glenmorangie at the same time. He said he hadn't found anything to shoot down our theory about Carpenter's influence on Lawrence, and he gave me the addresses of half-a-dozen old hicks who might have Carpenter letters. Unpublished manuscript material, that's what carries a Ph.D. thesis. You could be on a bum steer, concentrating on Lawrence's fiction. All his holographs'll be published or tied up in the States by now.'

'"Hole-o-graphs"? Some sort of pornographic print?'

'Don't push your luck. If you really don't know, I should have got a *triple-starred* First. Your notions on anti-rationalism and its links to anarchism and fascism were okay; but I sometimes think that you doing research on Lawrence'll be like putting an illiterate

135

vampire in charge of a blood bank. Talking of blood banks: Piggott invites us to a party tonight. His room, 8 p.m.; mostly the same people as last time.' He glanced at the door. 'Help you drown your sorrows, if any. Keep you off the streets.'

Casey walked in slowly and ordered his coffee. This was supposed to be a self-service place, but the girl at the counter still came scurrying to him, anxiously bearing a frothy glass. Perhaps it was because of his formidably weary and disgusted expression, or because he'd pass for a fastidious don in that black corduroy suit with the watch-chain across the waistcoat.

'You look as if you've been on the job all night', I jeered. 'Have you just travelled down?'

He raised an eyebrow at Jack and cleared his throat. 'I've been rendering my services to Cambridge all along.'

'Your landlady says you'd been gone a fortnight.'

'That's correct. I won't be returning to her ghetto.'

There was an odd silence, as if the other two were waiting for me to provide a cue I'd forgotten. I guessed they were expecting me to commiserate with Casey for getting only a II.i; but I charitably didn't mention the results. My guess, however, was evidently wrong. After sipping coffee for a while, Casey explained, reluctantly but with verbal nudging from Jack, that recent circumstances had brought him to 'a certain crisis in his arrangements' with Mrs Fletcher. He was about to take a lunch with her at which he'd have to explain that it was their final meeting. He fell silent, and Jack slowly shook his head.

'Well, that's no great problem, man', I told Casey. 'Say it with flowers.'

Which he did. In the Botanic Gardens on Bateman Street, Jack and I kept watch, while Casey drew his nail-scissors from their little leather pocket-case and at tedious length selected, snipped and arranged a tasteful bouquet of exotic blooms. He seemed too preoccupied to talk, ignoring our jocular quarrel about what the names of the things might be ('Venus Flytrap'? 'Deadly Night-shade'? 'Hemlock'?); and he didn't seem at ease; eventually he left us to march briskly towards Mrs Fletcher's.

'Wrap them in tissue-paper from a greengrocer's!', Jack shouted after the departing little figure.

I said: 'You know, so far as I'm still capable of any feelings after

136

three years in the company of you two, I'm beginning to feel sorry for that bloke. He's always spinning his webs, but it could be that he's trapped in them.'

Jack hummed a snatch of the Barcarolle (*'Belle nuit, O nuit d'amour'* from *The Tales of Hoffmann*: great film by Powell and Pressburger: we were fans of those directors). 'Casey doesn't need your charity, and nature doesn't support your analogy', he said. 'How's that for a finely-turned sentence?'

# Chapter 17

ENGLISH TRIPOS, PART II

Wednesday, 24 May 1961, 1.30 – 4.30

SPECIAL PERIOD OF ENGLISH LITERATURE FROM 1880
TO 1910

Answer Question 1 and THREE others.

1. Write brief notes on THREE of the following passages, showing how they represent or illustrate characteristics of the period:

...(*f*) I was brought up in the strictest school...; and when I was old enough to think for myself, I started on my journey of inquiry with little doubt about the general truth of what I had been taught; and with that feeling of the unpleasantness of being called an 'infidel' which, we are told, is so right and proper. Near my journey's end, I find myself in a condition of something more than mere doubt about these matters.

(T. H. HUXLEY.)

———

We spent the afternoon drinking cider by the river, and after opening-time we proceeded to the Mill. I vaguely recalled that the coach from Cheltenham arrived at 7.30, so I had time for a couple of pints. Alex Eastbourne was already in the Mill, and uninvited, he flopped into a chair at our table.

'Salutations', he said in his melodic public-school voice. Jack and I grunted, embarrassed. It was like a visit from someone diagnosed with cancer: you don't know whether to sound sympathetic or to try to act heartily as if you haven't heard of the diagnosis. Silence for a while.

'You've forgotten to congratulate me', he said, glancing at me with a smile like an apprehensive spaniel's.

'You're getting married?'

'No, I mean about Finals.'

'Don't say they've given you a pass, after all. A miscarriage of justice, that'd be.'

'You don't understand. I mean, congratulate me on my symbolic gesture.'

'Your *what*?' said Jack.

'He says he's been making his symbolic gesture.'

'His "symbolic" "gesture"?'

'An existential choice?'

'A leap into the void?'

'In fear and trembling?'

'An *acte gratuit*?'

'*Please* listen', he interrupted us. 'It takes courage, to walk out, but I *just* managed to do it.'

'Yeah, I'm sure', I said cheerfully. 'Like the man who just managed to save a gorgeous woman from being raped in the street. By a supreme effort of will, he succeeded in controlling himself.'

'Give the gent a chance to explain', said Jack.

'I've explained to Peter already, just before Finals started.'

'Tried to nobble me, more like', I grumbled. 'Miracle I passed at all, with you calling to preach sermons just when I'm in the middle of learning my notes.'

'I wanna hear about symbolic gestures', insisted Jack.

Eastbourne resumed, staring into space. 'I nearly funked it. The first day, I walked round and round, wondering whether I could do it, you see. Well, I did funk it for a while, through thinking of what my parents might say. I haven't gone home to face them yet... not yet... Yes, I went in for a while, but then, that first day, sitting in the examination hall, I felt – I *knew* I was right. I thought to myself, what matters can't just be the solitary sheet of paper one receives at the end; it must be how one has grown, spiritually, over the years. And after that, I stayed away. I still feel I've done what is right. It *must* be right.' He gave the beer-mat a gentle smile. 'Tolly's Ales', he read aloud.

'There's something to work on here', said Jack, rubbing his beefy hands together. 'Distinct possibilities. The last shall be first. (Bible and *Miss Julie*.) A new criterion of academic merit. People with

139

thirds and bare passes can say, "I came closest to a fail, out of idealism. Therefore, I'm really quite a first-class fellow." But are you sure you weren't simply rationalising away a panic?'

Eastbourne smiled at the mat, and twirled it round and round on its edge. 'I feel that I've done what is right.'

'Course you've done right', I said. 'What a noble sacrifice. It's like a cannibal deciding to abstain from celery. You can't lose. People like Jack and me, we don't get degrees for fun. We get them to end up with jobs a sight less badly-paid than our parents had. But look at you, with a father who's a millionaire, or near enough. You'll go back like the Prodigal Son, and out comes the fatted calf – '

'Degree or no degree', said Jack, 'by the time you're thirty, you'll be getting a salary – if you have to work at all – that'll make our pay look like chickenfeed.'

Eastbourne stopped twirling the beer-mat.

'Another thing', Jack continued. 'Places at university are given on a competitive basis.'

'So?', he said, puzzled. 'You can't claim I've robbed the taxpayer. You're the people receiving State Scholarships, not me.'

'We'll make it simple for you,' I said. 'Look. Suppose two men apply for one place. One man gets it, the other doesn't. All right so far?'

'So?'

'So by being in this University for three years,' said Jack, 'you've been keeping out some poor man –'

'Some poor bastard who'd have given his right arm –', I went on.

'– for the degree that you've flushed down the drain –'

'– flushed with pride –'

'– A flush in the pan!'

Eastbourne stood up, looking sick.

'If you want to make a symbolic gesture,' added Jack, 'get us two pints.'

But he went: slowly, preoccupied. We shook hands over this joint victory. Jack was shaking with laughter like a young Falstaff. 'There's one thing to be said for cannibalism: if people had to eat their enemies, there'd be no more wars.'

'I'm not quite with you, man.'

'Never mind,' he said. 'It's time we moved. Nearly half past seven. Nearly time for the party. And haven't you got to go to meet

140

your parents off the bus? (Three years ago, I'd have said "go *and* meet").'

'Christ, yeah.' I'd forgotten them. 'If I can install them at the hotel quick enough, I'll still be able to look in at the party on the way to Jan's. Don't steal all Piggott's Scotch before I get there.'

The table shook again. 'I'll leave you plenty – your need's greater than mine, tonight. You've got problems.'

'No trouble. My parents know how to be self-effacing, I'll say that. I'll fit everything in, somehow.'

'Mind how you go. You're staggering a bit already.'

———

When I reached the Drummer Street bus station, there were no buses. Just a couple of old folk sitting in the shelter, and nearby a gang of yobs yelling as they kicked a tin can along the gutter. Not a coach in sight. Then I saw that those old folk were my parents.

The shelter was empty, except for them. They sat as still as a pair of Henry Moore figures. My mother sat firmly upright, but my father was hunched by her side, gazing at the pavement. Their solitary suitcase stood neatly by their feet, and a lolly wrapper blew against it, stuck for a moment, and whirled free in the dusty breeze. They didn't notice it. Anyone could see at once that they'd been waiting there for a long, long time; past the stage of keen expectation, past the stage of irritated impatience, past the stage of weary worry.

I reminded myself to look genial: they couldn't help it if their arrival coincided with a party and my first chance in weeks to get to bed with Jan. 'Hello! Welcome!', I said. 'Haven't been here long, have you? Was the bus early?'

My father stood up stiffly, by stages, and held out a hand; he even mustered a smile.

'We've been here one hour and five minutes', said my mother as she struggled to her feet. She sniffed disapprovingly, smelling my breath.

'An hour and five minutes? Shouldn't the bus have been here at 7.30?'

'It came in at 6.30. The right time, by the time-table.'

I nearly said 'How was I to know?', but then remembered I was supposed to have come by bus myself yesterday.

At the Garden House hotel, they were slow to thaw out. I explained that here I'd booked them in at one of the best hotels in Cambridge; but all they said, without enthusiasm, was 'You shouldn't', and 'Any boarding house would have done'. My mother cheered up a little when I showed her the private bathroom (called *'en suite'*): she said she hadn't gone to the lavatory for five hours, and shut herself in there for five minutes.

I was puzzled by their response to the hotel. They couldn't ever have stayed in so posh a place before, with big glass doors and uniformed waiters and thick carpets, a place that made you want to tiptoe so you wouldn't mar it. I planned to spend on their stay the whole of my College English Prize (the Collins Prize, to be precise). Yet not a single Ooh or Aah. They just repeated quietly that I shouldn't have troubled; and in their room they unpacked that strapped case (with its candle-burn on the lid, from blackout nights) very slowly and carefully, while I sat on the dressing-table swinging my legs and glancing now and then at my – his spare – watch. The party would be under way; Jan would have been home from work a couple of hours by now. She'd be looking out of the window for me.

'I'd like to get you both a drink', I said. 'Or would you rather stay here for a while and put your feet up?'

'Of course you shall get us a drink, if you really want to', my mother replied. So I found myself leading them to the bar. I'd never seen them in a bar before, nor seen them drink anything stronger than a glass of cider, apart from the drop of port (always Cockburn's – 'it's pronounced *Co*-burn's', my mother would puritanically insist) at Christmas. They never went to pubs. Abstemiousness must be what differentiates the upper-working-class (skilled manual, with some middle-class aspirations) from the middle- and lower-working class and of course from Marx's *Lumpen*. Yet they sat at a glass-topped table in the bar of the Garden House and let me order two bottles of pale ale. And just as I was glancing at my watch again, they started urging me to go out and see my friends: they were sure I had my own plans, they said; and they themselves would be going to bed quite soon, because they were tired out by the journey.

I explained where I'd meet them on the coming day, after the ceremony, and hastened away. Only 8.30. It had all gone very

142

smoothly, really. As I'd told Jack, they at least knew how to be self-effacing.

———

I hadn't forgotten the resolution made during the previous night's inebriation, the resolution to make, unprompted, unexpectedly, an offer of marriage to Jan. The more I reflected on it, walking briskly up Mill Lane to College, the more it seemed a master-stroke. She'd be waiting more and more despondently, almost giving up hope; then suddenly I'd arrive and she'd receive a proposal out of the blue, delivered in cool, casual, throw-away style. I was about to rehearse the exact words I'd use, but then calculated that on this occasion it would be best to let the words formulate themselves at the very moment of meeting. If they lacked precision or neatness, that would demonstrate all the more the spontaneity and sincerity of my feelings. Lawrentian spontaneity. And of the sincerity of my feelings I was reasonably convinced; for if I didn't love her, how was it that the thought of proposing marriage did not seem alarming? The very fact that it seemed so natural a prospect guaranteed a sufficient if un-tempestuous emotional backing for the deed. We got along easily, simply, good-humouredly, without significant quarrels, without embarrassment; she knew the rancour of my socks, I knew the holeyness of her underwear, and without detraction. In short, it was doing what comes naturally (a Doris Day number?): a minute's thought proved it.

Therefore, to visit the party on the way would be little more than a bachelor's last gesture of irresponsibility. But no, not even irresponsibility, on reflection. If Arabella were there, I'd be able to round off matters neatly and completely. With the confidence imparted by my First, I could now make to her a generous speech on the lines of 'Sorry I stopped seeing you, but I'm sure you'll understand.' That First seemed to have given me the full courage of my moral convictions: I could now make the break cleanly explicit, whereas, before the results, something had inhibited me.

As at the previous party, Piggott's room was so crowded that people were clustered in the corridor outside, and, when I elbowed my way in through the throngs and the chatter, I recognised the bustling urgent background music: 'Boogie Stop Shuffle': the

143

Mingus band, with Booker Ervin on tenor. But instead of listening with respect, the chattering people were just chattering louder. Pausing to greet John Riley (ex-Crail), I nearly collided with a waiter; almost by reflex I took two full fizzing tall glasses from his tray; spoilt matters by saying 'For friends': a needless explanation that only a vulgar booze-lifter would bother to offer to a college servant. The waiter gave me a sardonic glance (as if to say 'You must be pissed but it's not for me to comment') and squeezed by, twisting and angling the clinking tray dextrously.

'Well done', said Arabella in her low sexy voice (Joan Greenwood came to mind, in *The Man in the White Suit*); at the same time, somebody's elbow boned me in the back so that I nearly emptied both the glasses down her ample cleavage. 'Do let me introduce you both. Lionel, this is Peter Green: you remember, he's that friend of Casey's I told you about. Pete, this is my fiancé, Lionel.'

His crushing handshake was a predictable cliché, and he beamed down at me as genially as he used to from the steel-framed photograph at her bed-side. 'Congratulations', I said hesitantly, unsure of my ground, and glad there was safety in a crowd. He wouldn't swing a fist at me in public, and in here there wasn't even *room* to swing. 'How long have you been engaged?'

'Oh, practically from childhood, you know, unofficially. Our fathers were partners in the same firm, so it's been brewing – if such pleasures brew – for ages.'

'Officially, for a month', said Arabella. 'Since the morning of the day your strange friend Casey turned up, actually. Didn't he tell you? I'm *sure* he did.'

'"Strange" is the word', said Lionel. 'The cheek of the man. – Care for a cigarette? Menthol. – Knocks on her door and promptly – you'd think he'd only have to glance at us to see he wasn't wanted – introduces himself as a senior acquaintance of yours, and then, just as if I weren't there, starts chatting her up with a story that a big bet hinges on whether she'll accept his invitation to a May Ball. You'd think the double ticket was a search-warrant, the way he held it out.'

'Oh, it wasn't *quite* as crude as that', she interjected, pinching his arm. 'It was a very civilised and polite and diplomatic sort of chatting-up, with lots of little throat-clearings; and when we

144

explained the situation to him and pointed out that naturally we'd already made *our* arrangements about the Ball, he didn't bat an eyelid; in fact, he seemed very interested in Lionel and in Lionel's career, and they found out that they both knew Leeds well, of all places; and that's how we ended up by taking him out for a run with us in the MG. But you'll know *all* about that run by now.'

'Oh sure', I replied, swigging down the Asti Spumante. 'Casey told me all about that farce.'

'Rather too ironic for a mere farce, don't you think?', she said.

'Seriously', he resumed, after turning briefly to beam at Arabella, 'Don't hold me responsible, old son. Man proposes, woman disposes.' He put his arm round her waist and murmured something about a bird in the hand, while there was an uproar of laughter from another group behind me. I recognised Dr Haggerty's cackle as Piggott called us over. One of Haggerty's sticks prodded my toe firmly while she asked me what I'd been doing in the vacation. 'Partly, sitting in a deck-chair,' I replied, 'and looking forward to inflicting myself on you and the rest of Cambridge for another three years.'

The puckered smile faded, she looked miserably reflective for a moment, and then she murmured up into my ear, slowly, as though she were selecting her words very carefully, 'You should not let your application to the Research Board deter you from applying elsewhere.'

'Some hopes', I said cheerfully. 'Some hopes.' I took her words as oblique sarcasm, and it wasn't till several months later that I understood how greatly she had over-estimated my ability to discriminate between sarcasm and informed advice. There were some Cambridge skills that were not in the syllabus. And in Piggott's crowded room, with the lights gleaming on the wine-flutes, with the Mingus cacophony competing with the prattling chatter, and my wrist-watch whispering 'Hurry to Jan's; go, now' – well, I wasn't in a position then to master that salutary skill.

Someone had stolen my bicycle from the College rack. Even with no leather to cover the spring-mesh of the saddle, someone had thought it worth stealing. (I shrugged: at least I'd had nine terms of use out of it since I'd rescued it at the police bike-auction.) Anyway, this meant that by the time I reached Midsummer Common on the way to Jan's, the sky was darkening and the fair was noisily busy: flashing coloured bulbs, a Babel of loudspeakers competing with the head-throbbing hum of the generators. Last night's huddle of caravans and carpentry had engineered this electric labyrinth of glitter, colour and stenches: oil and burnt rubber from Dodgems, the hot greasy rich aroma of hot-dogs, the infantile sweetness of pink candy-floss. A group of female teenagers – hardly teenagers – impeded me, their absurd paper hats saying 'Have a Go' and 'We're Swinging Tonight' and 'Do It Now'. Trying to push past them, I stumbled over a cable that snaked in trampled mud, and jostled a man who was hurling ping-pong balls at empty goldfish-bowls. Tunk-tunk-clack went the balls, bouncing from one globe-rim to the next, while above my head, in their transparent plastic envelopes, the trapped goldfish wriggled and zigzagged in the glare – relatives of the doomed fish in... in (ha: got it!) Cunninghame Graham's mordant story, commended by Jack.

When I eventually struggled through, I found myself on the side I'd started from, and had to struggle back. I was beginning to feel sick not in the belly but in the head: my head wanted to vomit the soup of light and noise and stench that sprayed into it, urged on by the shouts of shabby townsfolk. From a vibrating screened booth, a wall-eyed hag, like Sartre in a curly wig, thrust a rifle at me and said 'Try your luck, mister. Win a lovely vase for your girl-friend. Five shots a shilling, eight for one an' a tanner.' Below the row of swivelling targets were pyramids of ornamental junk: plaster geese and swans for walls, ugly ducklings, plastic bangles, tinny ashtrays, and stacks of flawed crockery, the rejected 'seconds' of the potteries.

Nevertheless, a few coconuts lurked, dark, solid and hairy, the only natural things to be seen. I thought I'd take one to Jan, a peace-offering for lateness: it'd make her grin that endearing toothy grin; I'd never taken her a present before (apart from the caterpillar). As I wasn't wearing my spectacles, it took me five minutes and six-bob's-worth of shots to secure one. But the Barcarolle came to mind reassuringly: *'Belle nuit, O nuit d'amour.'*

146

# Chapter 18

CRITICISM AND COMPOSITION

...1. Assign approximate dates to FIVE of the following passages, giving your reasons:

...*(b)*They parted without shaking hands: she had kept the interview, for his sake, in tints of the quietest grey. Yet she thrilled with happiness ere she reached her own house. Others had loved her in the past, if one may apply to their brief desires so grave a word, but those others had been 'ninnies' – young men who had nothing to do, old men who could find nobody better. And she had often 'loved', too, but only so far as the facts of sex demanded: mere yearnings for the masculine, to be dismissed for what they were worth, with a smile. Never before had her personality been touched. She was not young or very rich, and it amazed her that a man of any standing should take her seriously. As she sat trying to do her accounts in her empty house, amidst beautiful pictures and noble books, waves of emotion broke, as if a tide of passion was flowing through the night air. She shook her head, tried to concentrate her attention, and failed. In vain did she repeat: 'But I've been through this sort of thing before.'...

———

I rang the bell and arranged myself in a butler's pose with the coconut held aloft on three fingers.

The door opened promptly on Casey.

'Hi', I said. 'Hey, what the hell you doing *here*, Casey?'

'No', said Jan, at his side. 'Go back to the kitchen, Jim. Let *me* do it. Let me talk to him.' I looked over my shoulder, but there was no doubt about it – her 'him' was me; correction, was I. My arm began to tremble at the elbow, and I slowly, cautiously, lowered the coconut.

'I've brought you a nut', I explained; 'but I don't think there's any milk in it. It doesn't slop when I shake it.' I held it towards her and shook it, while confusion and incredulity befuddled me.

Casey backed down the narrow hall passage to the kitchen door and watched me with his arms folded, watching intently as if I were a potentially dangerous animal. Oddly, he was dressed informally: above the customary cord trousers was a white shirt with the sleeves rolled up. 'Hi', I said again, hopefully; but Jan led me into her room and shut the door. The bed-spring squealed like a tight fart as I sat down.

'Casey', I said. 'Uh... What's Casey doing here? Hey?'

She sat at the other end of the bed, puffing a tipped Woodbine and looking down at the frayed hole in the carpet.

'Christ, this is awful', she said at last. 'I don't know how to put it.' I could hear the fair-ground's loudspeakers in the distance, fading phrases of a dated pop song about honey and money. 'Lousy choice of background-music they lay on at this place. Look, Jan, what's Casey doing here? Has he come round to try to pick you up? I told you, that bloke tries to take anything that wears a skirt and moves. Run him out! Send him back to Mrs Fletcher.'

'You won't understand,' she said, 'but it's like this. I've been going out with Jim since before your Finals, and we're going to get married.'

'Balls, bullshit, and pull the other one! Stop this silly practical joke now, and let's go out and get drunk. I've got a First, I'm a genius, I've brought you a coconut, and the night is young. Come *on*, sort yourself out!'

She inhaled smoke hard, and just repeated more quietly what she'd said before: 'Jim and me, we're going to get married.'

The pattern I was staring at, I found, was composed of the frayed hole in the carpet and the speckled green lino beneath it. There seemed no good reason why the carpet should be so worn at that point. That's the only hole I'll get tonight, I thought, gently placing the coconut there. She isn't joking. Casey's got her. My pulse surged. Problem: what to do about it. Hollywood style would be to slap her face and stride away with a good dramatic slam of the door. Further

148

problem: How do you slap the face of someone who's sitting hunched and half-crouching, sideways to you, at the end of a bed, and, what's more, puffing a cigarette held close to the mouth? Alternative: a moralistic diatribe, make her feel guilty, make her feel repentant (improbable) but me righteous; then exit. Snag: Casey's in, I'm out. Further alternatives: try persuasion to get Casey out and me re-instated. Varieties of persuasion: (i) a Brando-esque near-inarticulate spiel, eloquent through its dulled tone and long pauses, expressive of deep feelings; (ii) rapidly articulate spiel, lucid, cool, implying my control of my feelings, my patient rationality (Trevor Howard style) – but perhaps alienating her through the seemingly forensic treatment. Further snags: (a) my head's beginning to spin, from the drinks I've had today; and (b) my bladder's full, but I can't go to the bog in these circumstances. It's worse than having to solve an exam problem in two minutes.

'It's a bastard', I said, surveying the alternatives.

'It's a bastard', she echoed without irony, to my surprise.

'Congratulations', I said for the third or fourth time that day.

There was a hole in the knee of her stocking, too. The pink skin bulged slightly there. I could imagine the smooth feel of that small pink bulge under my hand; and with a shock I realised that Casey must have had his thin bony hand there by now – why, and it must have groped up her thigh, and his delicate thin fingers must have paddled her vulva and tweaked her nipples; and his slow hard worm must have slid into her slime by now – once? In six weeks, he could have done it a hundred times; perhaps two hundred; why, the thought that he was competing with me would have made him screw again and again, even when he was sated and tiring: still, somehow, by summoning up imaginary mental orgies as he lay lightly on her, he'd have mustered a poke, a poke; and there she was, sitting quietly on the edge of the bed like a rational, sane, gentle, normal woman, and not half of that sweaty possessed comedy team, Beast with Two Backs, Incorporated.

I decided that hitting her could be postponed, for a minute or two. I did need to urinate. When my piss had stung me, wasn't that some mild form of clap I'd caught from her? 'May you be blest with issue', I said softly. (Ha: 'issue' prompted by notion of discharge.)

'Don't, Pete. Don't get bitter. Or theatrical.'

149

I was tempted to tell her about my big moral choice of rejecting Arabella, but I decided that might not work in my favour. The bed was comfy, my feet were tired, the room was rotating gently, pausing, rotating, and I wanted to lie back and shut my eyes – but that wouldn't do: the best pose was a hunched-forward one, like hers: tutorial attentiveness; and it relieved the bladder-pressure, too. The bed was soft. The beds i'th'East are soft, quote. I perceived the comforts of being a married research student: coming back knackered from the University Library to a kitchen where Jan would be grinning as she turned from the steaming stove: I could almost smell the stew: my stomach rumbled. Don't hit, not yet. See what the lie of the land is, try a little arguing.

'But how did all this come about, exactly? How did Casey pick you up in the first place?'

'Does it matter, now? You won't like it. For one thing, I knew about you and Arabella. I don't want you to think I was spying on you, or anything like that, but I knew. I was quite afraid of losing you, then. She used to bring her car into the garage from time to time for petrol or servicing. She's nice. We used to compare notes sometimes about what we did at the week-ends, the places we'd been to, pubs and so on; and after a while – you won't believe it, we giggled together like schoolgirls when we worked it out – then the manager came and told me off, because there were two cars queuing for petrol behind her Austin 7 – we worked out that one of the boys she'd been telling *me* about was the same one I'd been telling *her* about. Do you know, you're blushing. I've never seen you blush before, ever. Even round the back of your neck, too.'

'All right, all right. But what's this got to do with Casey?'

'Well, one Sunday she drove in with Lionel, and Jim was sitting on the back, on the luggage-rack over the petrol-tank. He was looking a bit windblown and sorry for himself, but he started talking to me about the work, and why did I waste my time in a job like that, and I said it was the first one I could get when I'd come to Cambridge with Jenny ("think of all those bright young men", she'd said), and I'd stayed in it, well, from force of habit. He said, I ought to get a better job, and away they went, and I didn't think any more of it. Then a few days later, he came out to the garage, just to tell me there was a job for an assistant at the Library. It needed four O levels, including

English language, and I'd got those; and, well, I won the job: I've started there. All because of Jim. That was what began it. I let him take me out a few times... and so it went on.'

'He gets you a job. You get him a wife. Bloody romantic, isn't it?'

'Wasn't *that* something, to find me a better job? You'd been going out with me the best part of a year, and you never called at the garage, or even phoned me there; you hardly ever asked about it. Consideration means *some*thing.'

'Consideration! Look, do you know why I came here this evening?'

'Well?'

I shut up. It might be a trump to say I'd come out to offer marriage; but if it didn't act as a trump for me, it would be one for Casey; it would complete his victory.

'Ah, forget it', I said. 'But anyway, get this into your head. Casey's got as much consideration as a rattle-snake. He's so mean, he has a wank before he goes into a brothel, to make sure he gets his money's-worth of time inside. When he sees a phone-box, he presses button B in the hope of retrieving someone else's tuppence. What's more, he's tricking you. Did you know, he's been practically living with a Mrs Fletcher for the last four months? How about that, then?'

'Perhaps he was. He isn't now. He said his goodbyes to her this morning. He even did *that* nicely, too. He took her some flowers.'

'Jesus wept. Poor bastard I am. I spend a chaste month at home, looking forward to getting back to you; I get a First, meaning that we can have three years together here, yeah, perhaps more too, if the ruling class postpones Armageddon; and I come trotting innocently out here like a lamb to the slaughter. Not a hint, not a tip. All those good times, and you rub them out; all those good Saturdays, and you scrub 'em off the record for that shrivelled little zombie; all –'

'You don't know him. He's got more kindness in his little finger than you've got all through. Look, Pete, we had good times. Don't spoil them now. I'm not going to start getting bitchy – but even now it's self, self, self, with you; "I" this and "I" that, all the time.'

'Self! Me – *selfish* – compared to Casey?'

'You and I had great Saturday nights. But what happened in between? Sometimes you saw Arabella; most of the time, you were working. You kept to a time-table. Well, all right; but you can't blame me if sometimes I felt I was just a – a *thing*: something switched on

151

when you needed it, and switched off when you didn't.'

'Just because I don't advertise my feelings, you think I haven't got any, that's the trouble. As soon as Finals were over, I saw you more often.'

'Oh yes, for a few days. Then comes the vacation, and off home you go. Jim stayed. He wanted to see me, so he stayed on. He cares for me... loves me.' (She blushed crimson as she said it, as if the phrase were an obscenity. I flinched: love was an embarrassing repressed entity.) 'You didn't even write – at least, nothing but a note, and then that might have been – well, it seemed as if you wrote *then* because you wanted somewhere to stay while you came up for your degree. You had to come up for that, didn't you? You wouldn't have come otherwise: you stayed at home all the other vacations. Oh, I didn't mean to go on like this. I know you'll feel bad, and I'm sorry; I am. But if you just try and look at it from my point of view, it won't seem so bad.'

I got up and walked out, my bladder being insistent. Casey was standing in the same place – far enough away not to hear the words of the talk, near enough to hear the tone and intervene if there was trouble. I thought of punching his nose hard, and stepped towards him. Instead of flinching, he actually stood his ground and clenched his fists; but I had a sudden incongruous recollection of him in RAF uniform two sizes too big for him, smiling, at J.S.S.L., Crail. All I could do was say, 'A happy gonorrhoea. It's *your* turn now.'

As I stepped out into the dark street, trembling slightly, he cleared his throat.

'Non-specific urethritis,' he responded.

I headed towards the foot-bridge, walking briskly, and the trembling in my legs abated. On the bridge, pausing to urinate, I found I was gripping a coconut under one arm. I lifted it – it didn't slop – and hurled it at the dim white swans below. There was a thud just before the splash, and a clamour of beating wings.

# Chapter 19

THE ENGLISH MORALISTS

Answer THREE or FOUR questions.
No moralist should be made the main subject of more than ONE
answer.

1. EITHER (a) Both Plato and Aristotle based morality on the
   notion that it is to our own ultimate good to act rightly.
   Explain and discuss this assertion.
   OR (b) Explain briefly Plato's doctrine of Forms and say what
   some of its implications are for ethics.

2. 'The basic moral question for Greek philosophy is not, What
   shall I do? but, What shall I be?' Discuss with reference to
   EITHER Plato OR Aristotle OR both.

3. Discuss the problem of self-control in the thought of
   EITHER Aristotle OR St. Paul....

---

The benches in the bus-station are cold and hard. That's what I found
out on the way back when some obscure association of ideas made
me sit there, while I submitted myself to a one-hour examination.

If my tangled wrack of feelings and thoughts-about-feelings and
thoughts-about-thoughts-about feelings had a centre, the centre might
have been called mortification.

Mortification, for example, at the fact that all the evidence had
been staring at me and I'd failed to understand it. I'd failed to

153

understand Arabella's and Lionel's last remarks at the party, Casey's business with the flowers this morning, and, worst of all, Jan's 'absence' the night before. While I'd been ringing the door-bell then, she must have been in there – probably with Casey; they had been possibly – probably – in bed. Just the other side of an eighth of an inch of glass and the drab window-curtain. She hadn't expected me back that night; Jenny must have been out with a boy-friend, and they were 'baby-sitting' – baby-making. The more I tried not to think about it, the more the scenario grew. Casey must have been sniggering to himself all the time – perhaps even watching me from behind the curtain... Mortification, mortification... I hadn't seen, I'd been thick, and now I was blitzed, rusticated, failed and felled: but how can anyone win a competition that he doesn't know exists?

The shelter faced Christ's, but the wind filled it with the greeny-yellow compound-aroma of trees and lavatories.

Failed: unclassed. Arabella and Jan had been collaborators in betrayal. The upper middle class had betrayed me through Arabella and Lionel; the working class had betrayed me through Jan and – at one remove – Casey. My very veins seemed to be part of the web of betrayals. My inadequate intelligence had sucked the blood out of my instincts; or my instincts had somehow poisoned my inadequate intelligence. Only the mortified eye of self-awareness eludes entanglement. 'Only the mortified eye of...'? Pretentious. Plain English says: 'Up shit creek without a paddle, I see.'

I sat huddled in the shelter, brooding. However, even the deepest and most inarticulate feelings sometimes demand to be shared, so I decided to visit Jack. At College, I was locked out, and had to climb the back wall (hand over hand up the lamp-post, foot over foot up the nearby brickwork). At Jack's room, he was sitting, drinking, in the door-stop duffel coat that now served as a dressing-gown, and he seemed to be expecting me. He poured a fresh glass of Scotch.

'The fucking world-conspiracy has victimised me yet again', I said, 'and Casey's organising it.'

'Machiavellian, isn't he? He waits till your attention's distracted by Finals and then he out-wits you in the sexual rat-race by stealing Miss Jan; even offers marriage as a bribe. Delayed decoding: brother, you're the duped victim of a covert plot.'

'That's about *it*.'

154

The table shook so that the glasses clinked around on it. Jack's hefty frame was shuddering with his endeavour to suppress laughter.

'You've got a sick sense of humour', I said.

He put his head back and laughed like a Falstaff, Orson Welles's Falstaff, laughed till he wept. 'Oh, Pete! You'll either make a diligent capitalist, or else you'll go around in ever-diminishing circles till you vanish up your own arse-hole! You've got all the right psychology – the possessive paranoia of a spoilt child, and hardly any sense of irony. Brother, you'll believe anything that makes you into the injured innocent. Just look at your socialism – it's about as skin-deep as Casey's fascism. Your socialism makes you feel happily hard-done-by, and his fascism's just the compensation of a little bloke from Leeds who'll be wearing false teeth by the time he's thirty. A couple of domestic years and a baby or two, and Casey'll be the most inoffensive, Labour-voting school-teacher you could ever meet. He's born for it. Born middle-aged. As far as I can make out, Miss Jan's just what he needs, and he knows it. Even *you* should have seen he's been withering away in his hunt for a nest – why, you know as well as I do, he's been pursuing anything in a skirt: waitresses, neurotic widows, tailors' dummies almost; and no bloody wonder: he's only got to look in a mirror and it puts the fear of death into him. Whereas you, you're just a both-and-neither man, janiform, and a chameleon, compared to that. A green thought in a green shade. And a small parcel.'

'You've lost me', I said, bewildered.

'Your loss, not mine, Mr Green. Man who's wrapped up in himself makes a very small parcel. Now have some of this Scotch I've purloined from Piggott, and tell me the whole sad story.'

———

The upstairs room at Carter's hire-shop isn't the place for grief and meditation. Jack and I arrived there in the morning, just as the newly-branded graduates from the first Senate-House round-up were stampeding in and stripping off their hired gowns, dinner suits, bands, stiff collars, shirts and the rest, while we struggled in the crowd to put on gear of more or less the right size, issued so rapidly that it was still warm from their bodies. The whole scrum looked like

155

the start of a queers' orgy or a film of Ovid's *Metamorphoses* directed by the Marx Brothers.

Then we had to trot through the streets to reach College in time for the formal lunch for graduates and graduands. The food was good; the wine (from the College's extensive cellars) excellent. Then, as a climax to the meal, an age-old ritual took place. A gallon-sized silver loving-cup was passed up and down the rows, so that everyone took a gulp from it. The ritual, involving a lot of bowing, was tricky. The man holding the cup has to utter a Latin blessing before he gulps, saying it first to the man on his right (who is standing, having passed the cup to him), and then to the man on his left (who rises to receive the blessing in turn). He takes a swig and then, bowing, hands the vast cup to the guy on his left, who returns the bow and in turn swigs while the man on his right remains standing, and the next guy on his left now stands up. And so on. Yes, I can see now how neatly it *should* have worked. Naturally, I made a complete mess of it, standing up and sitting down at the wrong times, forgetting to bow and garbling the incantation; and, before I could appreciate that the ritual was, among other things, a weight-lifting test, I'd spilt half the drink (mainly down my hired trousers) as I staggered beneath the weight of that silver urn. Some old don opposite assumed that if I was too drunk to stand straight I was too drunk to hear, and forthwith remarked loudly to his neighbours that it was the most incompetent exhibition he'd seen in forty years. Well, I leaned across and advised him that I had a fuckin' First and was willing to bet he hadn't, but, with people around him making hushing and shushing sounds at me, he didn't seem to notice.

At the elegant white Senate House, our procession had to queue inside for half an hour. It was stuffy there. I knew that somewhere in a gallery overhead, my parents were watching, but I didn't look up. I was concentrating on the floor, to keep it steady. If I looked away, it tried to undulate. The crocodile of students was four abreast, and at last it was the turn of my quartet to be presented. Piggott held out his hand in the traditional mystical udder-symbol, the four fingers of his right hand extended towards us. I, farthest from him, took his little finger; the man on my left took his third finger, and so on. Thus, fingerwise, he led us the last yard or so. (O'Connell's handshake

156

had been a texture-test.) There was a wide padded foot-stool, where you had to kneel, and beyond it was some aged stranger in brilliant robes, on a throne like the Pope. My name was called; I stepped forward unsteadily and knelt. It reminded me of church and childhood; and from distant habit I shut my eyes and bent my head in a praying pose, while the stranger recited incomprehensible magic spells in Latin, as if to mock me for only passing Latin O-level at the second go and having struggled with it during the Cambridge entrance-exams. Then Piggott hissed something, and hauled at my elbow, lifting me and directing me away. Another student took my place, and I walked carefully up the slightly undulating slope of the floor, towards a door where sunlight glared.

I had graduated.

———

I leaned against the white parapet of Silver Street Bridge. 'You see that quaint wooden bridge over there?'

'Ah', agreed my father.

'Yes, we do', said my mother carefully. 'It reminds me of the bridge on the Willow Pattern crockery.'

'Well, it's called the Newton Bridge of Queens' College. They say that it was designed by Sir Isaac Newton on special mathematical principles to be the first wooden bridge to be held together without nails or screws. Each part interlocked with the next. Every bit supported every bit. Okay. Now the story goes that one day, the Fellows of Queens' decided to take it apart to see how it worked, and when they came to put it back together again, it kept falling down. So, in the end, they had to put in lots of nails and screws to hold it together; and that's why you can see them now.'

'It just goes to show, you can't rely on other people to leave well alone', she said. 'But I wonder if that story is true.'

My father wrote 'Newton Bridge' with a pencil in his C.W.S. diary. 'They don't make things now as they did in the olden days', he said, writing in his neat copper-plate style, pressing more heavily on the down-stroke than the up.

It was five o'clock. I'd met my parents after the graduation ceremony (yes, they'd seen me, they said; I looked very smart; yes, I *had* been a bit unsteady getting up, but never mind). We'd walked

157

along the Backs in a sobering breeze. Memory of Jan and Casey throbbed with my headache. Twice my parents had sat down 'to admire the view', but from the way they sighed or said 'Ah, that's better' as they sat down, it was probably because they were tired. I prided myself on concealing my boredom during a walk along so familiar a route; I kept my temper, even though they repeatedly asked me the names of buildings that I couldn't name, or of trees that to me were just big trees.

I have a sensitive conscience, as is evident, but it is sometimes rather slow to operate. It actually took six years, by which time both of them had been cremated, before their manner that afternoon appeared to my conscience as probably that particular weariness of old age that comes when you see your child's upbringing completed, and that particular anti-climax that comes when you see that your child has become a patronising stranger inhabiting a different land in which, at best, you're a briefly tolerated tourist, and when you must even then, to be tolerated, alternately enact gratitude and self-effacement.

There were some shouted commands from the riverside behind me, and, in turning to see the cause of the shouts, I accidentally knocked diary and pencil from my father's hands. He bent down to pick them up, and two more pencils fell rattling onto the pavement from behind a folded handkerchief in the top pocket of his Sunday suit. 'Bugger – I mean drat it, I'm sorry', he said, stooping stiff-legged. His trilby hat fell off.

'Oh... Harry', she murmured, almost pitying rather than exasperated; she dusted the hat on her sleeve and settled it carefully on his head.

For relief from this embarrassing incident, I turned again to watch the men who were on the landing-stage between the Anchor and the Mill. One was crouching at the very edge, while the other scooped in the water with a long pole. As he lifted it up, I saw it had curly hooks, a triple hook, at the end. A policeman was directing them, while a small crowd gathered. 'Over to the right a bit. A bit more. Now. Now you've got it.'

The two men were sharing the pole, pulling it in hand over hand. There was a heavy soaked bundle just under the surface. The policeman reached down and held on; the others put down the pole and joined him, both groping up to the elbows in the water like eager

158

washer-women; and at last they heaved the whole body-bundle out and dumped it with a heavy splock on the planks. Water swilled out of the bundle and cascaded back into the river. The shirt might have been white once, but it was so saturated that the grey flesh showed through it, and the trousers were glossy black from their long soaking. One of the bare feet was criss-crossed by cuts.

'Oh my Lord', said my mother. 'The poor creature. He's gone, for sure. Don't watch, Peter. He's gone.'

'What's that?', said my father. He'd tucked his pencils away and had been still gazing at the Newton Bridge on the other side.

The cut foot was curious. (I was trying to memorise the details to tell Jack.) Some water-weed trailed out of the open mouth, as if the man had choked on green spaghetti; but I could still see plainly that the corpse was Eastbourne: an Eastbourne who must have waded out into the Mill Pool, cutting a foot on the broken glass from the beer-glasses that students over the years have tossed into the Cam there.

I'd got the account mentally word-perfect by eleven that evening when Jack returned to his room. He listened irritably for a while, and then said that he'd heard all about it from the barman at the Mill, who had found Eastbourne's jacket and shoes and socks on the bank that morning; which quite spoilt my account.

Next day, when we went to the Exam Office to retrieve our 'creative writing' submissions, we found that Eastbourne had never delivered them. They had vanished. So the examiners never saw the extract from my unfinished novel (as digressively plotless as reality), or Jack's subtle poems to outdo Wallace Stevens', or Casey's translations of Akhmatova. Our many weeks of intricate imaginative work had been wasted. The rule for this option was that if the examiners didn't like your stuff, you gained nothing but lost nothing. If they *did* like it, they could raise you; so, for example, someone on the borderline between II.ii. and II.i would rise into the II.i. category. Eastbourne, oozy-locked local Lycidas, whom I (with innocent naivety) had deemed naively innocent, now appeared to be a covert plotter or malicious saboteur who possibly – Jack thought probably – had deprived Casey of a First, and Jack and conceivably even me of starred Firsts.

––––––––––

# PART 2: FALMER, 1969: EXAMINING A CAMPUS

## Chapter 20

### CRITICISM AND COMPOSITION

... 1. Assign approximate dates to FIVE of the following passages, giving your reasons:

...*(f)* The various sects who have pretended to give lessons to instruct me in happiness have described their own particular sensations without considering ours, have only loaded their disciples with constraint, without adding to their real felicity. If I find pleasure in dancing, how ridiculous would it be in me to prescribe such an amusement for the entertainment of a cripple... General directions are therefore commonly useless... Every mind seems capable of entertaining a certain quantity of happiness, which no institutions can increase, no circumstances alter, and entirely independent on fortune. Let any man compare his present fortune with the past, and he will probably find himself upon the whole, neither better nor worse than formerly...

———

Yes, my conscience operates rather slowly, but it's sensitive enough. I began to appreciate my parents' end-of-the-road exhaustion and self-effacing pride. I began to realise it one evening, a year or so after my mother's cremation (she chose not to survive my father by more than a few months), when I was sitting on my bed with a girl whose name was – that's odd – whose name was – I can't recall it now. I think it was trisyllabic. She was one of my A-level students at the Tech.

160

Seducing one's A-level students is indeed, to use the cliché, like taking sweets from kids. That's partly why I no longer do it. There isn't much sense of achievement, once you've learnt the knack of escalating the approach from that of patient teacher, via coach-cum-father-confessor, to that of aesthetic-hedonistic collaborator, so to speak – and so to bed. Anyway, we were sitting there in my flat, and I was telling her about my graduation-time, and she said, 'Why, that's rotten: you must have killed him'; and I said 'What are you talking about? My father died quite naturally, years after'; and it turned out that she was talking about Eastbourne.

I chuckled tolerantly, and told her that her notion was typical of the faults in her essays, impressionistic, hasty, not enough homework. When she suggested that I might have been 'the last straw' for him, I explained that Finals had unbalanced him and that the ability to stay balanced under stress was one of the abilities that the exam-system valuably tested. But she continued to speculate morbidly, so I stopped listening and thought about my parents. A little nostalgia always makes me feel better, more relaxed; and after a while I began to kiss her neck and throat, gently, slowly, insistently.

Odd that I don't remember her name, because this I remember well, and this *did* seem important:

After all that talking and some long kissing, we got into bed (on the previous evening I'd made only cautious advances), and just as I was about to don the ribbed Durex Gossamer, she said: 'It's all right, I'm on the pill. You needn't bother with those old-fashioned things'; and she wriggled underneath me and into position. My tool quaked with surprise at the immediacy of the contact; but, or and, I couldn't, though I racked my brains, come to a climax. I had to fake one eventually, so as to have the pretext for a rest. She, having been lithely energetic, was glutted and placid, whereas I was puffing like a fat man running a race at pistol-point. No, it wasn't being out of condition that stole my climax, though, at sixteen, she admittedly had a dozen years' advantage over me; it was an obscure worry that had been prompted by her mentioning the pill, or by the way she'd made the remark – cheerful, confident, practical; or by the contact.

Oh, there's no need to phone the Principal. You could trust your daughter to me today; and she'll know how to take care of herself anyway. I've scarcely touched any of my students from that day to this. Since that evening with – whatever her name was – Miss Trisyllabic – I've slid into celibacy, a virtual sexlessness, of which the ease and tranquillity are such that my earlier goatish antics now seem a fevered series of nightmares.

No, that's not quite right: the rhythmic momentum and assonance of that last sentence seduced me into imprecision. (From 'my' to 'nightmares' – why, it's a fourteener; and 'seem' and 'series' probably engendered assonantally the 'fevered'. Expense of spirit, waste of shame; rats ravin down their proper bane.) It's difficult to put precisely what I myself don't yet fully understand. In part, it's connected with the way Lawrence's books have become boring to me, now that I see how he over-rated intensity and under-rated tranquillity. And certainly, in part, it's to do with the pill. There's no risk, no test of self, no sense of conquest, if the sexual relationship of a man and a woman has guaranteed sterility: Russian roulette gives no surge of adrenalin if you never release the safety-catch. There's another rough analogy that recurs to me: again, stealing sweets from kids. Suppose your sweet-stealer suddenly realises that he's trying to steal sweets in a land where the kids just grin back as though he's participating in a friendly game they understand well, and they hand him more sweets, and they've still got more sweets on them for all the other comers, so there's no rivalry, no rationing, no war-time shortage. Why, after a while, your sweet-thief would get plain bored with the game; he might even get sick of sweets and discover he was never really partial to 'em anyway. He'd valued not the sweets themselves but some sort of competitive prowess they seemed to prove.

By febrile Lawrentian standards, my present sexual – or sexless – state is doubtless one of life-denying corruption; but it seems remarkably like a state of grace. When I look along the bored rows of teen-age A-level students on a drowsy afternoon after I've explained for the umpteenth time the symbiotic relationship between Othello and Iago, or that Hamlet is really Amleth the hybrid (half the modern Hamlet, half the ancient Amlothi), or that, for Lucrece and Clarissa, loss of virginity entailed ultimate dishonour and led to suicide, – after all that, then 'state of grace' seems not a bad phrase for my knowledge that the flesh under the dresses of those yawning girls is just another fairly waterproof but ultimately perishable fabric.

162

I don't 'grind in the mill of an undelighted and servile copulation' (Milton). Happiness? No; more like 'blessèd P and Q', in my mother's phrase: peace and quiet; I've settled for that.

I used to be too fond of that word 'corruption'. For example, there was Felix Slattery, an English master at the Grammar School. I used to think of him as corrupt, merely because his lessons were like recitations: informative but mechanical; no spontaneous life. Well, if *he* was, so am *I*; and it's venial enough.

Obviously, I had to start teaching sooner than I expected.

In the September following graduation, Casey gained a post at a school in Haywards Heath and went to live there with Jan. The same month, I returned to Cambridge, all set to start research, and received a formal letter from the Board of Research Studies stating that the Chairman wished to speak to me at such-and-such a time in room such-and-such of the new English Faculty area on the Sidgwick Avenue site. The Chairman (the correct term in those days) was Haggerty; and she spoke clearly and inflexibly to the point. The point being that my application to pursue research had been rejected, and it was her 'invidious duty' to inform me of this.

There was a good view of Newnham's brown brick walls from her window. She repeated, in her refined public-school tones: 'Your application has been rejected.' After some moments, I heard myself say 'Why?' in a castrato pitch. The Board, she said, had been disturbed by the somewhat polemical, dogmatic style and approach. In other contexts, these features might be less disturbing, but, in a context of applications to undertake judicious, long-term scholarly work which might, through care and circumspection, contribute significantly to the fund of literary knowledge – in such a context, my outline was unsatisfactory. 'I won't be so unkind as to suggest that some of your paragraphs evoked the style of *Daily Worker* leading articles', she continued, smiling, 'but certain members of the Board may have thought so.' She read out a few samples. I remembered the confident mood I'd experienced after first befriending Arabella, who was so beautiful that a proud confidence, perhaps even arrogance, had for a few days wrecked the judicial balance that sexual gratification normally brought me.

'Furthermore', said Haggerty, 'Your proposal seems confused. Part of the time you talk as though "anti-rational primitivism", as you insist on calling it, – let's say the view that education is undesirable – is a *good* thing; and part of the time you seem to be saying that it leads to *The Plumed Serpent* and Fascism.' 'But some of the ideas are new,' I said; 'about the influence of Carpenter on Lawrence.'

She seemed to wince at my Gloucestershire accent ('Carrpinterr', 'Lahrrence'), then grunted and puckered her mouth. 'That was the third matter that gave the Board cause for concern. The ideas were sometimes remarkably similar to those in another application from your College, from a Mr John Hancock.' (Jack's full name sounded oddly formal.) 'I noted that Carpenter's *Civilisation: Its Cause and Cure* was almost as prominent in your proposal as in his, which was largely devoted to Carpenter. And since his application was received before yours, and since he has a consistently distinguished academic record (College Open Minor Scholarship, and a First in Prelims and Part I as well as Part II), and since he employed a cautious, scholarly presentation... almost excessively so... Therefore, while I would not allege plagiarism, your claims to originality became questionable. We have so many applications for so few places, you appreciate, that inevitably the applicants must be judged on a competitive basis. It is my duty to advise you that if you really wish to write on Lawrence and your "anti-rational primitivism", you must do so in your own spare time, and not as a registered research student.'

In short: with elocution-class lucidity, she gave me the bum's rush, the old heave-ho, the metaphorical boot up the arse. Craftily late, too. It was too late for me to apply for a Ph.D. course elsewhere; so I cut my losses and took a teaching post at this C.A.T. – 'College of Arts and Technology' – in London. (Thus, all my toil for a First resembled Crusoe's 'inexpressible labour' on his useless boat.)

I must have been a nerve-racking teacher to my A-level students at first: always nagging them about ways of out-ploying the examiners, of out-smarting their coeval students at other colleges and schools. But since then, over the years, and particularly since that night with... can't remember her name... the pill girl – since then I've outgrown that first immature belligerent enthusiasm. These days, I even have the absent-mindedness that goes with professional maturity: because one remembers what one emotionally invests, besieges, or hopes to use as ammunition; and I've no quarrel, now, with examiners, or

164

with texts. No quarrel, because for me there are no exams to come, no scholarships, no prizes. In the absence of the incentives I've been conditioned to require, I'm beginning to have some difficulty in remembering a wide range of texts and cribs from one term to the next. So I narrow the range, do more repetition-work, and teach calmly and systematically; and they yawn back, as I once yawned at that repetitive English master. They'll gradually come to understand, if and when they themselves start to teach.

They'll come to understand that originality is often over-rated, just as I over-rated the originality of Jack and Casey. What I learnt from them, in part, boils down to the war-time platitude: often, friendship is mainly a defensive response to siege conditions, and so it readily changes to neutrality or even hostility as the end of the siege is approached.

I've seen Jack and Casey only once since Finals. I was in Brighton on a day-trip, four years or so after Jack's doctorate had helped him to a lectureship at Sussex University.

Since graduating, I hadn't corresponded with the treacherous Casey. My correspondence with Jack petered out: after a while, he didn't reply to my letters. But while we were still in touch, I learnt from him that Casey had married and settled down with Jan (quite the family man, now), and her friend Jenny had married a divorced teacher at her school. So, as Jack pointed out, their covert plot (moving from Portsmouth to Cambridge to find intelligent husbands with secure jobs) had been successful.

Sussex University had opened in 1961 and received plenty of publicity in newspapers, particularly the new 'colour supplements'. Children of celebrities were studying there, in preference to Oxbridge: among them, Michael Attenborough, son of the famous Richard, and the glamorous blonde Jay twins, Helen and Catherine, daughters of Douglas Jay, the Labour front-bencher. The place seemed to be a liberal-and-left-wing contrast to the older universities, offering a 'new map of learning', characterised by the 'core and context' syllabus. For example, someone studying English would have to take appropriate contextual courses, usually in History and Philosophy, which would provide explanatory contexts for the central area of study. In theory, this 'inter-disciplinary' approach would make students more versatile, adaptable and flexible in outlook.

I had my doubts. At Cambridge, any students of English who were reasonably bright would naturally seek to explore history and philosophy. To know why Shakespeare's *Macbeth* is as it is, you soon find that it's designed to flatter the new monarch from Scotland, James I, who, in his *Daemonologie*, argued that witches really existed, wielded hellish powers, and should be extirpated. Again, in seeking to understand the radicalism of Rochester's 'Satyr against Mankind', you learn that the scepticism of Hobbes's *Leviathan* had been widely influential, and that Rochester was part of the reaction against the failed Puritan experiment.

It seemed to me, also, that if the Sussex students spent more time on contextuals, they'd have less time for the major course; so, if they were 'majoring' (a Yankeeism?) in English, their knowledge of English might become much patchier than was customary. It appeared that the teaching of science at Sussex was more conventional; but the University boasted an 'Arts-Science Scheme', presumably to bridge the gap between what C. P. Snow – soon assailed by Leavis – had termed 'the Two Cultures'.

Altogether, Sussex University seemed intriguingly experimental, and I wondered how Jack would adapt to it; so, having a free week-day, I took the train down to the campus, uninvited, impelled by curiosity. A sunny Thursday; and when I emerged from the narrow graffiti-scribbled subway from Falmer Station, the campus looked immediately attractive. Before me lay undulating park-land: lawns, a lake, lofty elms and dense bushes; and clusters of elegant modernist buildings, harmonised by their orange-brown brick walls, the plate-glass windows, and the high pale concrete arches. The bricks were set in thick creamy-yellow marzipanny mortar. In contrast to the walled, defensive colleges of Cambridge that seemed to say 'Hoi Polloi: Keep Out!', the open plan of this campus seemed to say: 'Welcome: you can't tell where countryside ends and academe begins; nor should you.' I remembered those late nights when, locked out of Pembroke, I'd had to sneak in via the rear wall in Tennis Court Road, climbing hand over hand up the lamp-post while simultaneously pressing foot over foot for leverage against the wall's nearby brickwork. So, at first sight, that Sussex campus seemed a vision of a spacious, welcoming, future: strikingly modernistic but reassuringly open and verdant. One big building at the entrance, Falmer House, even had room-size

166

rectangular holes in its upper storeys, so that you could see the sky through them, as if they were saying: 'We're letting fresh air into Academe.'

A minute of reflection, though, prompted misgivings. For instance, those rectangular gaps reminded me of the blitzed buildings I'd seen in war-time. Again, like Morris's Utopia in *News from Nowhere*, the design of this spacious campus seemed to be predicated on two notions: 1, that the weather of the future would be perpetually sunny; and, 2, that people of the future would be naturally honest. The Library had been opened by Her Majesty Queen Elizabeth II on September 13th, 1964, a plaque declared; but one glance at the building's flat roof with inset skylights told you that soon, if heavy rain fell, the staff would have to put plastic buckets in the foyer to catch the water dripping from above. Furthermore, if the steel rods to reinforce the campus's concrete had been exposed to wet weather previously, they would later corrode, expand, and crack their settings (and that predictable 'concrete cancer' duly arrived). As for the park-like openness of the campus: that would keep security guards busy. You could envisage how, on some dark winter's night, there could be a sudden rape among those conniving laurel-bushes, or a systematic burglary of two or three shops by a gang soon escaping on the convenient nearby motorway. At least, I observed, the graffiti on the Library's palimpsestic lavatory-wall showed promise: 'Nostalgia is not what it used to be, alas', above Blake's 'The tigers of wrath are wiser than the horses of instruction.'

Jack was giving a lecture in a series fashionably – if naively – entitled 'The Modern European Mind': a lecture on (surprise, surprise!) primitivism and anti-rationalism in modern writers, the topic of his doctoral thesis. Initially, as he acknowledged in the lecture, his thesis had concentrated on Edward Carpenter's influence on Lawrence, but his supervisor, Dr Haggerty, had persuaded him to marginalise Carpenter and make his study more widely-ranging. I recalled our former enthusiasm for *Civilisation: Its Cause and Cure*, which had declared civilisation a disease caused by the divisive fall into conscious knowledge – 'a temporary perversion'.

As Jack stood at the lectern, it seemed to me that his job had emasculated him: he'd become corpulent and flabby-looking, and each time he leaned over his script, his paunch made the lectern rock to

167

and fro. I'd expected him to improvise, but he read the lecture word-for-word from the script; and there were traces of his Geordie accent inflecting the pedantic phraseology (so that 'look' and 'away' became 'luke' and 'aweeah'), as though Caliban were failing in an attempt to imitate the elocution of Prospero. It was an erudite lecture: he'd done his homework, and students near me in that lofty tiered brick-and-concrete lecture-room scribbled busily when he began to quote unpublished stuff. He'd actually corresponded with Bertrand Russell, he revealed, and that eminent rationalist had privately conceded to Jack that in certain emotional moments he was a 'Satanic mystic', thus confirming what you might infer from the philosopher's vividly astute comments on *Heart of Darkness*, where he suggests that Conrad thought of civilised life as a dangerous walk on 'a thin crust of barely-cooled lava which at any moment might break'. So the Earl Russell was a relative of Mr Kurtz. Nevertheless, as the lecture proceeded (fifty minutes, fifty minutes and twenty seconds, fifty minutes and thirty seconds; how much longer?), Jack was so pedantically meticulous with his ifs and buts and other qualifications that towards the end, as I scratched some pleasantly-itchy dandruff from my thinning hair, I lost track. I began to feel bored then; and I told him so, afterwards, at some length, in his office in Arts Building A, overlooking a circular lily-pond where goldfish basked indolently.

He replied rather irritably, over coffee, that I'd failed to see the moral implications of his style: that he'd been deliberately meticulous in regard to definitions, qualifications, ambiguities, debatable judgements, and so forth, partly because of the nature of the subject, and largely in tactical opposition to the anti-rationalism which was becoming increasingly fashionable among a noisy and growing minority of students. That shut me up: Jack never seemed to lose an argument.

Then, suddenly thumping the coffee-table with his hefty hairy fist, he interjected furiously that he could break Haggerty's neck for deflecting him from Carpenter. The heavy square glass ash-tray hopscotched the table as, glaring wildly for a moment, he thumped. I flinched.

Recovering his breath and resuming his explanation, he told me that these anarchic students had recently led a successful boycott of the second-term examination, resulting in its abolition, for they had sympathetic allies among sentimental or cynical faculty-members:

*trahison des clercs.*

He was sorry he couldn't show me round the place, but I'd understand that he was very busy: he had two essays to mark before the next tutorial, at 2.15. And, alas, his lunch-time was already booked: he'd be having a working lunch with a fellow-examiner, his colleague Laurence Lerner (that's right: the critic and poet, creator of the poignant Merman). Incidentally, he remarked, Lerner had been a Pembroke undergraduate at Cambridge in the 1940s. Asa Briggs, from Worcester College, Oxford, was a founding father of Sussex University; another founder was David Daiches from Cambridge, now Dean of the English and American School here; and Piggott was here too, as a Professor of English. John Fulton, the first Vice-Chancellor, came from Oxford's Balliol College (Hardy's 'Belial'). Some journalists called Sussex University 'Balliol by the Sea', but 'Oxbridge at Brighton' was more accurate. I suggested to Jack that we might meet for a drink early in the evening, but he said he would be having a working dinner with a visiting poet from Pembroke (someone I'd never heard of, Timothy Longville, apparently a gifted associate of Prynne).

So we shook hands, past friendship having dwindled to present formality, and (jealously) I left Jack in the modish comfort of his Habitat-furnished office with its low, yellow-cushioned, rectangular pine chairs and its vista of the goldfish-pond on a terrace. In the distance loomed a Henry Moore sculpture, a bulky bronze.

I found a crowded smoky bar nearby (plate glass, orange brick, concrete arches); and, after nosing around for a conversation to which I might contribute, I was drawn towards a vociferous long-haired student. He sported a Zapata moustache (as modelled by Brando in *Viva Zapata!*); his hair hung in abundant ringlets over his shoulders, just like Rochester's in the perhaps-Huysmans painting; and he was wearing fancy dress: a hussar's red military jacket with golden epaulettes, above low-cut flared jeans. He was talking to a pretty female whose neat pink nipples graced a transparent blouse worn above a belted red mini-skirt; her slim long legs ended in little white plastic boots. Her arm was round his waist, and he was assuring her that in the new society, which was soon to be achieved by popular revolution, human nature would be 'radically and qualitatively completely fucking different'.

169

Naturally, I was obliged to intervene, to remind them that you cannot make a silk purse out of a sow's ear, that charity begins at home, and that, as far as I was concerned, I had achieved a social and political success if I managed to keep myself awake and competent for a whole day's teaching. They then argued at me energetically in turn, like a pair of tenor-players doing a chase chorus in a jazz routine, the clichés in this case deriving not from Illinois Jacquet and Flip Phillips but from Karl Marx and Herbert Marcuse, accompanied by pious allusions to the achievements of 'Fidel' (as they familiarly termed the Cuban autocrat) and of Chairman Mao.

Their accents, though not posh, were oddly indeterminate: you couldn't ascribe them to a class or, though southerly, to a particular region of the south; and their illiberal sentences were liberally sprinkled with casual obscenities. Both these students eagerly explained to me that universities like theirs would become paradigms of the new society: they'd become general assemblies of people, from all walks of life, who had entered freely to combine in practical and socially-relevant dialogues and confrontations, and, at the end of the collaboration, there'd be no exams and degrees, because, if there were, they would merely perpetuate the present 'liberal-capitalist bullshit, élitist exploitation, and subjection to the fucking military-industrial hegemony'. I advised them that in practice this ideal would convert the universities into holiday camps for the sons and daughters of the rich, for people who didn't *need* a degree in order to get a well-paid job. And so we wrangled repetitively.

'Radical change must begin here and now', they said, quoting freely: 'Subvert the fuckin' system from within'; 'There's no essential human nature'; '"Philosophers have only interpreted the world; the point, however, is to change it"' (Marx on Feuerbach); 'Sexual liberation makes general liberation'; '"Turn on, tune in, drop out"' (Timothy Leary); and even 'Cleanse the doors of perception' (Blake again, inspiring Aldous Huxley and Jim Morrison).

In response, I opined that Castro was doubtless prospering, as a dictator drawing a generous income from the Cuban tobacco and sugar trade, while Chairman Mao, an imperialist warlord who had conquered Tibet and had failed to conquer India, was starving millions of his people while becoming amply plump himself. I remarked that nobody was more conservative than a stoned pot-head;

170

that sexual liberation could entail new forms of exploitation of women; and that a hedonistic lifestyle needed and abetted capitalism: hadn't they read *Brave New World*?

They manifested disbelief, dismay and indignation.

Communication in that concrete-vaulted bar was impeded by noisy loudspeaker music: Bob Dylan whining his gibberish (given the gradual erosion of academic standards, some don will doubtless hail Dylan as a new Keats); then Jimi Hendrix repeating his irritating mondegreen in 'Purple Haze' ('Kiss the sky' or 'Kiss this guy'); and Mick Jagger in 'Stray Cat Blues' celebrating the joys of sex with a fifteen-year-old (so that if the nation continues its decline into decadence, they'll give him a knighthood one day). Even my namesake in Fleetwood Mac disloyally added his 'Black Magic Woman' to the cacophony. Consequently, I was obliged to raise my voice to make myself heard, which attracted further picturesque students: their throng resembled an audition for *The Pirates of Penzance* or for a Beatles' LP-sleeve to rival the 'Sergeant Pepper' classic. I bought an expensively large round (lager, their preference, but ale for me); and, to be fair to those students, they did in turn buy me a couple of beers – a good local real ale, Harvey's. I observed that it was wittily named after that huge eponymous rabbit, Harvey, who accompanies the alcoholic, played by James Stewart, in the famous film; but evidently that was long before their time.

At least we agreed that the U.S. intervention in Vietnam was misguided and would prove futile. (If Kennedy had read Kipling's 'Recessional', that might have forewarned him.) Otherwise, we seemed to disagree on everything. Indeed, I differed from them by deploring the 'red paint' incident, that much-publicised local demonstration when a couple of Sussex students, supposedly protesting against the Vietnam War, had flung red paint over a Press Attaché from the U.S. Embassy. I quoted my mum at the throng: 'Two wrongs don't make one right' – well, there's more sense in that maxim than in the whole of *L'Etre et le Néant*; and I cited J. S. Mill's defence (in *On Liberty*) of free speech; but the first lad retaliated with 'Everything reactionary is the same; if you don't hit it, it won't fall', from Chairman Mao's *Little Red Book.*

What with annoyance, argumentativeness, being out of practice at boozing, not having eaten anything that lunchtime, and having

171

passively inhaled clouds of sickly-sweet cigarette-fumes, I rapidly became inebriated. Once outside, in fresh breezy air, I began to spew here and there: vomited into a shallow rectangular moat that bordered the courtyard; and once I puked against a wall that bore a medallion stating that the building had won the award of the Royal Institute of British Architects. Designed by Sir Basil Spence, the place was; and my vomited breakfast spattered against the orangey masonry and spotted my black corduroy trousers and my black toe-caps, as if the bricks were spitting bitty spunk at me. Ha: theme: regurgitation. Hadn't Casey said that's what exams usually were?

The train back to London (Victoria) stopped for three minutes at Haywards Heath. I was still trying surreptitiously to wipe the puke off my shoes, rubbing them against the edge and underside of the seat opposite; so at first I didn't notice Casey. He stood on the platform, watching people step off a train that had come in alongside. A woman walking by flinched momentarily at a glance from that withered sardonic face; but then she looked down at the push-chair he was guarding, and in the push-chair, crowned with a red pointed cap, was a smirking innocent parody of Casey. His face was the same thin shape as Casey's, the staring expression similar; but pink, unlined and eighteen months old, fleshing the shape and expression into those of a complacent harmless gnome; and the woman, looking from the child back to Casey, smiled to herself and walked by.

Jan then stepped from the train and guided down another child, a grinning seven-year-old girl; Jan eagerly kissed the gnome and Casey; Casey solemnly kissed Jan and the seven-year-old; and they walked slowly down the platform to the exit, Casey wheeling the push-chair as carefully as if it held the Ark of the Covenant.

I attempted to inspect my feelings, sluggish, muddy, murky, but, in the general post-vomitory gloom, was unable to identify any. This was the consummation of my education, no doubt: a protracted examination seemed to have ended at last.

Well, I rubbed diligently and removed all the spattered vomit from my shoes, and most of it from my trousers; but the smell haunted those trousers for days, and, when I tried sponging them with Brobat disinfectant, the stuff burnt yellow-edged white blotches into the black corduroy; so those trousers went into the dustbin. Thanks to the 1944 Education Act, I could afford to throw them away and buy an identical pair. Now I need a watch and chain.

———————————

# PART 3: LONDON, 2011: EXAMINING A BODY

Civilisation...is a kind of disease.... Wherever we look today, in mansion or in slum, we see the features and hear the complaints of ill-health.... We are actually less capable of taking care of ourselves than the animals are.... When we come to analyse the conception of Disease, physical or mental, in society or in the individual, it evidently means, as already hinted once or twice, *loss of unity.*

> (Edward Carpenter: *Civilisation: Its Cause and Cure*, 1889; reprinted, 1921.)

## Chapter 21

Examinations ended, did I say?

They never end, in this life. They may even continue beyond it. If Christians are right, at death we are assessed by God, to determine our allocation to Heaven, Hell, or, if you are a Catholic, Purgatory.

And, before death, there are repeated examinations, tests, appraisals, assessments: by employers, friends, relatives, insurers, doctors. Self-examinations, too: looking back over life. In that Antonioni film *La Notte*, the jaded author – a jaded Mastroianni played him – says 'I no longer have inspirations, only recollections'.

Some of Casey's translations were eventually published in little literary magazines. There were numerous Akhmatova items. What surprised me was that he had also devoted much care to translations of the poetry of Osip Mandelshtam, the Jewish dissident writer, the so-called 'Acmeist', martyred by Stalin. Casey had even embraced, or subsided into, the Russian Orthodox faith. The tutors on the forces' Russian course at J.S.S.L. (Crail) had achieved another success.

Then one day in late 1980, Jack phoned me to say that Casey was dead. As he walked home from his usual pub to his wife and kids, two teenage muggers had apparently demanded his wallet. Casey fought them (his knuckles became grazed and bloody), was knocked down, received violent kicks to the head; and died in the gutter. In literary tragedies, I'd once written, deaths happen consolingly in Act 5; but this death, belonging to reality and not fiction, happened abruptly in Act 3. I didn't attend the funeral; I had too many commitments at work. (It might have been hypocritical to do so, too, for I sourly recalled his treachery.) Jack, his voice trembling with fury over the phone, had told me that if the assailants were ever caught, he would try to kill them. I recalled an occasion when, grunting and panting in a drunken nocturnal rage, he had selected several parked bikes and heaved them from the Garden House cast-iron bridge into the flowing Cam; and memory also showed me the two stupefied lads whose heads he had banged together. Casey's assailants were never brought to trial: the two main suspects, when bailed, vanished, and it was assumed that they had fled abroad.

I learnt that Jack, his shyness overcome by a congenial young woman, had abandoned poetry, after producing many verses even more arcane than those of his acquaintance J. H. Prynne (of Gonville and Caius). His *magnum opus*, written in collaboration with Laurence Wing, was *The Great Wall* (Newcastle: Janiform Press, 1970), every poem appearing in Chinese and English parallel texts: highly regarded by the Cambridge Group of anti-establishment poets.

One day in 1959, referring to a passing public-school lad of effeminate character, I'd remarked to Jack that the lad was (in the naval idiom) 'queer as a clockwork orange'; and Jack had promptly said: 'Good phrase. I could use it as the title of a novel.' In the event, he was beaten to it, three years later, by Anthony Burgess; and he didn't produce any novels himself. To compound the irony, between 1962 and 1964, while Jack was a research student, his landlord in Mill Road was a dour photographer from South Africa called Tom Sharpe (also ex-Pembroke), who eventually produced numerous popular satiric novels. Sharpe used the bathroom as a black-screened dark room for developing his photos, so sometimes Jack suffered a bladder-clenching delay if he needed the lavatory. Don't say he hasn't suffered for art.

Certainly, Jack in that period had a knack of encountering people who would one day be famed celebrities. One of them, at a Footlights party, was Germaine Greer, tall, wild-haired and loquacious, who had notoriously performed 'The Stripping Nun' at a Pembroke smoker (a cabaret). Another, also to be seen at Footlights gatherings, was the

175

eventual film-star, Miriam Margolyes: in 1960, she had played a plump posh-voiced Jocasta in a local performance of *Oedipus Rex.* A third was Clive James, later to be a popular writer and TV broadcaster, who once, from a high window in Pembroke's Old Court, jocularly emptied a bucket of water over Jack. Being accompanied by several rugby players, James had managed to repel Jack's ensuing furious flailing charge, though one of the bulky sportsmen had been tossed down a flight of stairs – an involuntary somersault with (thud, thud, *crunch*) a percussively untidy fibula-fracturing finale.

This roll-call of the illustrious reminded me that, at the Piggott party where I'd met Arabella, there had been one other spare female: a slight, fair-haired actress who had eloquently played the female lead in *Das kleine Teehaus* at the Arts Theatre: Margaret Drabble; but Arabella's outstanding amplitudes had deflected me from her. Casey, approaching swiftly, proffering Balkan Sobranie cigarettes, had secured an invitation to tea at Drabble's room, the Tower Room, at Newnham; but he had found her inviolably faithful to her fiancé. To excuse this uncharacteristic failure, Casey explained that he was preoccupied by his quest – soon successful – to complete the adulterous seduction of his landlady, Mrs Fletcher: a prudent insurance against rent-increases.

Jack had become devoted to scholarly research. He had published several volumes: the first an edition of the letters of Cunninghame Graham; the second a monograph on the topic of (ha!) *covert plots* in literary works. I eagerly scanned the monograph in a bookshop. He dealt with, among other works, Conrad's *Almayer's Folly* (showing how wily Abdulla's stratagem succeeds), Ibsen's *Vildanden* (*The Wild Duck*, ending with Old Ekdal's suicide) and Mann's *Der Tod in Venedig* (*Death in Venice* – a Venice haunted by the sly protean Dionysus). But no sign of any acknowledgement of Peter Green. I instructed my college library to buy the book (£40 from Harvester), and read it carefully, but there was no *trace* of an acknowledgement. Once again, I reflected sourly, a covert plot had ambushed me. When it came to a choice between friendship and competitive advantage, the competition, evidently, would always win.

As for Cunninghame Graham (alias Don Roberto): I could soon see why he'd chosen that bizarre fellow. He depicted him as an exemplary janiform personality: a courageous politician, jailed for his radical beliefs, who yet regarded political commitment with sceptical detachment, so that his career was a conscious artefact. Sometimes he resembled Don Quixote; sometimes he resembled Hamlet. Evidently Cunninghame Graham admired Turgenev; and Turgenev, author of 'Hamlet and Don Quixote' would have been proud of him. It all fitted together.

Jack later, when teaching at the Chinese University of Hong Kong, also edited a memorial volume of Casey's writings. The *Dictionary of Literary Biography* says that Casey's work 'owes little to (and is largely ignored by) the literary establishment' and expresses 'a profoundly spiritual preoccupation'. One item I grudgingly enjoyed was a rendering of Baudelaire's sonnet 'L'Albatros': Casey had made this translation in 1960 or 1961, as preparation for the Finals' translation paper. It went thus:


ALBATROSS


Those albatross, vast birds, on the ocean-run
Idly befriend ships gliding bitter gulfs.
The sailors often trap them, just for fun.

These rulers of azure realms, once dumped and decked,
Turn awkward and ashamed (their great white wings
Trail like pathetic oars), so quickly wrecked.

That former handsome flying voyager?
Behold: a clumsy oaf – an ugly clown!
Somebody teases his beak with a smoker's pipe;
Someone else mimics, by hobbling about, this soarer now dragged
down.

The Poet resembles the prince of thunder-clouds
Who, haunting storms, derides the archers' knack;
When exiled, grounded, jeerers all around,
His own gigantic pinions hold him back.


177

Of course, it's polemically romantic stuff; Casey outgrew it. What does the sonnet claim? Transcendent poet is demeaned and mocked by the vulgar throng of philistines: an easy Romantic-cum-Aesthetic topos. Privately, I prefer it to the Delphic subtleties and velleities of Casey's later work; and I jealously admire the clever details. The title-noun 'Albatross', for instance, could be singular or plural, so it thereby aids the transition from the plural of the first two triplets to the singular introduced in the first quatrain. Sometimes the phrasing is almost onomatopoeically deft: after the smooth suggestion of 'gliding... gulfs', the thuddiness of 'dumped and decked' is all the clumpier. Line 10 jerks us from the expected iambic pentameter into an awkwardly bumpy trochaic-and-iambic fourteener, to mimic the hobbling mimicker: you can even see the Chaplinesque figure's bobbing gait. 'Soarer' assonates aptly with 'haunting storms'. And there's a cumulative energy which makes you suspect that Casey himself must have felt at times 'exiled, grounded, jeerers all around'.

Students used to ask me, in tones ranging from the bored to the bitter, 'What's the *use* of the study of literature?'. I told them that Plato alleged that literature filled people with undesirable emotions, so he would have banned poets (other than toadies) from his republic. Then Aristotle, to save literature from such censorship, said that literature provides laxatives, healthily eliciting and purging emotions from us. Shelley and Shklovsky thought that good writing, being original, destroys habitual perception and valuably makes us see the world afresh. Nazis thought that attending *The Merchant of Venice* made people better Nazis. Marxists say that texts expose the contradictions engendered by capitalism. Divided and janiform people see their own divisions engagingly expressed (and sometimes temporarily resolved) on the page. Liberal teachers naturally like to suggest that admirable literary works impart liberal values.

Peter Green, however, expounds his own revolutionary theory of emotional and moral *depletion*. It is this: Because great novels, poems and plays are so rich in moral and emotional experiences, some readers will decide that they've been defeated in the competition: so they read with admiration, but become poorer morally and emotionally themselves. They're like football fans who, every Saturday, watch Premier-League football matches on television, while they, relaxing, are swigging beer as they slump on sofas. Those fans can appreciate the energy and vigour displayed on screen, but do they become more energetic and vigorous themselves? Of *course* not; they become fatter and flabbier by the week. And so it often is, morally and emotionally, with fans of literature. If you doubt that, look at the lives of teachers of Eng. Lit.: not, on the whole, an inspiring prospect. Quote me, examiners. I dare you.

I retired from teaching in 2002. I'd given up smoking and booze long before that. Almost incredulously, I recall how long and hard I smoked, and *what* I smoked. In school-years, there were other people's cigar-butts in my Woolworth's pipe, and my own cigarette-ends were incestuously recycled in Rizla papers by means of the fragile rolling-device. In the Navy, Pusser (i.e.'the purser', the invisible deity of naval order) supplied tar-laden blue-liners at five old pence for twenty: after collecting your pay on your hat at the first table, you pocketed the pay, donned the hat, saluted, and marched to the second table to buy your issue of 200. At College, I smoked Senior Service and dog-end roll-ups. An attempt to substitute snuff for tobacco ended in (a) sinusitis, (b) numerous orange-stained handkerchieves, and (c) an encounter in the Still & Sugarloaf with a furtive beady-eyed stranger whose proffered free sample of 'white snuff' made me reel and stagger. Almost incredulously, too, I recall how long and hard I boozed and what I boozed. In school-years, scrumpy; in the Navy, anything from Bass to rum (the daily tot) and *ersatz* Kraut Scotch; at College, mainly beer, but interspersed with gallon jars of Woodpecker or half-gallons of Strongbow. At the Angel pub once in '59, I'd drunk the yard of ale, competing with a Jesus man (John Blackwell, ex-Navy, at Secker & Warburg became Tom Sharpe's editor later). Jack was my caller, to warn me when the foam was about to surge from the ball up the barrel; and my gown, back to front, collected some of the spillage. The covert plot of yard-drinking is that, without a good caller, you imbibe so much windy froth that sheer internal air-pressure makes you choke and vomit. The glass yard, with its bulbous end, is craftily designed to maximise froth. The outcome that time: a draw, declared amid an elephantine cacophony of bestial belches from both the bloated contestants.

When I reflect on all that, I seem, as a survivor, to rival the cock-roach.

179

I have also mastered the art of keeping myself to myself. Damage limitation. One death on my conscience is more than enough. The score may be at least two. No, I've not led a heroic life. It's not the material of fiction. The heroic era has gone: that was my parents' era. They knew instinctively what J. S. Mill had taught: 'It is better to be a human being dissatisfied than a pig satisfied...'

Consider my dad: born 1897, son of a railway porter. Diligent pupil at school. In July 1912, when he was 15, he signed an indenture to become an apprentice in gentlemen's outfitting at the Co-op. The indenture specifies his wages for the next *six years*: year 1, six shillings per week; year 2, seven shillings per week; year 3, nine shillings; year 4, ten shillings; year 5, eleven shillings; year 6, fourteen shillings; and, during those years, 'the said Apprentice his Masters faithfully shall serve[,] their secrets keep'. A shilling was one-twentieth of a pound.

In September 1914, the Great War began. That war had long been planned by Kaiser Wilhelm II and the German High Command. Then in January 1915, on his eighteenth birthday, with the Co-op's permission, my father volunteered for the Army. He served in the 306th Brigade of the Royal Field Artillery in some of the worst battlefields, notably the Somme and Ypres (he called it 'Wipers'). His job was to lead horses laden with ammunition from the ammunition-dumps behind the lines to the troops manning the big guns. He did this through some of the worst barrages and foulest quagmires of that war. It's said that on the first day alone of the Battle of the Somme, 19,240 British soldiers were killed and 35,493 were wounded. 'After such knowledge, what forgiveness?' My father survived with a small scar from shrapnel in his neck, between helmet and collar. He wouldn't talk about the war afterwards, except privately to old comrades. To me, when I was a lad, he wouldn't say anything, in spite of all my nagging. Just 'It's too horrible to talk about'. One item he taught me: the historians refer to it as the 1914-*18* war, and, out of respect, he would use their phrase; but, to many soldiers, he explained, it was the 1914-*19* war. The Armistice of November 1918 was just a truce. The formal ending to the war did not occur until 28 June 1919 (in the Versailles Treaty, which helped to provoke the next world war). That timing meant a great deal to troops billeted in France, yearning to come home.

180

No, for good reason he wouldn't tell me about his war service; but sometimes, when he was talking to old comrades, I overheard details of the conversation. From this I learned that one of the treats in the trenches was a tin of heated jam, passed along, so that each man could take a spoonful. I learned that with a cigarette end, you could burn the lice out of the seams in your trousers. Once, leading a laden horse across the quagmire under fire, he had fallen through the muddy surface and found himself trapped up to his waist in the bloated reeking carcase of a dead horse that had been concealed by the mire. Another time, he had dragged back from No-Man's-Land to the relative safety of the duckboarded trench a wounded comrade: 'the red hole in his back was the size of a dinner-plate.' Any stress that I'd experienced during Finals was utterly negligible compared with what he must have experienced during that war. The term 'post-traumatic stress disorder' was unknown in those days.

My father returned from the Great War as a quiet, thoughtful, modest, restrained Christian gentleman, and resumed work at the Co-op. He attended Sunday services at nonconformist chapels, studied at evening classes, and befriended people whom others would avoid or ignore. For instance, one of those friends was Mr Trigg, a market gardener with a frequent stammer (a consequence of war-service), who lost his stammer when they talked. Another was Mr Munday, a bow-legged dwarf who was a deft tailor, sitting at (and sometimes on) a large table: my father took plenty of work round to his wide-windowed shop on the corner of Hewlett Road and Albion Street: suits to be adapted, that kind of thing. Father was equable and patient; swore hardly at all; didn't drink; smoked Woodbines or roll-ups, or occasionally a pipeful of Player's Navy Cut tobacco. ('Just to keep the flies off', he'd say, when lighting up outdoors.) He cycled to work in the grey suit that he wore there. At the end of the large carpeted Gentlemen's Outfitting Department in the High Street Co-op in Cheltenham, he stood behind the glass-topped counter, facing the big door to the landing and the lift, wearing his insignia and badge of rank, his tape measure, round his neck, like a mayoral chain of office.

He married in 1925; my sister was born two years later; and I was born in 1937, when my mother was forty.

Twenty years after he came home from France, the Second World War began. At 42, he was too old for conscription into the forces; but he contributed to 'the war effort', as it was called. He became a Fire Warden. This meant that after doing a full day's work, he would don the uniform and helmet, and spend nights at the shop, keeping watch from the roof, to notify the emergency services of enemy aircraft or of the site of bomb-explosions. He wore a heavy steel helmet with a white 'W' on the front, and was trained in the use of the stirrup-pump, to put out fires caused by incendiaries. In what little spare time he had, he would work on his allotment-patch near the top of Prestbury Road, on what had been the Co-op's sports-ground, growing rows of peas, beans, potatoes, cabbages and carrots, so that we were, for a large part of the year, self-supporting in vegetables. On the abandoned tennis court, weeds prised the tarmac, and the net sagged, bedraggled. Sometimes he would push his bike the two miles home, spade and fork tied neatly to the crossbar, steadying with left hand a heavy knobbly hessian sack of spuds balanced over the handlebars. 'Dig for Victory', said the government's posters, showing a booted foot shoving a spade-blade into soil; and he dug tirelessly for a victory of a personal familial kind. If he walked across grazing-land, any horses there would amble over and nuzzle up against him; and he would pat their manes and murmur to them.

When working at the shop, he was neat and deft: in seconds, he could tie the string symmetrically round a brown-paper parcel and finally, with a swift twirl of his wrist, snap the string: no need for scissors. And, literally, he would not hurt a fly. If, in the kitchen at home, a fly descended towards his lunch-plate, his hand would suddenly, quicker than the eye could see, snatch the fly, and hold it as it buzzed angrily between closed fingers and palm, while he walked to the door, where he released it, baffled but unscathed, into the side passage: 'Off you go, you varmint.' One sunny morning, as he mounted his bike to set off for work in his suit and trilby hat, I said, 'Why on earth do you wear a hat in this weather?'. He replied: 'To raise it to the ladies that I pass in the street.' Once in winter, when he had a cold, he blew his nose into a piece of tissue-paper and threw the paper on to the coal fire, where it briefly hissed. Sprawling in a soft chair, I looked up from the *Guardian*, and said 'Disgusting!'. He replied: 'What the rich man puts in his pocket, the poor man throws away.' At election days, he and his wife would walk to the polling station arm in arm, there vote against each other, and then walk back, arm in arm.

My mother had worked at Shirer's & Haddon's, near the High Street end of the Promenade: a dress shop and milliner's. Then, in the Great War, she volunteered for the Royal Navy, and worked as a switchboard operator at Portsmouth. (And that's why, forty years later, I was admitted to the Navy's Coder Branch for National Service. Which, in turn, is why, forty-five years later, I answered the Chekhov question in the Tragedy paper; and it partly explains how I learnt of my kindred, the superfluous men. *It all fits.*) After my mother's marriage, the housework and the fending for a husband and later two children were full-time arduous toil for her, in those days of coal fires, no central heating, no hot water supply, no refrigerator, no freezer, no dishwasher, no washing machine. It was a life-sentence with hard labour: endless repetitive work: washing the clothes entailed carrying the tub of boiling water from the hob of the spindly-legged rattly-doored gas-cooker to the shed where the laundry-work was done; mornings in winter, she'd be on her knees, raking the ashes from the grate and black-leading the tiles.

In the early weeks of the war, a man with a clipboard, from the Municipal Offices, knocked at the door one morning. He wanted to know how many people lived in the house (four) and how many bedrooms we had (three). He then said: 'You will be allocated three evacuees from Birmingham. Three girls. You or your husband should collect them from the L.M.S. station on Sunday afternoon.' Accordingly, on that Sunday afternoon, my father returned from the station with three Birmingham girls aged about ten. My mother then had to do the work not for a family of four but for a family of seven, which she did without complaint. At the grocery shop where she was registered, she might have to queue for half an hour to draw the precious rations.

After the war, sugar rationing lasted till September 1953; meat rationing till July 1954, the year before I won the Exhibition to Pembroke. When our carpets were threadbare, she bought a kit consisting of (i) a steel carpet-knitting grid which bolted on to the kitchen table, (ii) many yards of perforated coarse backing material, and (iii) countless balls of green wool. She then knitted, loop by loop, quarter-inch by quarter-inch, row by row, night after night, green carpets for three rooms and the staircase. Odysseus' Penelope

183

couldn't have done it: she'd have given up with a great howl of boredom and embraced with relief the nearest suitor.

It occurs to me now that the stress my mother underwent, in giving birth to me in 1937 when she was forty, must have surpassed a hundredfold any exam stress I'd felt in 1961.

Where I was concerned, my parents were always self-sacrificing and forgiving. I became proportionately selfish and inconsiderate. My parents' life was one of service and toil. Their terrace house usually seemed dark and rather gloomy to me. But on icy winter mornings, the lower part of my bedroom window would be frosted on the inside with miraculous fern-patterns, most delicate traceries of overlapping ferns with little fine fronds, overlapping rows of them, not quite symmetrical and therefore more cunningly imitative of real ferns, but ferns rendered miniature in the dimension of ice; so that it seemed sacrilegious when I scratched ice-dust-edged grooves through their filigreed delicacies with my finger-nail.

One day in 1964, after his retirement, my father chose to return for a day's stock-taking to help the staff at the Co-op. Apparently he went up and down a step-ladder, inspecting the stacks of shirts, coats, hats, and so forth, and calling out the quantities, qualities and brands to a younger man with a note-pad. That night, he had a heart attack. He said 'I'm all of a sweat', slowly got out of bed, put on a clean dry pair of pyjamas, returned to bed, and died in his wife's arms.

He had a life-long commitment to co-operation. To him the Co-op was not a chain of stores supported by its factories and farms; it was the tangible symbol of an ideal: the ideal of a world of peace and harmony, where the fruits of work were fairly shared by the workers. The basic idea of the Co-op was astute and simple: to convert capitalism into socialism by making every shopper a shareholder, receiving a share of the profits. This gentle revolution would transmute self-interest into altruism, and would gently subvert and dissolve economic exploitation. Well, that was the idea.

The churchyard elegy of Thomas Gray (Pembroke College, Cambridge, 1756-1771) comes to mind:

Some mute inglorious Milton here may rest,
Some Cromwell guiltless of his country's blood.

184

Within a few months of my father's funeral, my mother loyally chose to follow him.

———

My mother and father were brave, loving, strong in character, greatly industrious, uncomplaining and stoical. Their lifetimes were, for the most part, lifetimes of toil and worry. I sometimes attempt to imagine what my father underwent in the Great War, but imagination fails before the horror.

Compared with those lives, mine seems trivial, selfish and shabbily decadent. Alexander Pope says:

> We think our *Fathers* Fools, so *wise* we grow;
> Our *wiser Sons*, no doubt, will think *us* so.

———

185

# Chapter 22. London, 2011

## CRITICISM AND COMPOSITION

...4. Do you find that either of the following passages tends to give you a greater confidence than the other in the writer's distinction as a critic?

(a) Of Byron one can say, as of no other English poet of his eminence, that he added nothing to the language, that he discovered nothing in the sounds, and developed nothing in the meaning of individual words. I cannot think of any other poet of his distinction who might so easily have been an accomplished foreigner writing in English. The ordinary person talks English, but only a few people in each generation can write it...

(b) Has literature a function in the state, in the aggregation of humans, in the republic, in the *res publica*, which ought to mean the public convenience (despite the slime of bureaucracy and the execrable taste of the populace in selecting its rulers)? It has.

And this function is *not* the coercing or emotionally persuading, or bullying or suppressing people into the acceptance of any one set or any six sets of opinions as opposed to any other one set or half-dozen sets of opinions.

It has to do with the clarity and vigour of 'any and every' thought and opinion. It has to do with maintaining the very cleanliness of the tools, the health of the very matter of thought itself...

———

## FRENCH AND ITALIAN SET BOOKS AND UNSEEN TRANSLATION

...2. Comme un dernier rayon, comme un dernier zéphire
Anime la fin d'un beau jour,
Au pied de l'échefaud j'essaye encore ma lyre;
Peut-être est-ce bientôt mon tour...

———

Exams seem never to end.

I once wrote an essay for Piggott on a topic he'd advocated: 'onomastic determinism'. For instance, 'Hippolytus' means 'horse-broken', and in Euripides' tragedy with that title, it is the fate of Prince Hippolytus to be dragged to his death by his runaway horses: his name determines his destiny. Then there's Conrad's Razumov, in *Under Western Eyes*: his name means 'Son of Reason'; and he is led into corruption and disaster when he lets rationality defeat kindness. And me, Peter Green? 'Peter' means rock, and I'm destined to emulate Sisyphus, constantly labouring to bear and dump the rock labelled 'exams'; and as for the 'Green', well, when I look back over my past misreadings of events and people, I see that I was often green in judgement.

Physical examinations, for instance: I never imagined how intricate, extensive and intimate they could be.

I'd naively thought that the medical exam for National Service, at Gloucester in January 1956, had been the ultimate. You had to strip off and walk into a room where other stripped lads were being examined by doctors in white coats. The first doctor beckoned you behind an inadequate screen and instructed you to urinate into a vessel; behind him, a conniving tap trickled water patteringly into a shallow sink. Then you went round the room, being examined from every angle: you had to bend over so that two chuckling doctors could examine your arse-hole, for instance; then, from a strange picture-book, you had to read aloud numbers which emerged magically from the pointilliste abstract pictures, dots of all the colours of the rainbow. Finally, you sat in a leather chair to read and sign a form; as you stood up, your backside made a tearing noise when parting from the leather on which umpteen other perspiring bare bums had sat. I passed that exam 'Grade 1', in spite of having lungs already well kippered by cigarette-smoke.

Worse exams were to come.

On two occasions, early in January 2011, when about to urinate, I noticed that a little spurt of blood preceded the flow of urine. An unambiguous red sprinkle on the pan. Recalling Keats, who, on coughing blood, said 'I cannot be deceived in that colour; that drop of blood is my death-warrant', I assumed similarly that my two spurts presaged death, being, I supposed, symptoms of cancer in bladder or prostate. Websites confirmed these likely sources. Fifty years previously, when black crabs used to scurry across my dreams, an antibiotic had eventually cured the stinging N.S.U. that I'd caught from Jan; but there's no antibiotic for cancer.

The notion of death, I was mildly gratified to find, did not trouble me (apart from the need to do some planning). Indeed, the prospect of death had merits. The burden of guilt – about my vile conduct towards Eastbourne, towards my parents, towards many others – would at last be shed. Lethe, the river of Oblivion: that's attractive. The possibility of some kind of afterlife seemed extremely faint: I'd rate the chances as 0.01%. 'Do you believe in the life to come?': 'My life was always that.' (Beckett, *Endgame.*) According to a familiar story, religions offer stories about an after-life to help people overcome the fear of death and to enrich the priesthood. But who wants an after-life containing examinations set by some ultimate examiner: Pluto, Rhadamanthus, God (the One and Three), Allah, or the assessor of the reincarnative cycles of Buddhism? No, death as oblivion has its attractions. A Graham Greene heroine (Rose in *The Living Room*), about to commit suicide, says 'Please God, don't let school start again ever'. I say, 'Don't let exams start again ever.' One good mentor in such matters is Conrad's Singleton, the wise old salt who unreflectively steers with care: he says to the ailing, wailing Jimmy: 'Get on with your dying... don't raise a blamed fuss with us over that job. We can't help you.' Phrases from the 1961 translation paper arise: '*Peut-être est-ce bientôt mon tour...*'; or 'at the scaffold's foot, again I try the lyre'.

It's the *manner* of the approach to death which is, of course, the matter of concern: I had hoped it would be fairly painless and dignified, and would not entail a long decline into helplessness or

188

stupidity, into 'testy delirium or dull decrepitude' (that's Yeats, who thought injections of juice from monkeys would rejuvenate him). Please, corporeal self, not the horrors of Parkinson's or Alzheimer's; and not a stroke-induced incapacitation, of which I've had a couple of forewarnings.

The examination system, which, in 1961, I thought I had conquered, was poised to take a protracted revenge on me.

Its revenge proceeded as follows.

My GP arranged for me to visit the Urology Department of the local state hospital, he having first collected from me a sample of my golden urine in a grey papier-mâché receptacle, with Keatsian beaded bubbles winking at the brim. (Falstaff's physician offered a comment: 'The water itself was a good healthy water, but, for the party that owed it, he might have more diseases than he knew for'.) At the Urology Department, a little Indian doctor, after courteously apologetic preliminaries, inserted his greased latex-gloved hand through my tight anus and groped diligently inside my guts. As he did so, he recited Keats into my ear, since I'd told him I'd taught English literature: '"My heart aches, and a drowsy numbness pains / My sense," – please, sir, keep your knees bent – "as though of hemlock I had drunk" – bent!'

Signs of my old age: 1. I'm sometimes addressed as 'sir', as then. 2. Younger people, when giving me instructions, raise their voices and speak more slowly. 3. I readily forget what I was doing last week but remember with vividness events or even quotations of fifty or more years ago. The extracts I'd memorised for exams enter, as unheralded as Eastbourne. Suddenly making a guest-appearance between my ears: the ailing King of *All's Well*. In poignant world-weary tones, he recalls his dead friend:

'Let me not live', quoth he,
'After my flame lacks oil, to be the snuff
Of younger spirits, whose apprehensive senses
All but new things disdain...'.
I, after him, do after him wish too,
Since I nor wax nor honey can bring home,
I quickly were dissolvèd from my hive,
To give some labourers room.

189

A good epitome of some of my feelings. That's another function of literature: to epitomise feelings better than we could do, and thereby to give us greater conscious understanding of them. 'What oft was thought, but ne'er so well expressed.' (Then what happens? Sod's Law ensures that half the people who quote Pope's maxim garble its expression by substituting 'though' for 'but'.)

On February 1st, in the morning, I queued in the Haematology Department until it was my turn to have a blood sample taken from my arm. In the afternoon, at the local Nuffield hospital, I underwent an examination entitled 'Flexible Cystoscopy'. I had to don a backless gown, never a propitious omen, though I was told I could leave my socks on (M & S thermal, no longer the 'Indestructible' brand; and no whore to snigger, this time). The young surgeon, with a beaming middle-aged nurse in attendance, explained that, in order to make a thorough examination, he would insert up my penis a small camera on the end of a length of tubing.

*Up – my – penis – a – small – camera?*

No, he was not joking. 'I trust, then, that you will at least administer beforehand some potent anaesthetic', I said, in my best 'Indignant of Cheltenham Spa' manner. 'Well,' he replied, with a crocodilian grin, 'the end of the tube is coated with an anaesthetic jelly. That's the *good* news.' 'And what, might I enquire, is the *bad* news?' 'About thirty seconds elapse before the anaesthetic effect of the jelly is noticeable.'

Those thirty proved to be remarkably *long* seconds, verifying Bergson's thesis – and Conrad's, in *The Secret Agent* – about the elasticity of time. Towards the end of this ordeal, the surgeon invited me to observe, on his swivelling monitor-screen, the progress of the probe in my guts. There, on the bright screen, was a blue tube, the tube worming into me at that moment, apparently cushioned by crowding plump pink balloons, my innards. It was as though I had put my head up my own arse and could survey the well-lit experiment proceeding there. How's that for surrealism? Even Dalí couldn't have envisaged such a scenario. (Yes, Dalí, accent on syllable two: how infuriated he was on BBC television in 1954 when the interviewer insisted on calling him 'Mr *Dah*ley'. Little changes: BBC newsreaders today talk of '*Vlad*-imir' Putin, unaware it should be 'Vla-*di*-mir'. Nabokov suffered too: they called him '*Nab*-o-kov'.)

190

The resultant verdict was that my prostate was enlarged, and my P.S.A. score was 25. P.S.A. meant 'Prostate Specific Antigen'. The higher the score, the worse the outlook. The normal score for a man in his seventies should be (a website told me) 5; so 25 looked like a promising sign, if a speedy demise was my hope. Nevertheless, yet more examinations were required.

Feb. 22nd. In the morning, another blood sample was taken at the local state hospital. In the afternoon, I travelled down to Hurstwood Park and underwent a C.T. scan of my guts. On the way, I read in my *Daily Telegraph* an obituary for Arabella's Lionel, killed in a car-crash in Africa. He'd made his fortune in the City but then become a philanthropist, guided by his wife. They had travelled widely in Angola and Somalia, endowing special schools for orphans and for kids maimed by land-mines and acts of war. There was a photo of a fifty-eight-year-old Arabella, now white-haired but still beautiful, looking quizzically at the camera as she embraced several grinning Angolan children; Lionel, her benign Oberon, arms folded, gazing at her appreciatively. According to the obituarist, their marriage was childless; but they seemed to have achieved magnanimous compensation. And Arabella had died just a year before Lionel, of a brain tumour, after surgery. I imagined her white hair, once coppery-gold, being shorn for the operation; winced inwardly, and tried to repress memories.

In the Hurstwood Park waiting room, two of the other people, though young, were obese, densely tattooed, and wore rings and studs in their ears and faces: further signs of decadence. At St John's Junior School in war-time, out of three hundred kids, only one was fat: Paul Head, a lad we nicknamed 'Fat-Head'; and, since we were all subject to strict food-rationing, his fatness must have been caused by some glandular disorder. I recalled Alan Wills's portable breakfasts: occasionally his mum gave him an Oxo cube, which he nibbled on arrival at school. Today, I read, one third of English ten-year-olds (and one quarter of English adults) are overweight or obese; and some authorities blame the 'fast food' shops rather than the individuals who choose to eat to excess. Again, more and more people, like the young man and woman here, are spending money on adorning themselves with tattoos, or with flesh-penetrating rings and studs, which are usually far uglier than those worn in the past by

191

indigenes of Africa or Australia. It's an attempted regression to savagery which, if it deters potential employers, may help to ensure continuing dole-payments; and it mocks my interest in primitivism. I've seen a man whose face was tattooed with a spider's web, another fellow inscribed with a dotted line across his throat accompanied by the injunction 'Cut here'; and a woman whose forearm bore a skull entwined with roses and brambles. You'd think that they'd abstain from this self-defacement if they had any respect for the concentration-camp victims compulsorily tattooed with their captive-numbers by the Nazis. I recalled Celina Neville, an Auschwitz survivor, who in 1970 had rolled back the long sleeve of her floral dress to show me the indelible mauve digits in a neat line above her bony wrist.

Feb. 25th: I underwent a 'biopsy' at one of London's Nuffield hospitals. Another 'Keep your knees bent' examination. This time, a clipping device on a tube was forced up my anus, inch by inch. The anaesthetic? Believe it or not, it was merely *literary conversation*. Yes, honestly: *literary conversation*. As follows.

The surgeon engaged me in a discussion of our literary tastes. Conrad? He'd read *Heart of Darkness* at school, but didn't think much of it; too wordy. He liked Shakespeare's *Henry IV, Parts 1 and 2*, featuring Falstaff. Frankly, the literary work he most enjoyed these days was *Treasure Island*, which he was reading to his young son at bedtime. A rather intense pain suffused my guts. Then – pock! With a sudden intimate sharp painful stab, deep inside, a sample was pecked from my prostate. A long pause. Then – pock! Another sample: another intimate brief internal agony. Altogether, he took twelve samples, well spaced out. The protracted pocking and pecking evoked Prometheus. In the Greek legend, that educator of mankind (and anticipator of the crucified Jesus) is punished by being tethered to a rock in the icy Caucasus, while an eagle devours his liver, which is daily restored. Prometheus (which means 'Forethought', remember) is the defiant hero of Shelley's *Prometheus Unbound*, an A-level set text in 1953: he remains obdurate, defeats the tyrannical Zeus, and inaugurates the golden age of classless liberty throughout the universe; people become 'equal, unclassed, tribeless, and nationless'; cosmic rejoicing ensues, and – this being Shelley's version – the moon's snows melt. The aftermath of the pecking *I* received was relatively localised and less gratifying: guts felt bruised; blood would tinge my urine and streak my faeces; and the urinary bleeding would continue for nearly a month. I had to stuff sanitary towels into my pants. For the first time in my life, I experienced empathy with menstruating girls. 'And thus the whirligig of time brings in his revenges.'

Prometheus reminded me that Godwin, Shelley, Morris and S.P.G.B. propaganda had influenced my callow early political notions. The cashless, classless society. Then, it seemed logical; now, it seems barmy. Godwin sponged off Shelley; and Shelley deserted his young wife, so that she drowned herself in the Serpentine. Teachers used to claim that the study of literature made you more sensitive and humane; indeed, Shelley did, in his *Defence of Poetry*; but, if that were the case, why was it that so many eminent writers – including Shelley – were morally unsavoury? Sartre might call Genet a saint, but I wouldn't have trusted Genet near my wallet, any more than you'd have trusted Sartre to look after your teenage daughter. Some great writers are nasty; some great texts are nasty; but those texts endure because of their qualities of articulate intelligence, insight and imagination; they are not reducible to morality or politics: they exceed the moral and the political, and that's why moralists and politicians constantly try to control or contain them.

Perhaps. I got carried away there; teachers' mode. (As for composers, look at the views of Wagner or the life of Prokofiev: sometimes the relationship of the music to the man resembles that of a saintly child to an evil parent.)

April 12th: I was informed of some results. The biopsy had revealed cancerous growth in two areas of my prostate; indeed, the cancer was endeavouring to emerge from the prostate and embark on epicurean travels into tastier areas of my guts. I wasn't surprised. My P.S.A. score had risen rapidly from 24 to 27 and then to 37, a bad sign. My Gleason score (a gauge of the aggressiveness of the cancer) was 7 on the 1-to-10 scale. Indeed an aggressive guest. Life was gaining a quality of drama. I perceived that the Gleason scale must be named after Jacky Gleason, the distinguished comedian and actor who died of cancer. 'Cancer': the name recalled ill-fated Commander Crabb. The dynamic crab. Graffito in the heads at Victoria Barracks, Portsmouth, 1956: 'If you use these heads, don't stand on the seat. /

The crabs in here can jump ten feet.' And heads came to mind because Crabb was headless when they found his floating corpse at Chichester in 1957. A Russian rebuke.

April 24th: To the Nuffield Hospital again. First, a chest X-ray, done twice, as for some reason my lungs were larger than normal, and didn't fit the standard screen. 'Are you a singer?', the nurse asked. 'Not even in the bath,' I said; 'But I suppose teaching exercises the lungs; so perhaps it does some good, after all.'

Then to the M.R.I. Department. Once more, I had to undress and don a dressing-gown with the ominous draughty slit up the back; but a nurse told me I could keep on my socks *and* my underpants, which was encouraging. Next, she and another nurse arranged me on a narrow bed with a soft wedge-shaped support beneath my knees. Various sensors were stuck to my belly and abdomen. I was slid into the long hole in the plump white circular machine, like a torpedo going into a torpedo-tube, or an unwanted offspring being sent back into the womb.

To alleviate any claustrophobia, the narrow interior was brightly lit: I saw white plastic with a blue stripe running down it, and, an inch or two above my face, a three-hole grill through which cool air blew. Several times I was told to breathe in, breathe out, and then stay still with lungs empty – for about 15 seconds. The machine was noisy, and the noise varied from a hum to a pneumatic-drill hammering, and worse. At its most extreme, the pneumatic drill was accompanied by a shrill shrieking like a banshee chorus; much of the time, the din was that of a volcanic mountain trying to devour a distraught orchestra. The machine's cacophony was largely obscured, mercifully, by music piped through big well-padded headphones. These headphones were much like those I'd worn at HMS Royal Charlotte at Kiel in '57, with yellow balloony ear-pads, as I sat at the blue-grey B40 radio-receiver, listening to excited Russian pilots: '*Na boyevoi!*', they'd yell: 'On the bombing-run!': and I'd hope it was just practice.

Nurse Varinia had asked me beforehand which sort of music I preferred; I said classical, and what ensued was a pleasant popular selection, beginning with Handel's 'Hallelujah Chorus' (a king stood for it; I reclined for it; Jack and Casey had sat through the National Anthem in cinemas); then Elgar's 'Nimrod' (made my eyes prickle);

part of the Mozart clarinet concerto (Benny Goodman played that in *The Benny Goodman Story*: grinning Gene Krupa in his audience chewed gum: film, 1956); 'Summer' from Vivaldi's 'Four Seasons' (reminding me of the contemporaneous Couperin and an ethereal flautist on a sunny Newnham lawn); the finale of a Rachmaninov piano concerto (yes, the aphrodisiac selected by Tom Ewell, lusting for Marilyn Monroe in *The Seven Year Itch*; saw it with a pretty girlfriend at the Ritz-Essoldo in Cheltenham in 1955); then Pachelbel's 'Canon in D Major', its hypnotically coiling riff seeking in vain a Gillespie to soar from it, for Dizzy was silenced in 1993.

After the initial few minutes, the nurses had slid me out, so that a vein in my arm could be scratched open and a tiny funnel inserted; and through that a saline solution was pumped in, then fluid containing some relaxant. 'This will feel cool', Varinia said. The fluid was 20 milligrams of Buscopan (Hyoscine Butylbromide), to relax the stomach, gut and bladder. 'Will it make me want to urinate?', I asked. 'No', said Varinia; 'Everyone asks that.' Eventually, I emerged for the second and final time, having spent about half an hour in the machine and having made an untimeable journey into diverse constellations of music. There was a nurse on either side of me, so I said this was the nearest I had come to a three-in-a-bed situation: they weren't amused. Glossily bald and Audenly wrinkled, I was at least fifty years too old to be amusing.

I travelled back on the bus, and some teenage school-kids climbed boisterously on. The boys and girls seemed to be competing in uttering uncouthnesses: 'I'm fucking like, what the fuck you mean?', 'And she's like, fuck off you fucking cunt', etc. The use of 'I'm like' to mean 'I said' seems needlessly imprecise. As for the obscenities: they reminded me of my first day at St John's Junior School, 1942. In the asphalt playground at the end of the afternoon, I heard a lad from the Whaddon council-estate shout at another lad, 'I'm not focking doing it'. There was a word I hadn't heard before; so, when, at home an hour later, my mother told to come to the kitchen table for tea, I said 'I'm just focking coming', merely to try the word out. 'How *dare* you use that language!', she shouted. '*Never* use that word! It's straight to bed and no tea for you, my lad! Disgraceful!' And she hustled me upstairs and ordered me to get into my pyjamas and go to bed unfed. 'But mum,' I said, 'I don't know what it means.

195

What does the word mean?' Strangely, my logical request seemed to make her even more annoyed. I learnt the injustice of the world, which punishes a five-year-old child for mere linguistic experimentation and for innocently seeking to enlarge his vocabulary. Caliban had better comprehension.

On the last part of my return journey, between the bus stop and my flat, the crowds in the rainy streets, many emerging from the underground railway, seemed to be imitating Dante's and Eliot's throngs ('I had not thought death had undone so many'), and I recognised that, in spite of my undergraduate enjoyment of Lawrence and Blake, I was incorrigibly a denizen of London's 'chartered streets'. Brought up in a house which lacked a garden, I was now content to live in a flat which lacked even a window-box. Not a nasturtium or geranium to be seen. The view is of tower blocks, concrete, glass, rooftops, drabness; and the main relief is provided by an oddity nearby: from a length of rusty guttering along a roof-edge, a small dusty-green elder bush has managed to sprout. Nature feebly seeks to subvert culture – if 'culture' is what we call this dreary architectural wilderness, epitomising the God-forsaken: the realm of *deus absconditus*, the deity who departed after (in Conrad's words) 'seeing what a precious mess he's made of his only job'.

In the back yard of my home in Cheltenham, around 1942, a tendril of Virginia creeper had forced its way through the mortar between the red bricks of the wall from a garden on the other side; the attraction being a little more sunlight on our side; and it had spread. Years later, as a student, I had deemed that to be an allegory of someone winning a scholarship to university; now, the fact that it had tunnelled from a garden to a grim concrete yard seems to make a Carpenterian irony. Sunshine but sterility. Escape into a trap.

April 25, Easter Monday. As if to punish not only my scepticism regarding religion but also my callousness towards the sufferings of other people (Eastbourne, my parents, and other victims in my wake), this was the day when a pain in the prostate area began. That pain would continue during the coming months: variable, intermittent, often quite mild, and sometimes very unpleasant, like a hot corkscrew being twisted into the guts. Websites had given me the impression that prostate cancer was painless; but that impression was misleading. Common sense should have told me it was wrong. I'll try not to take pain-killers: I want to know what's happening; I want to know how much pain I can take. My life was too soft for too long.

3 May. Another examination, this time at the 'Nuclear Medicine Department' of the local state hospital. A petite young Indian nurse injected radio-active fluid into my arm ('tracer' she called it – bringing to mind wartime newsreels of Spitfires and Hurricanes firing at Dorniers and Messerschmitts), and told me to return in the afternoon. When I did so, I was taken into the scanning room. No need to undress, I was told, but I should remove all metal objects, so off came my belt. I lay on a narrow bed, where, though it seemed uncouth to do so, I was told to remain in my clothes and shoes. My ankles were strapped to keep them together; my hands were strapped to my sides; and I was told to keep very still. Bondage for the celibate; straitjacket for the passably sane. This scan took about 45 minutes altogether, with a few pauses. Half-way through, I said to the nurse, 'What about the metal clip on my trousers – won't that spoil the scan?' No, she said. After forty minutes, she said the scan was complete, but I should wait a few minutes in case it needed to be re-done; and soon she returned saying that it did indeed need to be re-done, and this time I *should* drop my trousers and pants beforehand. I might have known *that* was coming. Presumably to preserve my modesty, or perhaps to screen a vile sight, she then laid a sheet of paper across my loins. The scanner was positioned variously over my head, chest, pelvis, etc., while I lay on that narrow board, with a cushion under my knees. The machine buzzed busily to itself and gave occasional bleeps. It came in very low over my face once or twice. (On the wall was a list of instructions for doctors and nurses about lifting patients: the gist was, if in doubt, don't; and take every precaution: never lift a heavy weight. Reminded me of the winch in the Olivier film of *Henry V* – I saw it in 1945 – hoisting an armoured knight on to his horse.) I had thus received what was termed 'a Nuclear Medicine Whole Body Bone Scan'. A superstitious notion: this is punishment for all those times when I luxuriated in scopophiliac scansion of the naked Arabella's lissom whole body, as we lay together in her sunny room at Newnham. It fits.

Morning of Wednesday, May 4: Having obediently refrained from eating or drinking since 2200 on Tuesday, I proceeded to my GP's surgery to provide another blood sample. A further blood sample was

197

taken on May 6. As Lady Macbeth said of Duncan: 'Yet who would have thought the old man to have had so much blood in him?' Haggerty's account of Byron says he was killed by doctors who drew blood 'by the pound' from his veins; and that Robin Hood story I'd read in childhood had told me that Robin was murdered by a blood-taking prioress – yes, a prioress: that must have nurtured some embryonic scepticism.

In May, the so-called merry month, the time when Langland in the Malvern Hills contemplated a fair field full of folk, I noticed that when other people deemed the weather mild, I still found it cold. The London sun sheds on me 'more light than heat' (Polonius). At nights, my comforting bed-mate is no female but a woolly-covered rubber hot-water bottle; an improvement on the heavy and leaky stone bottle that in war-time my mother used to put in my bed, wrapped in an old sock for safety. Instead of air-raid sirens, the nocturnal streets now intermittently echo and re-echo to the wailing of ambulances and police-cars. Jan had always seemed warm. Perhaps this feeling of coldness is a cancer symptom. On 6 May, the oncologist told me that there were 'no major concerns' about a cyst-marked kidney; a nodule on my adrenal gland 'could perhaps be scanned again in some months' time'; the bone scan and chest X-ray had revealed nothing untoward. However, as I had already learnt, he remarked, the M.R.I. scan showed that the prostate was abnormal, harbouring cancerous growths which were endeavouring to spread. A 'panel of oncologists' (another examination board) would consider the various options for treating this cancer. Life was, albeit unenthusiastically, attempting to imitate art: here was a little drama, an element of suspense.

On May 14, I received a copy of a letter from the oncologist to my GP. It said in part:

> Diagnosis: T3a (on MRI), N0, M0 Gleason 7 (4+3) in two cores, PSA 37, localised carcinoma of the prostate.
> For neo-adjuvant hormone therapy with Bicalutamide 150 mg once a day.
> For radical radiotherapy to the prostate and seminal vesicles commencing September.

The letter (in delphic prose so medically functional that you could imagine choral wailing from the distressed shades of Pater, James and Wilde) added that the GP should prescribe the bicalutamide as soon as possible, remarking that this medication would be a better option than 'castration therapy with injections'.

'*Castration therapy*'? That's an oxymoron, if ever I heard one. And the medication list looked formidable. At least, for pensioners, there are no prescription charges. Ten years ago, I was taking no medication. But now my medication list reads thus:

At 0800: One aspirin, 75 mg. (that's a blood-thinner); one persantin retard, alias dipyridamole, 200 mg. (another blood-thinner); one tamsulosim pill, 400 micrograms (to relax the prostate and make urination easier).

At 1800, one persantin retard; one simvastatin (statin) tablet, 40 mg. (to reduce cholesterol); and one hormone pill, bicalutamide, 150 mg. (to reduce activity in the prostate).

As the blood-thinners indicate, I've had a couple of strokes recently. Only mild ones: they made me giddy, so that I fell down; and they slurred my speech for an hour or two. In the event, trivial. Perhaps punishment for my sin of verbal pride (ha: logophilia).

The hormone pill seemed to have some beneficial effects. Less often did I have to rush impetuously to a lavatory in response to a sudden peremptory demand from the bladder. (I remembered how Jan's N.S.U. made her hasten into the Blue Boar.) For a while, the pain in the prostate seemed milder. On the other hand, my nipple areas became sensitive and bruised-feeling: I seemed to be growing little breasts (a punishment for all those times when, as a teenager, I had heavy-handedly groped some girl's flinching delicate bosom); my armpits itched and shed hair, and generally hair seemed to be vanishing from my chest and legs – it's just as well that my head is bald as a white bar-billiard-ball on the Mill's table; and it seemed that my testicles were shrinking. Perhaps I'll gain the insights of the hermaphroditic Teiresias of Ovid's *Metamorphoses* and Eliot's *The Waste Land.*

The baldness seems a punishment for those many months when, as a student, I didn't wash my hair but just added Brylcreem, so that sometimes when I tried to comb the hair, my solid gluey quiff would snap the comb in half; and behold, I'm still thinking in metaphysical terms of crime and punishment, even though it's nearly seventy years since a cane-wielding headmistress, Miss MacDonald, assured her school-children that Satan's hell-fires were infinitely more painful than the punishment she was about to inflict on Alan Wills or some other hapless little victim. Again and again she slashed their palms.

This autumn, then, I'm to undergo two months of radiation treatment 'of the prostate and seminal vesicles' at the Cancer Unit of the local state hospital. In plain English: fried guts. Ironic that I used to worry so much, in the 1960s, about atmospheric radiation from nuclear tests; but perhaps my carcinoma (Greek *karkinos*, crab) is a consequence of them. Crabs had scurried through my nightmares. The oncologist (Greek *onkos*, tumour) informed me that possible side effects of the treatment included impotence and incontinence.

'Impotence'? Bring it on. I outgrew sex in the 1970s, when it became a decadent national obsession, and when it became so readily available as to lose value: a debased currency. Making everyone a winner merely destroys the contest, rendering it pointless. My greatest orgasm was the mental orgasm hugely induced and greedily sucked out by the voracious Cambridge Final Examination in English, 1961. I've long been liberated from the sexual servitude which has enthralled and subjugated so many, all slaves of Circe and dupes of Dionysus. (On that distant Saturday afternoon with Arabella, my very phrase '*slimy* haven' implied some distaste.) One day, compulsory celibacy may be the salvation of this over-populated planet. The breeding of race-horses is a scientific skill entailing long-term planning and promethean forethought; the breeding of humans is a carnal blundering, so that most babies are an accidental by-product of the janiform beast with two backs. Vendice says he was begotten by 'some stirring dish' at a 'gluttonous dinner'. At least, being childless, I'm not transmitting to posterity my genes, with their freight of myopia, flat-footedness and egotism: there's altruism for you.

'Incontinence'? There would be moral justice in that, and a thematic irony. I recalled my disgust when little Patrick's reeking crappy bum was being wiped clean by Jenny, and remembered the thematically-attuned nurse in *Agamemnon* who grumbles about baby Orestes' unpredictable excretions; and, for the first time, I thought of

200

the number of times my patient mother must have washed my nappies when I was a wailing incontinent infant. Mothers had to use durable towelling nappies in those days, not the environment-polluting disposables used today. The older I become, the more the patterns in my life emerge clearly into visibility and reach a neat, if ironic, completion. They try to vindicate Alexander Pope: 'All Chance, Direction which thou canst not see.'

The oncologist specified other side-effects: I would, almost certainly, experience not only lethargy but also some inflammation of bladder and bowels. I asked whether the treatment killed the cancer or merely prolonged it. He said that in 70% of cases, patients survived for another five years; and, in the other 30%, they did not necessarily face speedy death. (I noted his 'not necessarily'.) I'm reminded that in fiction, the central lives culminate usually in climax; in reality, usually in anti-climax.

Tragic deaths: Act 5; everyday deaths, Act 1 or 3 or 8 or 10. Well past Act 5, ineluctably *real*, I sometimes gloat at my ontological superiority to fiction and its consolatory plot-culminations; at other times, I wince as I find that partly I've been plotted, or as I recognise that my span has been longer than those of morally-superior people.

For the radiation session, your bladder is supposed to be 'comfortably full': that's another oxymoron, in my view. And if it is indeed 'comfortable' when you enter the waiting room, it may not be so comfortable should there be a delay; and, if you then visit the lavatory, you are supposed next to drink water from the dispenser and allow twenty minutes for the liquid to descend.

I would wait an unpredictable time (perhaps an hour, perhaps two minutes) in the room with the intermittently-gurgling water-dispenser, the walls bearing brightly-lit photos of rural views. (Sometimes there were three or four other people waiting with me, sometimes a dozen. They often seemed subdued, tense and preoccupied.) One photo showed the Rottingdean windmill facing the sea, the very mill that Lawrence had called 'stately but a bit ridiculous' when he had cycled down from London to Brighton and on to Rottingdean in May 1909. Another memory stirred, and I suddenly recognised that my mother would have made a fine sister for Mrs Morel in *Sons and Lovers*: they were akin in pride, courage and devotion; yes, and even in that incidental moment when she holds the smoothing-iron close to her cheek, 'listening, as it were, to the heat', her mouth 'closed tight from suffering and disillusion and self-denial'. Precisely evocative. But Mrs Morel eventually employed a servant; my mother could never have afforded one, and in any case would have been too proudly self-reliant.

Boswell said: 'A man should not live more than he can record, as a farmer should not have a larger crop than he can gather in.' I'd retained the undergraduate habit of note-taking. I therefore noted, meticulously, an absurdity for connoisseurs: a confused and confusing message on the waiting-room wall, which declared:

> Today's Radiotherapy Treatment Rooms
> are running behind schedule
> by approximately:-
> Treatment Room 2: On Time
> Treatment Room 3: On Time

(The wording did not vary from one week to the next.) Nearby, a board was festooned with notices and racks of leaflets, some entitled: 'Coping with Hair Loss'; 'Breast Cancer'; 'Rectal Cancer'; 'Coping with Advanced Cancer'; 'Controlling Cancer Pain'. Posters were headed: 'Living with cancer is expensive' and 'Any questions on your cancer in any language'; and another notice said: 'Please assist radiotherapy staff by placing litter and used drinking cups in the rubbish bins provided. Thank you.' For relief and refuge from such prosy prose (well-meaning voice of witheringly prosaic reality), memory proffered some of the snatches of poetry I'd learnt for exam purposes. The first offering, with suitable irony, was the Duke in *Measure for Measure* saying:

> Reason thus with life:
> If I do lose thee, I do lose a thing
> That none but fools would keep: a breath thou art,
> Servile to all the skyey influences
> That dost this habitation, where thou keep'st,
> Hourly afflict...

Here I was distracted by a copy of the *Daily Mail*, abandoned on

202

an adjacent seat, which, beneath the headline 'Golden Oldie', told me that a Gloucestershire great-grandfather, 74-year-old Alan Wills, had won eight million pounds in the National Lottery rollover. It was Alan of St John's Junior School and the GCHQ building-site. His lined face grinned at me from the page, and he was quoted as saying that some of the money would be spent on a cruise for himself and his wife, and some would buy a far better education than he'd had for the youngsters in his family (nine grand-children and fifteen great-grand-children). Thus, one individual from my primary school had achieved fame, albeit transitory. Shakespeare's deranged Timon arose in memory, the Timon praised by Karl Marx for denouncing gold:

This yellow slave
Will knit and break religions, bless th'accursed,
Make the hoar leprosy adored, place thieves,
And give them title, knee, and approbation,
With senators on the bench.

If Marx had seen those purple bruises on young Alan's palm, he'd have conceded that sometimes wealth was a just compensation. Perhaps a deity delighted by euphony and poetic justice had transmuted weals into wealth: Fortuna turned her wheel and Wills's weals. Life's lottery.

Then I was called into the 'Linear Accelerator' radiation area; and I obediently dropped my trousers and pants, pulled my shirt up round my chest, and reclined on the narrow sacrificial board of the great curved machine named 'Elekta' (to punish punsters – 'Mourning Becomes Elekta'). Exposing my tool reminded me of Arabella's deft ministrations, half a century ago. The ministrations I received now were as erotic as cold tapioca. One nurse placed a rectangle of kitchen paper over my genitalia, and the other nurse then prodded and kneaded my flabby buttocks into position with cool firm hands. The machine's over-arching scanner made ruminative clopping and clacking noises, like the lurking Triffids in the BBC film (1981 I think; monochrome; I missed the recent adaptation). The two nurses exchanged arcane information about the location of the scanner, relative to marks on my abdomen: '80 point 5': 'Yes'; 'Laterally positive 5 point 9': 'Yes.' (At a preliminary session, three little black guide-marks had been tattooed down there; perhaps a punishment for my dislike of voluntarily tattooed people.) Just before the machine started its penetrating work, the nurses scurried away out of sight.

Their haste to escape the dangerous radiation made me feel kinship with martyrs on the rack or sacrificial victims on an altar. Poor Iphigenia; poor Tess at Stonehenge; ...poor Jan when sore. And the compulsory prostration is punishment for all the mornings when, as a teenager or student, I wallowed in bed until 10 a.m. This board is a Bed of Procrustes too: I'm being trimmed (internally) to fit better. In 1961, there was no scurrying away: we were all being impartially doused in radioactive fallout from the distant test-sites, American, Russian, British, French. The number of cancers resulting must have been vast: even mine now, perhaps. Yes, 1961, when I refused to take Jan to a May Ball: that was a stupid and mean-spirited mistake... But she became a belle of the Pembroke ball, of course, thanks to Casey's double ticket and a borrowed dress.

The scanner examined me. A glass-covered central disc, three feet in diameter, ornamented with red and green lights and a 360-degree scale, was set in the middle of the cream-and-grey steel and plastic arch of the machine. After the initial clopping and rattling noises, the room was pierced by repeated high-pitched whistling, some kind of warning: bosun's pipe whistles. (One evening at Victoria Barracks in April 1956, I'd been ordered by P.O. Feasey to scamper along the chilly corridors ahead of the inspecting officer, Jimmy the One, blowing the pipe piercingly to alert each mess-room to the impending inspection: a pusser ritual. If you clench and unclench your hand over the perforated ball of the curved steel instrument, the pitch can be varied excruciatingly.) Then the arch slowly rotated through an arc of 180 degrees from right to left over my abdomen, and, within that arch, the central head swivelled like an inquisitive Martian, and emitted its penetrating radiation (reminding me briefly of *The War of the Worlds* and lingeringly of my selfish penetrations of young women long ago). The arch also made bleeping and buzzing noises interspersed by, as it moved, a slushy grinding noise. The head irradiated my prostate gland from the right: two bursts lasting about ten and four seconds respectively; then, from directly above, two bursts; then from the left, two more bursts. In effect, my cancer was being micro-waved. Fried in its own poisonous goo; a sizzling toadstool.

204

Each of these sessions took about eight minutes. They reminded me that in 1898, as an amusement at a party in Glasgow, Joseph Conrad's hand had been X-rayed in a machine operated by Dr John McIntyre: I remembered seeing the resultant bone-photo in a volume of Conrad's letters. That X-ray probably engendered his science-fiction novel, *The Inheritors*, written with F. M. Hueffer; yes, Hueffer, who later had the courage to fight for Britain during the Great War while retaining that German surname. Only afterwards did he become 'Ford Madox Ford'. And only after National Service did I, recruited to C.N.D., seek to register as a conscientious objector, to the amusement of the desk-bound police constable whom I had assumed to be the relevant official for such registration. 'But son, if you've *done* your National Service, what's the *bloody point*, forgive my French?'

One day, as I lay ready on the board, trousers down, shirt up, a nurse remarked that I was wearing a tie; but I usually do. 'I like to keep up appearances', I explained, and promptly remembered, remorsefully, my father wearing his trilby as he cycled to work.

She responded with a story. This man goes to the doctor and says: 'I'm feeling generally unwell.' The doctor gives him a thorough examination and says, 'I have bad news for you: you will be dead within a month.' The man shouts: 'I demand a second opinion!'. The doctor replies: 'You are also remarkably ugly.'

So I offered her Blake's aphorism, uttered on what he deemed to be his hundredth birthday: 'If I'd known I was gonna live this long, I'd have taken better care of myself.' (No, not William Blake this time; Eubie Blake, the jazz pianist and composer.) She responded with Woody Allen's: 'I'm not afraid of death; I just prefer to be somewhere else when it happens.' I winced, recalling my avoidance of Casey's funeral. Conscience is superstition's story-teller.

That night, on television, I saw a documentary programme on the changing fortunes of Sussex University. No sign of Jack. There were clips and stills of the early hopeful days: Asa Briggs, the Jay twins, parties, demonstrations, Vietnam protests, red paint, sit-ins. We were reminded that Denis Hobden, aided by students, was elected as Labour M.P. for Brighton Kemptown in 1964: the first Labour M.P. to be elected in Sussex: just seven votes decided it; Tories blamed the University.

Later came the Thatcher era. It seemed that in 1980-81, Prime Minister Thatcher had taken revenge on this left-leaning university by cutting its financial subsidy by more than 20%, and since then the university had experienced recurrent financial difficulties. In the competition to recruit students, the 'new map of learning' had been torn up: instead of the 'core and context' approach, the place had restored traditional departments, so that courses were now more 'job-orientated', as the 'spokesperson' put it. The unpopular Arts-Science scheme had undergone fatal (ha:) entropy.

Meanwhile, the 'concrete cancer' which had infected the early buildings had apparently been eradicated. The Library had more than doubled in size, and its roof no longer leaked into rows of yellow plastic buckets. Some of the campus's lakes and ponds had been filled in, to reduce maintenance-costs or on 'health and safety' grounds. The Henry Moore had vanished. Although the elm trees had succumbed to the Dutch disease, ash trees seemed to be thriving. As though seeking safety in numbers, the university was investing in vast new buildings: for accommodation, for seminar rooms, lecture rooms and offices. Consequently, to the north of the big boiler-house, the vista was a gaunt array of massive functional structures. Another speaker offered assurances that the examination-system, once a cause of dissension, remained firmly in place; and he noted that, in English, the proportion of firsts and upper-seconds had increased remarkably since the 1960s. To provide a sardonic comment, a camera-man had entered a lavatory in the Arts Building to film a toilet-roll holder on which some student wit had inscribed with felt pen 'Collect your B.A. degree here.' The programme concluded with two interviews: one with a dour jobless graduate who was drawing the dole, the other with a jubilant graduate who was now working for the BBC.

The same day, the *Martlet*, the alumni-and-now-also-alumnae magazine of Pembroke College, Cambridge, informed me that the College's 'Development Fund', to which past graduates contribute, had raised over twenty-four million pounds. I remembered the ham sandwiches that Piggott had bought for Jan, and resolved to send a modest donation.

Piggott had died of a stroke in 1996. The obituary that I saw claimed that 'he belonged to the generation that took *Finnegans Wake*

206

off to war'. I learned that he was a hero of World War II: he had served with the Special Operations Executive in North Africa, India and Europe, and had become a *chevalier* of the *Légion d'honneur*, being awarded the *Croix de guerre* by the French government. The S.O.E. specialised in notoriously dangerous work: espionage, sabotage, and the priming of resistance groups. If I'd only *known*; how much more respectfully I'd have regarded him. He never talked about his war service; nor did my father. Those men believed that reticent modesty was a virtue: a mode of self-denial implying altruism. Among many young people today, that belief seems not to exist. Boastfulness, crowing, arrogance, naïve triumphalism: you see them on football pitches, on tennis courts, cricket grounds; on TV talent shows; among politicians. It's part of the decadence. Well, I sometimes think that; other times I put such thoughts in ironic quotation-marks and add 'says agèd hypocrite'.

Piggott's colleague at Cambridge and Sussex, David Daiches, died ten years after him, in 2006. I heard he'd done important war-service in Washington, not all of it in the public domain. Crafty plotter. Another death I winced to read about was Heckstall-Smith's, in 2004: thirty years after Graham Bond had been killed by a train at an underground station. Falstaff's 'chimes at midnight' came to mind, accompanied by distorted echoes of frenetic sax duets, and by Daiches smoothly and affectionately reading 'smooth pillows' from a Sidney sonnet... Yes, the sonnet 'Come, Sleep, O Sleep, the certain knot of peace'.

*Requiescant in pace*, with the plural *-ant*.

Haggerty, 1907-1972, had published another book on Byron, two on Shelley, and one, I had noted bitterly, on *Carpenter and Lawrence*, to critical acclaim, in 1970. Edward Carpenter, that resourceful foe of civilisation, that sandalled Uranian graduate of Trinity Hall, had evidently helped her to a Professorship, awarded a year after the book's publication. Gleeful reviewers noted the irony that Lawrence, once thought a champion of virile heterosexuality, had been so pervasively influenced by the homosexual libertarian. Obituarists praised Haggerty's study for revealing the remarkably extensive influence of Carpenter's ideas on Lawrence's, particularly the notion of humanity's redeemable fall into the divided and diseased state known as civilisation, a condition in which the hypertrophy of mental

207

consciousness entailed the suppression of the healthily instinctual. 'Revelatory', said the *T.L.S.*

I had under-estimated Haggerty's guile.

I'd been so keen on detecting covert plots in *literature* that I'd overlooked covert plots in *life*. The real-life versions had repeatedly laid ironic ambushes for me; so the world-conspiracy theory now looked more plausible than the 'Sod's Law' alternative. 'Savage Man alone does Man betray', murmured Rochester in memory's ear. Arabella, Jan and Casey had fooled me; Eastbourne had sabotaged Jack, Casey and me; I'd been plagiarised by Jack; and both Jack and I had been Hag-ridden. In Haggerty, the competition for promotion had vanquished honesty and, ironically, the examples of moral courage set by Lawrence and Carpenter.

The treacherous Haggerty had, however, died in mysterious circumstances: evidently, she had broken her neck in falling downstairs at her block of flats. What made the incident mysterious was that, according to her acquaintances, she always used the lift. Nevertheless: 'Unfortunate accident', the coroner had concluded. Jack's voice, uttering sardonically the phrase 'Act of God', came to mind. As did his hefty fist, thumping the coffee table at Sussex University. And as did, briefly, that phrase 'covert plot', flitting into memory like an ominous bat at dusk; guiltily, I batted it away. A batty suspicion. (I don't know what became of Jack; so he thereby gains ontological superiority to a fictional character. That's life.)

I had also misjudged the famous F. R. Leavis. I used to think that the quietness of his lecture-room voice was calculated to induce a conspiratorial atmosphere, and that his open-necked shirts in all weathers were a Lawrentian affectation. Obituaries of Leavis in 1978 taught me, however, that he had served gallantly with the Friends' Ambulance Unit on the western front during the Great War, and there his lungs had been damaged by poison gas: hence the quiet voice and the open collars. *Mea culpa.*

And at least Leavis was sufficiently the democrat to write in reasonably clear English about the human worth of literature. Between the 1970s and 1990s, literary studies were invaded by vile anti-democratic jargon-bound theories: structuralism, post-structuralism, deconstruction: usually recycling sceptical notions so old that they'd have made Socrates groan. These arrogantly derivative theorists included Paul de Man (who in war-time had written anti-Semitic propaganda), Louis Althusser (who strangled his wife and successfully pleaded insanity), Barthes, Derrida and Foucault. They sometimes claimed that literature referred to nothing outside itself, that language had no purchase on reality, that the true author is the reader, and the text should mean whatever any reader takes it to mean. Many lecturers and students obediently recited this drivel, even though it opposed not only common sense but also feminism and Marxism, which were trying to make a comeback. Heard about the post-structuralist bank manager? He cashes your cheque and puts your money into his own pocket, since the reader is the true author.

Nothing endures; and nothing's sacred. Jack had predicted that in years to come, after we three had achieved our justly-deserved literary fame, the Mill's outer wall and the Still & Sugarloaf's entrance would bear blue commemorative plaques, to inform tourists and our pilgrims that he, Casey and I, now renowned cultural eminences, had played bar-billiards within. The plaques, installed by English Heritage, would be unveiled by suitable delegations: at the Mill, by the Prime Minister, accompanied by the Culture Secretary and the Poet Laureate, applauded by the appreciative representatives of most nations retaining pretensions to civilisation, and protected from jealous placard-bearing demonstrators by a white-gloved armed guard-of-honour from the Royal Navy and the Royal Air Force. Overhead, exactly on time, the Battle of Britain flight (an Avro Lancaster accompanied by a Spitfire and a Hurricane) would roar across the respectfully serene skies. The ceremony at the Still & Sugarloaf, taking advantage of the scale of the Market Place, would be somewhat more elaborate, including a public performance of Beethoven's Ninth by the Royal Philharmonic Orchestra (conducted by Sir Malcolm Sargent), augmented by massed choirs and a frenzied bevy of topless go-go dancers.

But the last time I visited Cambridge, the Still & Sugarloaf had vanished: the site was occupied by a Marks & Spencer shop.

Other changes, too, were depressing. Granta Place, in 1961 a pretty row of 17th-century riverside cottages with petite doorways and windows, had been largely demolished to make way for a harshly modernistic building to house a 'University Centre' (with facilities for graduates, conferences, etc.). Boasting a 'Concrete Society

209

Commendation', it brutally dominated the river near the Mill Pool, where Arabella and I had once swum, and where Alex Eastbourne had drowned. The Mill pub and the pool remained; but nearby, the Garden House Hotel, where I'd booked my parents in, had become vastly enlarged as a Hilton hotel. St Cat's and numerous other colleges now housed steel-and-concrete additions which were so lacking in local character that they might have been transported from Berlin or Bangkok.

Jack was right about Borges and Quixote, too. That story, 'Pierre Menard, Author of the *Quixote*', says that even if you re-create precisely the past, thinking you are repeating it unchanged, the simulacrum, being in a different context, is transformed. A once-colloquial style becomes quaintly archaic. My undergraduate encounters with Arabella, which then seemed riskily bold, now seem, when recollected, to be testimony to a time of fearful inhibition, bound with briars. Then, original research for an essay implied days of work; now it implies a few minutes mouse-clicking at a computer. Mouse-click? 'Snap!' would exclaim the war-time spring-trap in the pantry at home, breaking the neck of a bulgy-eyed cheese-seeker.

My final radiation session occurs next week. They call it 'radiotherapy', but that term seems optimistic if not hubristic. The principle of the Elekta, I realise, is admirably symbolic. *It examines, in order to destroy what it examines. It appraises, and kills what it appraises.* Like the snakes of Laocoön, ironies entangle me.

As a precaution, and to make it easier for any relative who would have to tidy my flat when I die, I've been taking books to charity shops, and putting into the recycling-bin heaps of papers. To Oxfam I've delivered Hamlet, Don Quixote, Heathcliff, Prometheus, Ivanov, and Mr Kurtz: a bizarrely picturesque gang, now all co-operating as conscripts in the service of charity; so perhaps Kurtz, transmuted into medicine, will return to the ravaged Congo after all: didn't he declare 'I will return'?

My sister is 84, living far away; so I wouldn't wish to inflict on her the job of tidying the flat. Citizen Kane's workmen burnt his beloved 'Rosebud'; Faustus tardily offered to burn his books; Prospero drowned his magician's manual; and Peter Green, fan of Caliban, merely recycles as pulp his stale teaching-notes and copiously-annotated set texts.

The aesthete Axel said: 'As for living, our servants will do that for us.' I say: 'As for loving, my heroes have done that for me.' Romeo, Troilus, Antony: they show me what I could never attain; while Aguecheek, Thersites and Caliban show me aspects of what I have become. Vicarious life provides a derisory chorus. Between my ears all six parade: incongruous prancing dancers in top-hats and tailcoats, pointing their silver-topped canes accusingly at me; the tune being Gillespie's 'The Champ', the choreography by Berkeley (Busby, not Bishop), and the footwork mostly nifty – except, of course, that Caliban, at the end of the row, is clumsily out of step, lurching, stumbling: another flat-footed beneficiary of compulsory education. But perhaps he's satirising my jiving with Jan at Miller's on those distant Saturday nights. And now she'll be a white-haired widow.

At the back of my filing cabinet, I found a file containing my Final Examination question-papers, still marked with hasty ball-point-pen comments, ticks and deletions. How difficult the questions now looked, and how formidably arcane seemed so many of the quotations for comment! If I were to take that exam this week, I'd fail it. The ticks and crosses on the white borders made Eastbourne's cross-wounded foot flicker into my visual memory, and a surge of guilt induced some kind of cataleptic trance: when I looked at the clock, I found I'd been motionless for twenty minutes; like that time I'd dozed in the exam-room. 'Be sure your sins will find you out', my mother used to say. Eastbourne's quoted exhortation ('Woe to the man', etc., etc.) seems, in retrospect, to have served effectively as a curse. Another pattern emerges into completion. Mind-forg'd manacles clink and lock.

Seeking a temporary exorcism, I selected some redemptional music. I still retain a record player that plays LPs; so on went the Wanda Landowska harpsichord record I'd bought with Bafs in the Naafi shop in Kiel in 1957 and carried back to England in my kit-bag. Well padded by socks and pants, the LP had survived the overnight crossing by dank throbbing troopship-ferry from the Hook of Holland to Harwich. I always took great care of my gramophone records: their grooved vinyl will outlive my lined flesh. The Landowska selection includes Couperin's 'Les Barricades mystérieuses': preserved by my underwear, the music of the pure civilisation that the world glimpses but never achieves.

The H.M.V. sleeve-note says of that Couperin title: 'This would seem to be a technical joke, the continuous suspensions being a mysterious barricade to the basic harmony.' That's what I've been examining as I look back on my life: 'continuous suspensions'. Turgenev's Tchulkaturin said: 'Sinking into nothing, I cease to be superfluous': so even that superfluous man achieved his 'basic harmony'; and one of my tardily-perceived achievements has been to extend the futile tradition of which he was part. We superfluous men (corrupted by education, critical, sterile) have survived from the nineteenth century to the twenty-first. Survival of the unfittest.

Into a big brown cardboard box went those yellowing question-papers, together with files of notes that I'd used when teaching. Landowska's harpsichord was variously plangent, poignant and defiant. Other items in that filing cabinet included my O and A level certificates, my degree certificate, and a brownish newspaper-cutting listing the results of the 1961 English exam. In those days at Cambridge, the percentages of students in the different classes for the B.A. in English were: Class I: 6%; Class II.i: 37%; Class II.ii: 38%; Class III: 18%; Pass: 0.5%; Fail (an estimate): 0.5%. I looked up the English results for 2010, nearly 50 years later, and saw clear evidence of the decline in educational standards, of the corruption of examiners, and of the devaluation of degrees, largely as a result of political and financial pressure. The 2010 results were: Class 1: 24.5%; Class II.i: 71.4%; Class II.ii: 4.1%; Class III: none; Fail: none. Ha! Absurd. Human intelligence has not soared; therefore, standards must have sunk. It's not just at Cambridge, or only in that subject. Whether it's A level or doctoral level, whether it's an Oxbridge college or a lowly comprehensive school, standards are declining: a dire consequence of the enforced commercialisation of education. Institutionalised cheating.

And *I'm* guilty there, too. When I became an examiner at my C.A.T., I tried to maintain rigorous standards; but this endeavour made me unpopular with colleagues and students. Numerous students appealed against my marking, saying they were being 'victimised' by 'anomalous' grades. Irate colleagues argued that the survival of the C.A.T. (and thus our jobs) depended on the College's ability to attract funding and students, and that, in turn, depended on the ease with which students would be able to obtain 'above average' grades.

So, eventually, I conformed; and now, you can depend on it, virtually all students receive 'above average' grades – even when their essays, as the spelling shows, have been downloaded from American websites; and yes, even when their essays cite uncritically an out-of-date litany of those jargonish theorists (Barthes, Bakhtin, Althusser, de Man, Derrida, Foucault) who were either self-contradictory or were recycling Plato. Having advised us to disregard the author, Barthes signed his essay and claimed copyright for it.

A decadent culture is one in which various forms of cheating seem normal. Every couple of months I receive emails from firms in the U.K. and abroad which, guessing that I may be a student, promise me that, for a price, all the written work can be supplied to enable me to obtain exactly the B.A., or the M.A., or the D.Phil. that I desire. 'The material supplied will be original and guaranteed to defeat any known plagiarism test.' Ironically, every couple of months I also receive emails from the same or similar firms, which, guessing that I may be an academic, assure me that I can earn good money by supplying the written work for candidates for the B.A., M.A. or D.Phil.. I must, however, promise that the work I supply will be original and not plagiarised; furthermore, I must be prepared to 'adapt' my style to that of the candidate who, ultimately, is paying for my services. (This means, presumably, that I make my style as uncouth as his or hers; sorry, hers or his.) According to reports in various newspapers, academic cheating in England is now a multi-million-pound industry.

Furthermore, the British taxpayer now provides students with 'loans' worth £9000 per annum. Many of those 'loans' will never be repaid. I read that numerous students from France or Italy or Greece, for instance, go home and don't repay. Even if they could afford to repay, they can't be pursued for repayments. Mad Hatter economics. Our 'culture' of cheating – I envisage the culture of a multiplying mould – has infected sports, of course: even the most admired footballers foul, or dive to imply they've been fouled; and increasingly football seems less a contest of team against team than a contest between one millionaire-owner and another. Meanwhile, cycling champions, athletes and body-builders take illegal drugs: erythropoietin, growth hormones, cortisone, steroids and testosterone. Some able competitors claim disability allowances. Among school-children, girls as young as twelve digitally alter their online images in

213

order to look more attractive. Women fake their appearance by using botulinum toxin, or collagen, or silicone breast-enlargers. Men dye their hair and buy Viagra or penis-enlargers. Men and women resort to surgery to alter radically their appearance; in Africa, however, starvation still does the job. Law and order? Recently, policemen have been jailed for rape and theft; and even judges have sometimes been revealed as crafty lawbreakers. Bankers who have presided over banking disasters retire with pensions worth millions of pounds. Millionaires and multi-national companies cheat the tax-collector.

As for British politicians: these days, they routinely break the promises made in their election manifestos. Not long ago, furthermore, the *Daily Telegraph* demonstrated that the vast majority of British M.P.s had been assiduously fiddling their expenses. Whatever their avowed political allegiance, and whether they were cabinet ministers or back-benchers, their deepest allegiance was to their own bank-balance. Accordingly, they made the taxpayer pay for bath plugs, mouse-traps, second homes, porn films, wallpaper, and so forth. Shameless, large-scale cheating. In a cashless society, they'd steal carrots from allotment-patches. Cunninghame Graham had founded the Labour Party, but he was soon so disgusted by the selfish behaviour of Labour M.P.s that he said they'd do more good if they came to Parliament 'drunk and tumbling about on the floor'. William Morris was partly right, after all: in his Utopia, the Houses of Parliament have become a dung-heap. Casey had taught me that the exam system would make capitalism seem natural and inevitable; these days, his claim doesn't seem so eccentric: Russia and even China now toe the Casey line.

At elections recently, I'm guided by that anarchist graffito of the 1960s: 'Why vote for the bastards? It only encourages them.' The Duke in *Measure for Measure* complains that he has 'seen corruption boil and bubble / Till it o'er-run the stew'; I begin to sympathise with that erratic autocrat; though Pompey Bum and Barnardine are the characters who usually win my sympathy. Literary friends don't let you down: Rochester, Swift, Voltaire, Maupassant, Graham, Conrad, Hardy: *they* understand. I don't need to say 'The country's going to the dogs'; that would insult dogs. But I haven't wholly become the kind of moaning old reactionary I used to mock; on the contrary,

214

Conrad's maxim (if taken in context) seems increasingly apt: '*Je respecte les extrêmes anarchistes*': a noble Pole writing to an aristocratic Scot (Graham) in French, at that time the appropriate language of philosophical scepticism. As an American critic said: 'Conrad's view of history is skeptical and disillusioned, which, for us, today, must mean *true*.'

When I'd calmed, after this rhapsody infused with senile rancour, I continued to empty the filing-cabinet. At the back, I found some sheets of lined paper bearing notes that my father had made, around 1945, for a speech to colleagues, entitled 'History of a Shopman'. Copper-plate handwriting; immaculate grammar, punctuation and spelling. Part of it read:

> After the 1914-19 War, there were those of us who sought to increase our knowledge by courses of study relating to our work. What were the facilities for learning our jobs?
>
> Classes in book-keeping;
> Classes in salesmanship;
> Classes in knowledge of goods;
> Classes in Cooperation.
>
> *But* there was little to stimulate interest in these classes.
>
> What happened was that a notice went to each shop saying that Mr. Kennan was holding a class on Cooperation, or that Mr. So-and-So was holding a class on Book-keeping – usually at Gloucester; with the result that a very small percentage of employees attended classes.
>
> I think that it can be truthfully said that the technical knowledge gained by attending classes gives one a greater interest in the daily round. But is that all that one should look for? What effect in the past has the quality of knowledge had in regard to promotion to the better paid posts within the Society?
>
> If it is true that there are none among us capable of filling the better paid posts within the Society, then I am afraid very great reflection must be cast upon the past educational policy of the Society.

He was for many years 'First Hand' (approximately, 'foreman') at the shop, but, though he was liked and trusted, and though he had assiduously attended evening classes, he never succeeded in being promoted to Manager. Repeatedly, the Board appointed an outsider. He felt that the co-operative spirit was being sapped by unfair competition for promotion. There's a familiar irony.

My father and I span three centuries, from 1897, when Queen Victoria, Empress of India, ruled the greatest empire the world had ever known, to now in 2011, when the U.K.'s national debt is colossal (one thousand billion pounds) and is increasing every day, and when much of our sovereignty has been surrendered to the European Union, an organisation so corrupt financially that, for many years, no firm of accountants has dared to approve its accounts. I've no faith in the independence party called UKIP, either. Youth is wasted on the young, and politics are devastated by the politicians, carcinogens of the body politic.

'Just listen to yourself', says the last relic of my doubleness. 'You sound at times like a parody of the grumbling old man. Whatever became of the fine discriminations, the subtle qualifications, which, according to Leavis and his ilk, the study of English Literature was supposed to elicit and to nourish?' As I've indicated, the best I can do these days, when I consider my stock of opinions, is simply to put quotation-marks round all of them, to imply the possibility of valid alternative opinions that I don't have the inclination to try to seek and to formulate. Such an inclination, though eleemosynary, would be supererogatory. Ha! I always wanted to use those two inabordable adjectives; now I've done so, at last. The *nunc dimittis*, which we had to memorise at Junior School in 1946, provides an applauding chorus: a memory-din of raucously-chanting children: 'Lord, now lettest thou thy servant depart in peace...'. As for 'inabordable', that's a tribute to Conrad's vocabulary in *The Nigger of the 'Narcissus'*: 'inabordable as a hedgehog': spikily resistant, like that title today.

If, now, I really make the effort, I can concede that some politicians may have been decent: the Attlee government of 1945-50, probably, which promoted the National Health Service and the questionable boon of university entrance for working-class kids. And, of course, some things have improved: living standards, greatly; children are no longer caned in schools; women are gaining the rights that Cunninghame Graham and Carpenter used to advocate; and

216

'paralympic games' are established. Among trivial changes, men use deodorants now; and loo paper – sorry, lavatory paper – is soft, instead of being the torn-up newspapers of the 1940s or the abrasively shiny San Izal paper of the 1950s (liked only by comb-and-paper soloists). How's *that* for the sensitive discrimination that the critical study of literature was supposed to induce?

I stacked, in the three-foot-high cardboard box, heaps of old material from the filing-cabinet, together with numerous books that would be worthless at the Oxfam shop: notably, a tattered yellow-covered souvenir of my naval Russian course at J.S.S.L.: *A New Russian Grammar in Two Parts* by Anna H. Semeonoff (London: Dent, 1934, reprinted 1946; issued to me in July 1956, at Crail; teachers' names come to mind: Galko; Gladkowski; Dmitri Makaroff, a.k.a. the Muse of Fire, extinguished decades ago).

It was joined by a grimy blue-backed *Naval Ratings Handbook* (*sic* – no apostrophe on *Ratings*; London, Admiralty, 1954; issued to me in March 1956), which fell open at page 72: 'At the supreme test in battle it is usual and natural for officers and men to feel a little afraid, dazed and abnormal.' My father had faced that test, day after day, year after year; and I had never done so; nor had I shown him any understanding. I had learnt plenty of quotations and gained worthy paper qualifications, but sometimes there seemed to be various absences from my range of talents: one being common sense; the other being an ability to love. Yet, in 1961, hadn't I at least booked my parents into the impressive Garden House Hotel? But when I went to the reception-desk to pay their bill, the receptionist told me that my father had paid it already, before departing. And he wouldn't let me refund his money. Within a year, that rather attractive hotel had been damaged by rioting left-wing students; three years later, he was dead; and, in 1972, the hotel was rebuilt on a large scale after a fire. Muddly reality and plotty fiction are snared by irony into perennial mutual ambush. Ha: *Ave Ianus.*

At the back of one drawer, I found a postcard-sized picture in a cheap heavy metal frame that had become tarnished and rusty: John Wilmot, Lord Rochester. He was now much younger than he used to be, but still looking at me with sardonic and world-weary under-shadowed eyes, as, with fastidious thumb and forefinger, he holds the laurel wreath over the head of the little monkey, which, in turn, offers

217

him a page torn from a plum-coloured volume. Even with my blurred sight, I noticed a detail I had previously missed or had forgotten. That monkey, sitting on a couple of smartly-bound tomes, lets his tail cunningly curl down and round, so as to point directly at the sheaf of inscribed manuscripts that Rochester is holding in his left hand. The writing is far too small to be legible (and even my good right eye seems these days to be cobwebbed by what *King Lear*'s Edgar called 'the web and the pin'), but I'd still bet my bus-pass that it's the opening passage of the 'Satyr', in which the poet declares:

> I'd be a Dog, a Monkey, or a Bear,
> Or any thing but that vain Animal,
> Who is so proud of being rational...

A later passage, also memorised in 1960, came predictably and bitterly to mind:

> Then Old Age, and Experience, hand in hand,
> Lead him to Death, and make him understand,
> After a Search so painful, and so long,
> That all his Life he has been in the wrong.

To compensate for weak memory, in the period 1953 to 1961 I deliberately memorised two quotations per night. These days, I can't remember what I did this time last week; but those quotations bubble and ferment in my pill-steeped brain.

Tenderly, reluctantly, I consigned young Rochester and his astute monkey to the big box that was already heavy with books and papers. When I attempted to lift it, at first it seemed to be nailed to the floor, like (metaphorically) the feet of that Greek chorus in *Agamemnon* when their netted master shouts for rescue, or (literally) poor infant Oedipus fettered on Mount Kithairon – nailed by his name, 'Swollenfoot', in onomastic determinism. How about 'Peter Green' again? In my salad days I was green in judgement. Peter: *petra*: rock: Sisyphus perpetually rolling the rock of exams. The result: yes, the last of the superfluous men, the impotent critics: Timon, Thersites, Tchulkaturin, Rudin, Cherbutykin, Decoud, Vladimir, and now Peter: petering out. Let's have ironic background music: Chopin's Funeral

March, with Cornel Wilde miming at the piano. (*A Song to Remember*: film I saw in 1945, the year the Poles were betrayed.)

Heaving the box up, using a knee as well as arms, and clutching it to my chest and belly, I lurched under the weight, and the burden seemed to murmur 'Books: 'tis a dull and endless strife; / Let Nature be your teacher' (Wordsworth, *Lyrical Ballads*, 1798) and 'Thought is a disease of flesh' (Hardy, *Return of the Native*, 1878).

Literary culture: what *is* it, really? A ceaselessly-examined and endlessly-examining part of the entertainment industry? Or an entertaining part of the examination industry?

And why do governments try to pack more and more young people into universities? (1) It pays the governments to do so, because graduates usually pay more income tax than non-graduates. (2) Passably intelligent young people are extracted from the working class, so that the working class (what's left of it) loses shrewd potential leaders. Result: decline of proletariat into *Lumpenproletariat*. (3) It reduces the number of the unemployed. (4) As Casey suggested, the competitive exam ethos attunes the youngster to the competitive capitalist economy; so, generally, a more acquiescent populace results: internationally, capitalism is increasingly regarded as natural and inevitable. Carpenter's shade would sob.

On the stairs, returning breathless from the waspy recycling-bin just now, I felt giddy ('like a sheep stricken with the gid', H. G. Wells); sat down for a while, and crawled, literally crawled, swaying, back to my flat. (Director: suspend the camera six feet overhead, looking down on this black-suited creeping quadruped, kin of the beetle of Kafka's *Metamorphosis.*) Then severe head-ache flickered: lurid forked pain-lightning, nauseating; and I violently vomited, spattering my trousers, yet again. Arabella's velvet bed-cover came to mind; so did Casey, who also wore black corduroy: he'd said 'You treat an exam as a pretext for regurgitation'. As, stinking, I slump, huddled, at the computer, trying to complete these notes, the head-ache returns to this reasoning engine. Engine fingers engine.

It would be ironic if a stork strike, sorry, *stroke* were to kill me now, after all the expenditure on examinations and cancer treatment. Cerebral haemorrhage: a crimson brainstorm. 'G2G', kids text; no swan-song. No novel to show, either; but at least the 'Pay As You Earn' deductions from my salary have ensured that, during the decades, I have refunded with interest the money that the taxpayers provided for my education. Therefore, if anyone examines my life, the result may not be failure. A past sorry *pass*, perhaps; though without honours.

Discuss.

---

# PART 4: POST MORTEM: BRIGHTON, 2013: EXAMINING *FINAL EXAM*

The olfactory details constituted the first tactful warning. From the outset, the narrative repeatedly told you what the protagonist was smelling: his fingers, Arabella, corridors, food, et cetera. What else were you told? That he was a heavy smoker. Consider. If indeed he smoked as much as was said, his sense of smell would have been thoroughly dulled. (But I'm sure you passed *that* part of the exam, having perceived the anomaly.)

Thus, the whole story was a traditional amalgam of fact and fiction. Those quotations from 1961 exam papers are accurate; but I cannot vouch for the answers. I lack my protagonist's ingenuous craftiness, such as it is; on the other hand, as you see, I have outlived him, and here, ineluctably fantasmic, will continue to do so. (Cancer, strokes? *His* problems, not mine.) One unlikely descriptive detail, the plastic combs that snap, being defeated by Peter's gluey hair: that, I can testify, is factual, as are his attendant flies. Body mocks mind: you couldn't have missed *that* theme.

All the main characters are amalgams. Jack, for example. In his appearance and perspicacity, he resembles an actual undergraduate of Pembroke in the period 1958-1961, who could have come from Newcastle-upon-Tyne. It ought to be said, however, that his character on the whole (upbringing, kleptomania and other idiosyncrasies) and career were borrowed from several other people, one of whom was a sentry at Victoria Barracks, Portsmouth, in 1956. Just as Jack's Falstaffian laughter came from Orson Welles in *Chimes at Midnight*, the suggestion of his derangement came from Welles in *The Third Man*. The narrative implies that Jack is guilty of at least one grave crime; but, if anyone is guilty of it, it is I, aided by femicidal Hänsel. Other features derive from fiction: for instance, Jack had learnt his finger-snapping from (as you should have

221

recalled) Fielding's Parson Adams. Easy:II.ii-ish.

Casey, too, is based on several people. One of them, a gentle and gifted poet, was indeed brutally killed while on his way home. He is sometimes, in my mind, commemorated by Shakespeare's innocent Cinna, torn by the Roman mob. Casey's Machiavellian characteristics derive from three other real people and at least two fictional characters. The Baudelaire translation was not committed by Casey. Of the four women who, by literary parthenogenesis, engendered Arabella, two are (at the time of writing) still alive; but the coppery-gold hair is now silver. The main source of Jan was, when I last received apposite verifiable information, quite well, and happily married; furthermore, her son graduated from Sussex University. The car named 'Mr Toad', in honour of the enthusiastic motorist in *The Wind in the Willows*, was hers and not Arabella's; and it was a big Triumph convertible with running-boards, not an Austin 7. Toad reminds me that (unlike my namesake) the symbolic crabs, flies, wasps and swans performed with tact and discretion. Indeed, if you registered the craftiness of the adjective 'crabby' in Chapter 1, or subsequently noted the 'absent swan-song' motif, you may presume that you deserve an upper second at least.

Piggott? His congenial characteristics derive from a supervisor and director of studies in English at Pembroke College in the novel's period; he did become a Professor of English at Sussex University. I don't recall any uncongenial characteristics in the rendering, but if there are any, they derive from me. Haggerty, like Eastbourne and Farthingale, is an impurely fictional creation: as her nickname and crutches indicate, her ancestors are the broomstick-borne witches of folk-tale, pursued by Rochester, whose 'Satyr against Mankind' says:

> So charming Oyntments make an Old *Witch* flie,
> And bear a Crippled Carcass through the Skie.

Indeed, Rochester and his monkey are somewhat more reliable than is my wretched protagonist, usurper of my name, whose opinions do not always tally with mine, and who (as you saw) is doomed to demonstrate that an aspiring mind is imprisoned in a primitive body.

I cannot use the prudent formulation employed by litigation-wary authors: 'All the characters in this book are fictional, and any resemblance to a living person is purely coincidental.' Some real people make appearances in these pages, and there I have been reasonably accurate, though they sometimes did not do exactly what they are described as doing. Like Morecambe at the piano, I have employed all the right notes, but not necessarily in the correct order. Dr Leavis, however, did seem to wear an open-necked shirt all the year round; and Professor C. S. Lewis did lecture at Cambridge in that period, and really gave a very dramatic rendition of the Green Knight. (They wouldn't have envisaged that eventually Leavis would be enacted on television by Ian Holm, and Lewis on the cinema-screen by Anthony Hopkins.) In related cases, where I have not achieved strict accuracy, I have espoused scrupulous benignity. If you perceived that the moral heroes of the narrative are those founders of the co-operative movement, the Rochdale Pioneers mentioned in Chapter 5, you may (at your peril) award yourself a First.

Two quotations come to mind. They make a sufficiently apt conclusion. One is from *Serious Reflections During the Life and Surprising Adventures of Robinson Crusoe... Written by Himself*:

> I, *Robinson Crusoe*, being at this time in perfect and sound mind and memory,... do affirm, that the story, though allegorical, is also historical.

The second is from – of course – Rochester:

> Our *Sphere* of Action is life's happiness,
> And he who thinks Beyond, thinks like an *Ass*.

223

Printed in Great Britain
by Amazon

13968046R00132